THE AIRLIFT

THE AIRLIFT

VICTORIES, MYTHS, AND THE BERLIN BLOCKADE

JOSEPH PEARSON

For James Helgeson

First published 2025

The History Press
97 St George's Place, Cheltenham,
Gloucestershire, GL50 3QB
www.thehistorypress.co.uk

© Joseph Pearson, 2025

The right of Joseph Pearson to be identified as the Author
of this work has been asserted in accordance with the
Copyright, Designs and Patents Act 1988.

All rights reserved. No part of this book may be reprinted
or reproduced or utilised in any form or by any electronic,
mechanical or other means, now known or hereafter invented,
including photocopying and recording, or in any information
storage or retrieval system, without the permission in writing
from the Publishers.

British Library Cataloguing in Publication Data.
A catalogue record for this book is available from the British Library.

ISBN 978 1 80399 822 0

Typesetting and origination by The History Press
Printed and bound in Great Britain by TJ Books, Padstow, Cornwall.

The History Press proudly supports
Trees for Life
www.treesforlife.org.uk

EU Authorised Representative: Easy Access System Europe
Mustamäe tee 50, 10621 Tallinn, Estonia
gpst.request@easproject.com

CONTENTS

Author's Note 9
I   Introduction 11

Enemy Backstories
II   Roar 23
III   The Unforgivable 32
IV   Enemy of My Enemy 45
V   The Revolutionary 53

Winter–Summer 1948
VI   The Breakdown 65
VII   Crisis 80
VIII   Champagne 101

Summer–Autumn 1948
IX   Culture War 115
X   Through the Iron Curtain 131
XI   Students in the Ruins 144
XII   Sweet Victories 157

Winter–Spring 1948–49
XIII   In the French Quarter 183
XIV   New Year 198
XV   Wolves in Sheep's Clothing 209
XVI   The Hollywood Version 220

After 1949
XVII Reflections   237

Timeline   250
Acknowledgements   252
Bibliography   254
Notes   263
Index   284

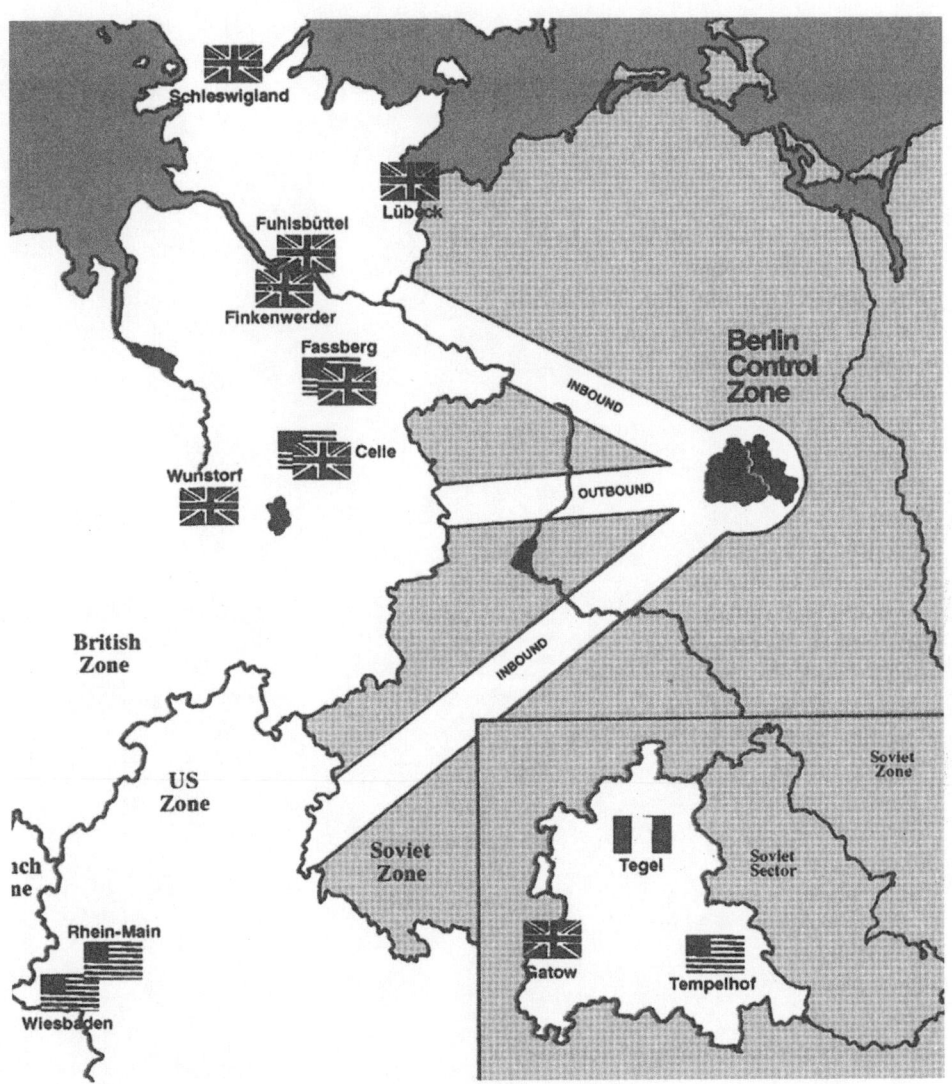

Air Force bases and corridors map. US Department of Defense, 1948. (Public domain)

AUTHOR'S NOTE

What follows reads like fiction, but it is not.

The stories in this book are unembellished. They were uncovered through primary sources, such as interviews, and cross-referenced in the archive. Even descriptions of interiors and locations – down to the day's weather – are taken from documentary material, while dialogue is quoted from records such as transcripts.

Apart from wishing that readers experience this history vividly and accurately, I wanted to write a book that corrected a Cold War myth of the Berlin Blockade.

When I began this project, we were still emerging from the COVID-19 lockdown. It was a state of exception that limited freedom and daily choices, and I wanted to find comparable moments in Berlin's history. A blockaded city, choked by a foreign army – rather than a virus – with no way in or out except by air, fit the bill.

As I researched this work, increasingly I could not square the story I had learned and believed – that Berlin, apart from air routes, was completely sealed by the Soviets between June 1948 and May 1949 – with my historical witnesses' evidence that land crossings were commonplace. In effect, Berlin was not blockaded.

Most works, relying on English-language sources, perpetuate an Airlift legend critiqued in recent German historical research, and discredited by documents I studied in the National Archives in London. In these pages, it will become clear that this fabrication emerged from nascent Cold War propaganda and solidified as an accepted fact. Throughout this book, including its title, the use of the term 'Berlin Blockade' should be taken with this qualification – as something people talk about, but that did not strictly happen.

A correction does not diminish the contributions of the Berliners, and the Western Allies who refused to abandon Berlin under Soviet pressure. This useful myth played a vital role in commandeering support to push back Stalin. A sense of urgency for a common cause united Germans and the Western Allies, overcoming the enmity of the Second World War.

This book goes into production as the United States questions its commitments to European security and the spirit of the Airlift. The friendships built during the operation were also military alliances whose deterrence secured four generations of peace on the European continent.

Joseph Pearson
Berlin, 18 August 2025

I

INTRODUCTION

1

For a year, Berlin was a city with few lights, and a loud roar.

Looking from a plane window on such a night was Kenneth Hawk Slaker, an American pilot who had flown during the war. Below, the city was half-darkened. He later wrote how his navigation lights created an 'eerie glow' in the 'thick murky night', and how 'heavy rain hammered itself to pieces' on the windshield of his cockpit. But, as he flew the DC-3 between Wiesbaden and Berlin-Tempelhof airports, it was the roar of his engines that kept him awake.[1]

Slaker had dropped bombs on the Germans. He had learned to hate the enemy, but now he transported flour and coal packed in heavy bags. Before midnight, Slaker reduced the throttle and descended to release the load not on the homes of the frightened Berliners but on a runway to feed and power a city. The enemy was now the Soviets and, after only a few weeks in Germany, on 14 September 1948, Kenneth Slaker's DC-3 crashed behind the new Iron Curtain.

On the ground below Slaker lived a journalist behind an apartment window in the neighbourhood of Steglitz. Ruth Andreas-Friedrich had lost her husband – an orchestra conductor, shot in his car at a checkpoint by the Americans. Except she was the kind who knew how to move on. Her flatmate, Heike, kept her company. Ruth was almost 50 and had stubbornly seen Germany through four forms of government and two world wars. She even remembered the Kaiser from her teens. But she had never experienced a period like this one.

At midnight, there was still no light, radio, or electricity for cooking. Most Berliners had already gone to bed at dusk because their homes were cold and dark and only the beds were warm. Then they woke abruptly to their alarm clocks, in time for the two hours of power between midnight and 2 a.m.

Ruth and Heike didn't sleep; they sat and waited, tapping their way through the apartment 'like blind people', watching the candles burn down as the minutes crept 'like snails' – or so she wrote in her diary. They discussed the blockade in the dark: would Berlin hold on? What would it be like under Stalin instead of the Americans? Just another form of government to add to the list? They agreed that it all came down to who could provide electricity. And to nerves. Ruth had plenty, of course. But Heike had lost hers and was so tired she began to cry. And then, all at once, the women spoke with one voice: 'Light!'

Candles were snuffed; the two got busy, laughing as they bustled about, rushing to the stove, washing stockings, ironing blouses, all the time listening to the Radio in the American Sector, or RIAS. It sent out the news every hour, and all around the city people tuned in to a pro-Yankee cabaret. Berliners made coffee into the early hours – real coffee carried to them by American planes, not the ersatz from chicory and ground acorns that was heavier to transport. They made meals for the next day from dehydrated ingredients – desiccated flavourless vegetables, powdered potatoes – which would keep warm in a box lined with feathers. For 120 minutes, life felt better. The women even felt like heroes. Champions of democracy! As Ruth said, it was a question of nerves.[2]

The radio could not block out the roar. The *brummende Flugzeuge*. The roaring aircraft. *Brummen*: a word that better mimicked the sound, associated first with war but now with peace. Allied planes had bombed the city for years, casting the inhabitants into shelters or burying them in tile and brick. But now, many of those same pilots were landing at airfields around the Western Quarter of Berlin, or even on lakes, for another purpose. *Das Brummen* sounded the same but felt different.

Meanwhile, Henry Ries, 30 years old, was often coasting through the borough of Schöneberg in his black Chrysler, imported from the States. He was so well-dressed, one would never guess his origins. The American with the one-hundred-dollar-a-week salary was a native of Berlin who had escaped Hitler, fled to New York, and returned in a US uniform, eventually becoming a staff photographer for the *New York Times*.[3]

Ries photographed Berliners' everyday lives. He coasted past untouched elegant façades and the crenulated peaks of bombed houses.

His camera might peer right into the innards of a half-gutted home at the end of the street, with candles in the windows or shadowy figures sloped in the doorway. There, the deep focus could illuminate a patch of rubble like a moraine.

Ries was skilled at photographing dim light. One of his most famous photographs was the perspective from under the belly of an American plane, looking towards an elliptical queue of aircraft stalled by in-rolling fog at Tempelhof. That same winter mist hung over the city façades, broken and intact. Years before, Ries had lost his family.

Now, on Martin-Luther-Straße, the U-Bahn station was only operating for a few hours to save electricity. Here, paths were cleared between the small avalanches from the broken buildings. Eerie in the dark, Rathaus Schöneberg's carcass served as the West's administrative offices from early 1949. But the façade was blurry as the fog rolled in thick. Ries's car sliced through this penumbra, not towards home, but to a party.

Up above, in one of those Rathaus city offices, a man worked late. A Turkish fez might hang from the hook behind the door, a cane dangling from the desk edge, Ernst Reuter's head alongside documents in English, German, French, and Russian. He had been elected mayor of the city and perhaps had fallen asleep at his desk. But now the aquiline figure might wake with a start, soaring to the old casement windows to look up at the sky. Except the man of 60 capered with the help of his cane.

The fog seeped over the craggy edges into the Hof; half of the building had been bombed. The sky, thick with cloud, hung low over the metropolis, etched by the low moon tonight, the underbelly illuminated.

What was it that had woken him up? Not the silent seeping of the fog. Not the noise but the ceasing of noise: of aeroplanes that no longer flew in this weather. The roar that had become normal, even at night – white noise protecting sleep cycles – had stopped. Before, *das Brummen* would have sent them to a bomb shelter, but today, it was silence that suggested danger. Only when the roar resumed could Reuter hobble back to his desk and keep working, or fall asleep.[4]

Henry Ries turned the corner and motored through Kreuzberg, down Mehringdamm, towards Tempelhof, the airfield where the planes had resumed taking off and landing every three minutes. From somewhere in the airport – perhaps the officers' open mess – was the sound of swing music. A shift had just ended; the radar and the Allied logistics staff were getting off work. They had cigarettes and chocolate that they traded for every kind of pleasure. And there would be women.

When Berlin was at war, it was a city of women, with German men stationed at the front. Now occupied by the Western Allies, Berlin was still full of females on the ground, because their soldiers did not return. Meanwhile, thousands of uniformed men arrived from the sky. The thirty thousand administrators and soldiers posted in Berlin were also almost all males. The meeting of heaven and earth was a perfect storm.

The planes landed, unloaded, and departed. The roar grew intense as another plane rose sharply from the airfield. The storm of noise was Ken Slaker, his plane now lighter, having dropped its load of flour and coal, returning through the Western corridor, past midnight, through the 'wet black night' over the Berlin lakes towards Wiesbaden.

Far below, Henry heard the music from the open window. He changed gears. He gained speed.

2

The runways are still here, and so is the old terminal. But today, the fastest speeds allowed down the paved surface are achieved by bicycle. That the Cold War ended in Berlin, with the fall of the Wall in 1989, is common knowledge. But few remember it began here too – its first serious conflict was the 1948–49 Berlin Airlift. However, the runways of Tempelhof Airport, now the world's largest inner-city park, won't tell you this story just on their own.

Pedalling down the decommissioned airstrips, with their painted lines and numbers, can still cause a shiver – the illicit thrill of being where you shouldn't. Of having climbed a perimeter fence. As if the rules have not yet been invalidated. Hold your arms out as wide as possible – as the directional signs flit by to each side – and imagine looking through an aircraft window. There's the feeling a plane could come barrelling down the runway at any moment.

Many Berliners think of Tempelhof as a backdrop to their Sunday afternoons. The terminal's horseshoe, seen across the broken asphalt, is a setting for selfies on rollerblades or picnic blankets. But those who consider what happened here – and notice the weeds invading the cracks on the tarmac – can begin to imagine how the ruins of the twentieth century will look to future archaeologists.

Tempelhof's terminal was built and used by the Nazis. It was one of the largest buildings in the world, almost a mile long, with 3.2 million sq ft of surface area. Hitler intended it, with its towering limestone façades, to be a dramatic entry point to his capital from the air.

He would be outraged that, after the war, it became a US Air Force base.

3

After the defeat of the Nazis in 1945, the victorious powers occupied Germany, and each carved its zone. In the West were the Americans, British, and French. In the East was the counterweight: the Soviet Union.[5]

This division in Germany was imitated in the old capital, Berlin, also divided into sectors, drawn along the 1920 municipal neighbourhood boundaries. It became a quartered city. In western Berlin, the French occupied the northern neighbourhoods (Wedding and Reinickendorf). The British took the western centre (such as Charlottenburg and Zoo Station), and the Americans occupied the South (Kreuzberg and areas like leafy, bourgeois Zehlendorf). These zones were connected to the rump of West Germany by land and air. While oral agreements governed land traffic, written agreements guaranteed air traffic. The Soviets had the East (including the historic centre of Mitte, the neighbourhoods of Prenzlauer Berg and Friedrichshain, and other districts contiguous to their occupied territory surrounding Berlin).

West Germany and East Germany were not yet formalised as countries. One Germany still operated under all four occupied powers. In Berlin, the inter-allied government authority was called the Kommandatura and first met on 11 July 1945.

At first, the powers thought they could work together. But cohabitation was soon nightmarish because of their opposing ideological and economic systems – the East under Stalinism, the West under the free market. By the spring of 1948, the Western Allies had ceased to see the Soviets as a trusted partner, understanding – as they watched civil war in the Balkans and a coup in Prague – that their former ally was expansionary and its economic strategies incompatible with the West's desire to expand markets. Not least, the West believed that life under Stalinism was an ordeal and democracy a better way of living.

Joseph Stalin, from his side, was weary of tolerating President Harry S. Truman's capitalist atoll in his sea of red and was tempted to starve Berlin and then draw it under his hegemony. After all, the city was closer to the Soviet border than to Paris. And the Soviets had superior land power, with twice as many troops in the East. What the United States had – that the Soviets had not yet developed (it was tested on 29 August 1949) – was an atomic bomb. Western democracy and Stalinism jockeyed dangerously to extend their spheres of influence.

On 24 June 1948, Stalin made his move. He obstructed Berlin by land and water to squeeze out the West with the 'Berlin Blockade'. How would the West react? Truman insisted they could not set a precedent of retreat. A Europe that rolled over for Stalin put everywhere else at risk. Experience with Soviet Russia was that if you gave an inch they took a thousand miles. Vienna – also divided by the Allied powers – or Germany beyond the Elbe could be next on Stalin's list.

An airlift is the emergency transport of supplies by plane. The British, French, and Americans took the Soviets by surprise when they launched this feat of logistics: the largest air operation in history, centred on the US airport at Tempelhof, the British one at Gatow, and eventually the French zone's Tegel. It was a project that almost everyone expected to fail. It was also fraught with risk. A false move – a transport aircraft shot down by Russian fighters – might even risk the atomic drop that some trigger-ready US generals wanted.

But the Berlin Airlift was an enormous success. From 24 June 1948 to 12 May 1949, it delivered 2.3 million US short tons of supplies on 278,000 flights using air corridors. They flew from West Germany, over Soviet territory, into the Western sectors of the city, using the only avenues for which there were agreements. A little over 2 million people in West Berlin were eventually stocked from the air.

The spectacular operation became a symbol of freedom and was a propaganda coup for the Western Allies. It delivered dividends that redrew and reinforced the lines of friend and enemy that would define the Cold War era.

4

Tempelhof, the 'mother of all airports' (to quote architect Norman Foster), was built to last. Except it didn't, at least not as an airport. These days, touring its halls, former waiting areas, and abandoned security checkpoints, one feels as if the gates of a deposed monarch's palace have been thrown open. Tempelhof houses refugees or hosts music festivals, not DC-3s. The hollow feeling about its disused hangars is perfect for a techno party. It's hard to imagine it once chock-full of military purpose: American brass, radio controllers, and crews rushing to unload coal and flour that pilots transported to supply the city, with aircraft landing and taking off every three minutes.

But the past persists in Tempelhof's present. Not just because developers have not torn up the airfield and demolished its buildings. But because of something more intangible. One sees it in how people use the park, projects it into families flying their kites. Events in this airfield formed their educations, civil liberties, and quality of life. How Germans position themselves in the world today – in relation to Europe, Britain, and America – is also about Tempelhof. I understand it in the very fact that a Canadian like me can have spent most of his adult life living in Berlin, among the enemy his grandfather fought as a soldier in Europe just eighty years before.

In 1948, a large swathe of the political spectrum in Berlin – from conservatives to social democrats – got behind the word 'freedom'. It is a word whose meaning has been cheapened by the Cold Warriors who emerged from the crisis – the Berlin Airlift set the tone for the generations to come. But it had an obvious meaning back then, as the West pushed back against Stalinist totalitarianism, and Tempelhof succeeded in its role airlifting supplies to Berlin. If they had not succeeded, life in the Reich's former capital, and perhaps all of Europe, would have taken a different turn. When I visit Tempelhof, joining my German friends along its disused runways, cycling among the taxiways and ramps, and arrows that pointed aircraft to the sky, I feel that we are still living at the edge of democracy – that threats are not so far away.

The West succeeded, however, against Stalin in Berlin with means only justified by the ends. A struggle with the German left mirrored the Red Scare at home in the States. Former Nazis worked on the Airlift as the Allies tore up post-war agreements to establish West Germany. Histories of the crisis idolise Western pilots who saved a blockaded city, with its women and children, from starvation – but this is an enduring myth.

For Berlin was, as will be shown, never completely sealed. The Airlift became a propaganda performance meant to draw a line between East and West – to bring Americans and West Germans onto the same team as the Cold War exploded.

5

There are many ways to tell the Airlift's story. This book concerns how Germans, who had been the West's foes, became friends. The first victory may have come in 1945 when the Allied powers pummelled Germany into submission. But the sweet victory came three years later when the Western powers conquered the hearts of their former enemy. Airmen who had spent the war dropping bombs on Berlin now risked their lives dropping chocolate bars, and Germans looked to the skies not with dread and hatred but with hope and admiration. But it is also about how new battle lines were drawn. The Berlin Airlift wrote the playbook of the Cold War and still influences Western thinking and diplomacy with Russia.

This book is, however, not a straightforward military or political account. Historian Natalie Zemon Davis is the famous example of a historian who explained her research through characters. She unravelled the quotidian lives of a sixteenth-century peasant, Martin Guerre (and that of his imposter), as if they were a novel – retrieving the past in all its bright colours. She called this an 'adventure with a different way of telling about the past'. She felt she had 'uncovered the true face of the past' and its 'stubborn vitality'.[6]

This book, too, focuses on all the textures of everyday history and finds that, during the Airlift, individual lives intersected with momentous struggles. Their experiences illuminate the atmospheres of the city and the sky over it – and the looming threat of war between East and West. The people one meets in these pages stand in for the many: in the air, making decisions, struggling to survive, and winning hearts and minds.

Most of these stories are told here for the first time in a book in English and, in some cases, in any language. When one reads history, one struggles with the consequence of time passing and that our existences are brief on earth. There is pathos in that these lives could have easily disappeared from memory. As Walter Benjamin elucidated, 'for every image of the past that is not recognized by the present as one of its own concerns threatens to disappear irretrievably'. So, we weave a line of understanding between generations – the historian's relation to former lives is what Davis calls a 'compact sealed in the blood of birth and death'. The reader's act of bringing these forgotten lives back into conversation is something akin to saving souls.

The emphasis on the otherwise lost individual with whom one might identify – what made them a living, sensitive human – means that, while this is a comprehensive history of the Airlift operation, it is not a blow-by-blow geopolitical and logistical account. One learns 'what happened' and about the important turning points – a timeline is included as a reference at the end of this book – but the history is told from the ground up. The focus is not on the beads of the chronological rosary but instead on what the Airlift meant to particular people, which helps one understand better why it mattered at all.

We begin with our first four characters. Each of their backstories merits time – and going back in time – to know them as individuals and give contour to the tensions between the East, the West, and Germany. Pilot Kenneth Slaker and photographer Henry Ries despised Germany. Ruth Andreas-Friedrich and Ernst Reuter despised the Soviets. In June 1948, these tensions exploded with the isolating of Berlin and the West's decision to act. But new friendships arose out of this triangle of acrimony. As the Airlift chronology moves from autumn to winter to its conclusion in the summer of 1949, the focus will turn to other witnesses – Soviets investigating a 'secret army', a rowdy flight engineer, a troop of student actors, a little girl chasing falling chocolate, farmers betrayed by the French, a Hollywood actor, and others. These Airlift stories intimate how implacable foes became friends.

ENEMY BACKSTORIES

II

ROAR

1

During the war, from the height of his B-17 bomber, Ken Slaker killed a lot of Germans.[1] At first, he had strong reservations. After all, he was a Presbyterian who had won a Bible contest as a teenager. He drank orange juice at the bar when the others drank beer. When quoting the old crack about American troops being 'overfed, overpaid and over here', he would omit the word 'oversexed'. And when he joined up to fly bombing runs over the Mediterranean in the Second World War, he was shocked by his commanders' foul language and the lusty names painted on his buddies' aircraft. His B-17 – which he signed for after Pearl Harbor at the age of only 22 – bore instead the name of his newborn daughter, Elaine.

Ken described his enemy as 'atheists out to take over the United States', but he had nothing personal against the Germans or the Italians. Not at first. Ken's family were of German extraction: farm people from Elderton, Pennsylvania, near Pittsburgh. The rolling countryside looks like parts of Germany, and perhaps his ancestors wanted a place that resembled home. Slaker is, after all, an anglicising of Schleicher, and the family is possibly related to the Prussian General Kurt von Schleicher, murdered by Hitler during the Night of the Long Knives. Slaker said proudly: 'Of all my fifty missions, I never did bomb Germany itself. My bombs were always on Germans in Italy, North Africa, southern France, which makes me feel pretty good because my ancestors came from there.' Unsurprisingly, he had a moral objection to accepting a Distinguished Flying Cross, 'for killing people', as he put it bluntly. Even after the war, when offered one, he replied: 'If I'd accept it now, I'd be a hypocrite.'

But halfway through his service, one mission changed his attitude towards Germany. In short succession, he lost two of his cadet school friends, Lieutenants Simpson and Shirmer. They all shared the same room for a year, and he described his buddies as family.

Slaker watched with horror at Shirmer's plane plummeting, as the other men bailed out, chutes popping over the Mediterranean. On the radio, Slaker got a hold of the falling pilot, trapped in the burning aircraft, 'Shirmer, you get out of there. You know you can do it.'

But Shirmer replied, 'Ken, I can hardly move. I just can't.'

Just before Shirmer hit the water, he told his friend: 'Slaker, give the Nazis hell.'

Ken was used to men 'losing an arm or a leg or one of each', but he was unprepared for this. He quickly volunteered to fly twenty-five more missions: 'That's when I changed my attitude. From then on, I gave them all hell. It became a real war. I'd lost two buddies. It became personal. It became my war.'

Slaker's battle was launched from bases in Morocco with the 12th Air Force, bombing Mediterranean ships and ports. The dogfights at high altitude were cinematographic, as were gruesome bombings of Italian cities, as he took out a historic square in Palermo and pounded the small island of Pantelleria into submission. The B-17, called the Flying Fortress, was a workhorse of a plane that dropped more bombs on Europe in the Second World War than any other. 'If you ever visit Sicily', his crew warned him, 'don't tell them you're a pilot.' When the Germans retreated to the mainland across the narrow Strait of Messina, his B-17 picked them off from 1,500ft, and there were a lot of dead. He'd hit munition ships crammed with explosives coming down to supply Rommel in North Africa. Nothing remained but towering ash, amidst flak so thick he said he could not see the sky. From above, Slaker spied planes like his own burn as he set airfields on fire.

After his fifty bombing runs, Slaker returned to the States with hardly an injury, except for eighteen cavities, as there was no toothpaste. But the war marked him. He returned to find his mother on her deathbed. On the edge of tears, he said: 'It's tough, after losing your buddies and seeing everybody killed, and coming home and losing your mother.' But he had his wife and Elaine, and they found their way to Omaha, Nebraska, at an Air Force base where he was now promoted to captain and Base Operations Officer. Life promised, for a short time, to settle down.

The last thing he expected was that four years later, in June 1948, he'd be ordered back across the Atlantic, this time to Germany, for the opposite of *his* war. It was a reversal for hundreds of pilots like Slaker, who found themselves sick at heart. After everything they had seen and done, these men who had served their country, lost their buddies, and given the Nazis hell were now asked to feed their enemy instead of bombing them.

2

When asked why he wanted to become a pilot, Ken Slaker said it was because he saved up 25 cents when he was 9. It was a lot of money for a child in 1930. Not that he knew a quarter would make him a lieutenant colonel in the US Army Air Corps. On an airstrip near town, a Ford Trimotor propeller plane was on show, and Ken paid his quarter to go up, do a loop of the field, and come down. He was so excited he said: 'I'm going to be a pilot.' But he never thought – even after cadet school – about becoming a bomber pilot.

Slaker became a very good flyer. He could take on dirt runways, land in tight fields, dodge flak and enemy aircraft. He could operate in cold temperatures – because it got down to minus forty up there. He'd break up the ice inside his oxygen mask, fitted so tight he never grew a beard. But after these challenges, he wasn't prepared for the piece of shit they offered him to fly into Berlin in August 1948, less than two months after the Airlift began.

The American DC-3 – or C-47 in its military version – was a classic, with all the good and bad that comes with that moniker. The aircraft, called the Dakota (Douglas Aircraft Company Transport Aircraft) by the RAF, had been a victim of its success. When American safety authorities banned wood in planes, the metal DC-3 filled the need between 1936 and 1942: more than six hundred DC-3s and more than ten thousand C-47s were built quickly. With their 64ft length and 95ft wingspan, they could carry thirty passengers, two on each side of the aisle. Chances are it was the first aircraft most people had ever taken. During the war, planes made for civilian use were converted into C-47s to drop bombs, carry cargo and troops, and go on spying missions. Then after the war, demobbed, they reverted to commercial aircraft. There were so many DC-3s, they became cheap and available. With their dual piston engines, they had advantages: they could fly in and out of tight fields, manage most surfaces, such as dirt and grass, and so were useful when landing in Berlin's Tempelhof with its steep approach and pierced steel planking runway.[2]

But these old planes, which had seen combat, were also relatively slow, had no pressurised cabin, and many were falling apart. For the Airlift's mission, the DC-4 (or C-54 Skymaster) was a better choice: it could carry almost 10 tons of cargo compared to the DC-3's measly 3. And the DC-4 could fly 50 per cent faster. But in June 1948, there were only two DC-4s in Europe, something that would change.

To transport cargo to Berlin, these planes could not fly as they were. They needed to be modified. Aircraft were requisitioned from all over the world, and one C-54, a league apart from Slaker's rust bucket, happened to be a flagship carrier for American Airlines. The London nightclub Ciro had two planes, meant to bring guests down to parties on the Riviera, requisitioned. The luxury seats and fine carpeting, dividers, cargo heads, decorations, along with anything else unnecessary, were ripped out – and the ground crew installed straps to hold down cargo.

Of all the 380 aircraft used during the Airlift, Slaker and his co-pilot, Lieutenant Clarence Steber, were assigned a rusty gooney bird. The designers of the Airlift, General William H. Tunner and the US Military Governor General Lucius Clay, worried the operation would litter the ground with destroyed aircraft. Perhaps they'd seen this DC-3.

The pilots walked around it that day after it had just been taken out of storage in Munich, presumably because it was not intended to fly again. It was painted sandy pink, camouflage that indicated it had wartime service somewhere in the desert. The men kicked the tyres, looked around it and said, 'Oh my god.'

They were surprised when both engines started.

3

That night, on 14 September 1948, they filled the DC-3 with many fuel reservoirs, 55 gallons each. With this explosive load, Slaker and Steber climbed into the fuselage. The plane had already flown them to Tempelhof and back to Wiesbaden three times – a miracle. They had no flight engineer or navigator: the extra weight was used for cargo.

Flights went out around the clock in four six-hour blocks (from 6 a.m. to 12 p.m., 12 p.m. to 6 p.m., etc.), with seventy planes participating in each. The blocks were subdivided: one group landing and refuelling while the other flew. They were further subdivided in the air: the thirty-two planes, three minutes apart, flew at five different heights with approximately 8 miles between each over the 275-mile distance. This unbroken chain in fixed distance maintained a consistent speed to land as many planes as logistically possible within the time block. The precision was facilitated by using pilots trained by the demands of war.

These planes circulated into Berlin from different airfields in Western Germany. The American planes would arrive via a southern corridor from airfields around Frankfurt, Rhein-Main and Wiesbaden. Both the Americans and Brits used Faßberg and Celle in the British zone. British planes would also come through a northern corridor closer to Hamburg, from Wunstorf, Fuhlsbüttel, Lübeck. Planes exited through the middle corridor to return, and they could fly faster because they had lighter cargo. The aircraft were so closely packed that, if a plane missed its landing, there was no time for a reattempt. It returned immediately through the middle corridor because any delay, any error, risked a domino effect.

The men flew at night. Slaker put on his parachute in advance, something he got used to doing each time because he was a tall man at 6ft 2in. Otherwise, he didn't trust he'd have the time to fit it correctly in an emergency. He took the cushions out of the cockpit, again because of his height, and sat on the right as the co-pilot. The regular pilot was always on the left, and then Slaker and Steber swapped for the flight home.

The ground crew checked the twin propellers, and then the pilots, tightly fit in the nose of the cockpit, snapped the magneto switches located above the windshield to start the Wright Cyclone engines. When the DC-3 was first brought into service, there were concerns about it having only two engines. In the event of a failure, a third would have allowed it to land.

Now, packed with duffle bags and boxes, burlap sacks, and gallons of petrol, the aircraft rattled and lifted, heavy. The aeroplane ahead was a speck, even if only three minutes away. The chatter from the radar station, the rundown of the weather — 59°F (15°C), partly cloudy, clearing to the east — kept them awake.

Sleeping was not allowed, but everyone took turns doing it. The men got tired of flying continuous runs with constant concentration. They took any moment they could to doze as the DC-3 followed the earth's crust, and Germany – a mess of rubble, suffering, and hunger – faded into a chessboard of greens made sharper by the evening light.

They climbed to 3,200ft over Darmstadt, 6,500ft at Aschaffenburg, and then took the usual 30-degree turn to Fulda. Slaker had studied a topographical map for rivers and mountains but today there was too much cloud, and they couldn't see where they crossed the line that marked the claims of the victorious powers. Later, there would be no lights in the Russian sector, and they would rely on their compass. The controls told them by degrees which way to rattle forward; they stuck to them because going off track meant risking being shot down. The whole jalopy shuttered in the roar – perhaps only air pressure kept the collage of metal together.

And then, the clouds wisped away to the recognisable shapes of the half-city and the lakes, indicating they had flown far enough east to arrive in the West again. Their plane followed the silvery thread of the one before, precisely distanced, towards the landing strip. The side door cracked ajar, and the city roofs raced below – all the jagged remains of courtyards blown open, and streets cleared into rising piles of war rubble, like snow drifts, where so many hungry walkers staggered on an evening in September that felt like late summer. The plane roared and echoed over a seven-storey building that was too close for comfort, perhaps only 17ft, with skid marks on the roof.

The DC-3 then made its final approach through a shaft over the graves of St Thomas Cemetery. Apartments were to each side of the cemetery, constructions that also rose right up against the runway. Neighbours in the windows could see the plunging aircraft, perhaps even glimpse the trembling pilots, who came in more steeply than they had been trained, another plane almost chasing their rudder.

No matter the landing's precision, there was what they could not control – men still unloading on the runway, a forgotten shovel or ladder to strip the DC-3's wheels, as it screamed down 1.3 miles of metal planking. The aircraft lurched and chimed, dust rose in the cabin, the controllers' voices moved in and out, and the plane shuddered in resignation to turn into the taxiway. It was time to let the next machine, already landing, barrel in.

The trucks rushed up, one with a bib that said 'Follow Me'. Follow, towards the building's overhang, to unload quickly, to meet the jeep sporting snacks. Follow to wonder at the prettiest girls in Berlin who serve them, with faces enjoyed for thirty minutes at most – not enough to do much when sitting on an airfield's tarmac. Unfolded before the pilots was the great arc of the building. Tempelhof: packed with mechanics, logistics, controllers, and officers.

But the pilots might never set foot inside the beast; instead, they quickly loaded up again, switched places in the cockpit, and rattled back into the air as the sun went down at 8 p.m. Dusk moved between the clouds, gaps to a deep violet sky. The aircraft was so light now it glided, clean about the airfield's crater, the rim of Tempelhof a crust. The landing lights blinked. The controls were feather-light as they soared over the Grunewald and the lakes – the Schlachtensee and the Wannsee – as they slipped into the faster middle corridor. They pierced the enemy's zone, with its darkening forests and waters, towards yet another distant landing in Wiesbaden, and another quick turnaround. They were ever-flying, ever-sleepy, always touching but never staying, as the sky darkened, and light crept from the ground – as all the hours in the air became a blur.

4

On the second flight out of Wiesbaden that evening, they were loaded with sacks of flour instead of petrol. It was only slightly better than flying coal from the Ruhr, which accounted for two-thirds of the cargo, to keep the city running with electricity and heat. As Slaker said, 'They loaded us solid.' The men changed places again in the cockpit, so Ken was co-piloting, and they flew off east in the dark.

As the men gained altitude, air pressed through the gaps in the fuselage, so dust rose from the sacks. Flour mixed with the coal previously transported in the cylinder, white dust and black powder filling the corners of their eyes, entering their breaths. The radio changed, garbled with Soviet interference that sounded like their dusty chests would later when a doctor with a stethoscope asked them to breathe. Heavy above foreign territory, hundreds of miles distant from Wiesbaden, they dragged their load over rolling forests and farms where the East stored more food than could be imagined in the city ahead.

Wind rattled the metal wingspan, rain shed over the windscreen, and flooded through the cracks, soaking their clothes. The fuselage was an aluminium drain. Moisture gave pilots haemorrhoids, rashes. The controls, already corroded by coal and flour, now thickened with gum. They dared not pry the doors open at that height to dispel the fug.

Without warning, deep in Soviet airspace, it happened. *Das Brummen*: the sound that accompanied their flight, that roar, ceased. It was replaced by the scream of air.

Both engines had quit. Steber's hands raced over the controls.

They were heavily loaded, and nothing was holding them up. Another aeroplane was just three minutes behind.

The frenzied conversation was something that Slaker later recounted, word for word:

He cried, 'What's happening?'

'Kid, I don't know!'

The two engines were supplied by separate fuel tanks. How could they both quit at the same time? Not because of ice. Look at all the water. The temperature outside was only 57°F (14°C).

'We're dropping down!'

'Kid, what's the altitude?'

'We're dropping fast!'

They were at less than 5,000ft, and Ken knew the map. They were above the Harz Mountains, rising to 4,200ft – the way down was shorter than they expected.

Steber tried one last emergency procedure. If it didn't work, they would have to get out.

Ken raced over the flour sacks and laid out his buddy's parachute.

Steber still couldn't get the plane started. He abandoned the cockpit, so it was unmanned.

Bounding over the cargo, he fumbled with his chute.

Ken tugged at the door. It flew off, and parts of the fuselage went with it, ripped by speed and pressure.

Steber cried, 'For god's sake, get out. This thing is going to crash anytime!'

Ken dived first, into the rain and the dark, pulling the rip cord, the chute opening immediately.

Then he saw 'a million stars'.

5

Later, Slaker would recount:

> That was the last of it. When I came to, I was suffering from amnesia. I didn't even know anything. I was just looking around. Then there was the shock reaction with my brain coming back. And I saw it was daybreak. I had been unconscious for five hours, having landed on my back, my legs paralysed. But luckily in a potato field that had just been harvested. It was muddy. Stupid me: I'd had my tongue between my teeth and cut it halfway through. My head was bleeding. And what now? US intelligence had told us, if you end up in [enemy] territory, 'what you do is up to you'.

He thought about it.

If it were up to him, he would die trying to escape through the Iron Curtain.

Finally, there was sensation in his legs, and he could stand, shake, and get them moving. He disguised his parachute with mud and looked around.

It was just dawn. At the rim of the field was the highland, and the woods – those thick German woods of the Brothers Grimm, dark and otherworldly, where anything can happen. They could be full of Soviet troops.

In the Boy Scouts, Ken had learned that, if he were lost in the forest, he could find his way out by following the tree trunks, because the side with moss on it was north.

The pilot – stunned, wounded, and streaked with blood and mud – staggered through the potato field to the edge of the spruce forest, and parted into its thicket of whorled branches and cones.

He would make his way through the mountains, from forest to forest, from tree to tree. Following the moss, Kenneth Slaker would stride west.

III

THE UNFORGIVABLE

1

On 29 August 1945, Henry Ries took a photograph on his return to Berlin after a seven-year absence. It was of American troops lowering the Stars and Stripes before the US Headquarters in Berlin, its façade fronted by top-heavy Scots pines. Seven helmeted officers seemed tiny. They grappled at the fly end of the enormous flag as it descended. Perhaps they were making a mistake – the unwieldy banner is not supposed to touch the ground. A superior rushed towards the group, one hand outstretched.

The half-obscured building was one of the Nazis' first monumental Berlin projects, built in 1937 on Kronprinzenallee to house a division of the German Luftwaffe – with all the austere classicism of the brief empire. Behind its looming casement windows, the US occupying forces would make many of the most important decisions of the Berlin Airlift.

Henry Ries, 27 years old, was in his US uniform, a military photographer and translator dispatched to Berlin from London. He had had his first substantial meal with his fellow soldiers. His clothes were clean and pressed. In front of this building in the neighbourhood of Zehlendorf, he had also saluted the US flag as it lowered to a trumpet call. Except then, before the flagpole, he turned the other way, towards the Berlin street.[1]

Ries was keenly aware of the space he held between two worlds. Born in 1917 to a Jewish family in Berlin, he was educated there before fleeing the Nazis to America in 1937. Ries had escaped the extermination of his relatives. Seeing his new country's flag dominating the Nazis' old power centres must have given him some satisfaction. But the scene in the other direction was what 'he would never forget', what stayed with him his whole life – he described it as a photograph he wished he had taken.

A beggar stopped before him at the compound's edge. He had only one arm, with which he pulled a rickety three-wheeled cart full of old clothes. Leaning against the conveyance, he dragged his grey cap from his head and examined the asphalt.

Behind the man was destruction — all that had happened to Berlin in Ries's absence. This was not the city Ries remembered. He would write of the strangeness of wandering a place familiar but now destroyed: Europe's largest metropolis reduced to more than 3 billion cubic feet of rubble — a quarter of it obliterated, with large parts unrecognisable. More than half a million apartments were gutted, making 1.5 million homeless. The pre-war population was reduced by half. From the air, the city appeared like crags of egg cartons. From the ground, it was all craters, rats, flies, and it stank. The parks were cut down — even the seats of park benches were stolen for heat.

So much defeat generated gruesome material for the press. Touched with more than a little *Schadenfreude*, Ries's journalist colleagues toured Berlin like a haunted house. Collie Small, writing for the general interest magazine *Collier's* — one of America's most widely circulating — painted a sensational, apocalyptic picture. His city abounded with rumours of babies ground up for sausage and young women hanging from butcher hooks. Famine made zombies of the locals, 'easily confused and frequently wander[ing] uncertainly into the paths of oncoming automobiles'. In schoolrooms, the children did not have the energy to learn. At work, there were industrial accidents. Sex was traded for food. People ate boiled roots, mice, cats, and dogs, and foraged garbage that poisoned them. Berliners without soap reeked as they huddled for warmth, sharing beds. One morning in the Old Garrison Church, the authorities discovered corpses 'sprawled grotesquely on the stone floors'. The coffins had been stolen for fuel. It was the resting place of some two hundred Prussian officers, many of whom fought with Frederick the Great. None of these horrors made the Berliners worthy of compassion, opined Small. Rather, he lamented their alternating self-pity, cut-throat stealing, and everyday betrayals. He wrote: 'for sheer meanness, Berlin is unsurpassed by any other city in the world'.[2]

Ries was not so decided. He described the defeated Berliners passing on the sidewalk as haggard, suspicious, and hungry. But the photographer's feelings were complex toward this one-armed beggar, who would reappear repeatedly in his writings. The two men stood across from one another, the well-fed and pressed American staring directly at the impoverished German who looked only at his feet.³

What a photograph of the scene would not reveal was what Ries was thinking, but we know from his memoirs that he had a lot of questions. He scoured the man, first wondering how old he must be: 35 or 65? He could not tell. Then, harder questions came to the surface – as Ries later wrote, 'questions that popped into my head that have been bothering me ever since'.

What kind of person had the other been during the war? 'Was the old man a Nazi, was he even directly involved in the murder of the Jews?' 'Had he taken part or just watched as Jews were threatened, mistreated, abducted and murdered?' 'What did he know, or did he not want to know? Was I justified in condemning this unknown man? … Or had he perhaps acted humanely?'

Ries ultimately distilled his moment of confrontation with the German into two related questions: 'Who is he?' and 'Who am I?' For both, he was left without answers. He could not pry this information just by staring at the other human being, just as a photograph can only tell so much.

Not having answers 'tormented' the photographer with his own relationship to Berlin. Before him was not an easily dismissible chamber of horrors, but rather the crevasse of identity. In his autobiography, *Ich war ein Berliner* [I Was a Berliner], Ries wrote: 'I realized that I too had once been a citizen of this city and had witnessed the beginning of the disaster before I was "denationalized" … It was not easy for me to remain an observer rather than a judge.'

His widow Wanda Ries, now in a seniors' home at the leafy edge of Berlin, recounted that 'this moment when he saw the one-armed man was decisive. It exposed his two sides: was he a judge or an observer? Henry was a responsible, feeling person. He wanted to know. What did he see? Who was he?'⁴ Ries wrote he did not want to be a Berliner anymore: 'I arrived in the city that I had left seven years earlier, a city that I had never wanted to set foot in again.'

There were a few ironies that spun out from what happened next. The man who never wanted to return to Berlin would stay another five years. First as a conscript in his US Army uniform, he would later make his career of choice in the city as a staff photographer for the *New York Times*.

Ries's time in Berlin made him famous, especially in the German-speaking world. He became *the* photographer of the Berlin Airlift.[5] As he would later say, his success as an artist was 'baptised by the waters of the Spree', the city's river.[6] Ries captured the images that excited both Berliners and the New Yorkers precisely because he saw the city from inside and outside.

As his widow observed, he was connected to his subjects: 'Everyday people were what really interested him. That's where you see the reality.' Although he worked for the *New York Times*, Ries surprisingly did not think of himself as a photojournalist: 'Basically, I'm not that interested in important events. I'm not a news photographer. I'm interested in people.' And yet, it was a news event where he made his mark.

The one-armed man moved on with his cart, and the photographer was left alone until he too left the frame. He would go out into the city he once knew – looking, judging, making new friends, and meeting old enemies – asking if he could forgive the Germans. In the previous fifteen years, he had endured the unforgivable.

2

In 1933, Heinz (aka Henry) was brought to the front of the class.

Hitler had swept to power, and the new teacher was there to teach Nazi Race Theory to students of the Schiller-Realgymnasium.[7] The 15-year-old Ries catalogued the man wearing a swastika on his left lapel. Henry thought he looked Jewish – perhaps even the caricature of a Jew, with his dark eyes and hair. As Ries later wrote, the man had called Heinz forward, wanting 'to explain Nazi-propagated theory using a living subject'.

The two men, one an adult and the other an adolescent, now stood before the class. The teacher indicated his subject: 'Compared to the rest of you, Ries seems to be the best example of an Aryan young man.'

Ries explained how the teacher proceeded to 'point to my straight nose, the shape of my ethnic earlobes, the musical back of the head and similar typically "Aryan" features'. Heinz, after all, was blond-haired, with blue eyes, with a 'name that gives nothing away'.

The classroom was suppressing their giggles. As Ries returned to his seat, he asked if he might add some information to the discussion. Ries was not shy.

The teacher said that he could.

'I am a full Jew,' replied Ries.

The class erupted in laughter. The Nazi was beside himself with anger.

Ries did not last long at the high school, leaving it at the end of that year. Dropping out would have been unusual given he came from a wealthy, educated family that owned a laundry factory and lived behind a Jugendstil glass and wood door on Meinekestraße 12 in the old-money neighbourhood of Charlottenburg.[8] Heinz loved literature, music, and the arts. He had received private music instruction. He ran exuberantly through the city at night, after concerts at the Philharmonie, and owned two expensive Leica cameras, which he'd use to photograph passers-by down Unter den Linden to the Brandenburg Gate. The family attended high holidays but 'felt more German than Jewish' – or 'Jewish without giving it much thought', as Ries wrote – until the Nazis made it something to think about. Soon, there were police visiting, harassing the family, and even sending young Ries to prison without charges for a few nights.

The stubborn father, Max, had come to Berlin from Silesia and was adamant about remaining in Germany, repeating, 'things will definitely get better soon'. When Heinz's older brother, Kurt, decided to leave Berlin for Brazil in 1936, his father smacked him straight across the face. As Wanda Ries explained, 'Max didn't want Henry to leave either – he was very German in this regard: he felt you didn't leave your country. But Henry had been imprisoned and suspected war was coming.' It would be his grandmother, not his father, who would finally give him the money to go abroad.

Unable to study, Ries began to work, joining a firm specialising in the installation of radio antennae on the roofs of Berlin. The firm was staffed by Jewish men who had lost their jobs under the Nazis: 'almost all of them academics, factory owners, civil servants, all well-bred but completely inexperienced in radio technology'. Ries was the youngest.

A series of images, worthy of a series of movie stills, shows the young man balanced on a rooftop trying to install a Siemens antenna. His sleeves are rolled up, and his thirties haircut is slicked at the top and taper-faded at the back and sides. The sloping roof had hooks built in, so a ladder could be attached, to climb up during roof repairs.

Heinz found himself on one of these ladders when one of the hooks broke suddenly, sending him plummeting from the peak: 'The ladder slowly slid down the roof with me until it came to a stop in the gutter. At the same moment when I could reach another hook within arm's length, the gutter gave way.' As the ladder crashed into the street below, Heinz hung from the roof edge until the safety rope was passed to him, which he hooked to his belt.

Ries explained later, 'I climbed back onto the roof. I had been very calm the whole time, but when I was safe, my knees started to shake. My rescuer even had to hold me in the elevator.'

Ries later acknowledged that he'd been lucky throughout his life, even though he did not believe in luck. One can imagine the panoramic view over the pre-war city and the young Jewish man hanging precariously from a roof. In 1937, he left Germany for New York City.

3

Ries wanted to be an American, but America did not make it easy for young Ries.

He departed for New York on 7 October 1937. It was the first time he had ever left Berlin, with only 10 dollars in his pocket, 'two heavy pieces of luggage, a trunk full of darkroom equipment, and two Leicas'. Once disembarked without problems through US customs, he found his way by taxi into the broad boulevards of Uptown Manhattan, with his bags half-hanging out the window, unloading in Morningside Heights a few blocks from Columbia University: Broadway and West 112th.

In his autobiography, Ries described a long night of farewell sex with three different girlfriends:

> On my last night in pre-war Berlin ... Uschi visited me from five to seven and Victoria from nine to eleven. The rest of the night was dedicated to Hazel in her little room at the 'Hotel zur Scala'. The next day, I reached the port of Bremen in a daze, where I staggered onto the 'SS Bremen' – and met another woman!

In New York, when he was introduced to his six roommates in the boarding house he was amazed by the rules: 'We got to know each other in the hallway and the kitchen, but please don't touch! Slowly but surely, I began to miss the sexual permissiveness of the Berliners.'

His widow Wanda told me that some people who read her late husband's autobiography were shocked by his frankness, 'but they are not Berliners. He was a very handsome man who knew how to be convincing. He was a warm, human person who moved others. Women were aware of it. And he was always a more assertive person than me. I was the one always grabbed by life. But he grabbed life!'

American puritanism was the least of Ries's problems. He had to fight to stay in America. The visa with which he had entered allowed him only one year in the country. Henry did not find a way to remain, so he faced the worst possible outcome.

Henry never expected to escape the Nazis as a Jew, only to be forced to apply for another immigrant visa – but back in Germany. He did not think he'd have to face Nazi officers again, who harassed him at the port on his arrival by steamer. Nor did he anticipate his permission to emigrate would be denied by a hostile US Consul in Berlin, who systematically prevented Jews from getting visas (this unsung villain was Avra M. Warren, pilloried in 1958 by the Berlin Chief Rabbi in his testimony to the Holocaust Museum Yad Vashem as the 'greatest misfortune for the Jews in Berlin'[9]). Nor did he expect, exasperated as he escaped Germany a second time, that he would almost be booted off his return boat to New York by a Nazi crew, suspicious he was using the same tourist visa for a second entry. Eventually, Heinz found his way to the US Consul in Cuba and made his successful application to emigrate.

Making a living would also be tough: he sold vacuum cleaners and worked long hours in a sweatshop dealing with scrap metal. Meanwhile, the November Pogrom (Kristallnacht) exploded in Berlin, and Ries watched from New York, thinking how his grandmother, aunt, and little sister were still in the city (his mother had died in 1930). Inexplicably, his father Max had already exited the country with a new wife, leaving the others behind. Getting his sister out soon became a full-time job that cost money and energy. With the help of the Quakers – after what he described as a nineteen-month 'ping-pong game' between the life of a young woman and the infamous US Consul in Berlin – Steffi too finally arrived in New York in March 1941, just a half-year before the systematic deportation of Jews from the Reich. Her brother had saved her life.

America's entry into the war in December 1941 then turned Ries – still considered German by US authorities – into an 'enemy alien'. He had his radio and Leicas confiscated, as they could be used for spying.

He wrote, 'From Ries the Jew in Germany, I was now Heinz the Nazi.' His status prevented him from serving in the US Army despite repeated attempts. Only when he stubbornly, assertively, banged down the door of the Chief of Manpower at the Pentagon in Washington D.C., did the tide begin to turn:

'What's your name?' Heinz? Are you German?', the chief officer asked him.

He explained his situation.

And the chief shouted: 'So you're no God-damned Nazi?'

'I'm Jewish.'

The chief was beside himself, 'But we are crying for healthy young men!'

Ries wrote: 'From then on everything was very easy: on May 18, 1943 enlistment in the army; on May 25 Fort Devens; on June 17: Private Henry Ries becomes an American citizen.'

Dispatched to an aerial photography unit based in Bengal (Ries would quip, 'I was sent to India for speaking such excellent German'), he spent the war stitching together military images for military reconnaissance. It was there that he wrote in a letter to the United States on 21 January 1945 that 'while I am at the subject of photography, I like to mention that I have made up my mind to stick to this type of work after the war ... I always found great difficulty in deciding a future course, wavering between a number of possibilities, never finding a decision. Well, I have made it, and I shall stick to it.'[10]

This was a time when he began to change his identity. Wanda Ries explained to me:

> He wanted to be an American. There was no question about returning to the country. He's drawn a line under that. *Strich*. Then he had been shocked by his efforts to get into the Army and his rejection. Shocked that he had to give up his camera and radio, that they thought he could have been a spy. All this convinced him. And then Pearl Harbor was a wake-up moment. He wanted to fight. He changed his name when he enlisted and wanted to be seen and accepted as an American and accept himself as one. All his life, he preferred to speak English over German. The way he spoke changed in both places: his voice was always lighter in New York, more baritone. And he loved the English language and spoke it without accent. At heart, he was a New Yorker, but at the

back of his mind, you could still find a Berliner – that Jewish mixed with Berliner sense of humour.

This is how Henry Ries donned a US uniform. He thought he'd never have to see the Brandenburg Gate again. But he was wrong. On 29 March 1945, Ries requested a transfer from his wartime post in India. What he did not expect was that the ODI (Office of the Director of Intelligence) would commandeer his language skills to work through an archive of secret Nazi documents, and that he would do this in Berlin.

It was on 29 August that he flew into the city that he 'never wanted to set foot in again'.

4

In June 1945, US troops were detonating explosives through a mountainside at Hallein, Austria. They were looking for Heinrich Himmler's top-secret papers, reportedly buried in the salt mine there. Hallein had been a subcamp of Dachau just over 100 miles distant, and documents were said to have been taken from the main concentration camp and hidden under the mountain before Germany fell to the Allies. That Villa Trapp – a secondary residence of the pedantic, unemotional SS leader (and former home of the singing family) – was 12 miles away in Salzburg supported the suspicion.

After days of blasting, the soldiers emerged into a secret underground room. The walls were lined with large metal lockers containing the papers. These were loaded onto a truck and eventually sent to the Seventh Army Document Center in Berlin.[11]

The thirty-six wooden boxes, Ries explained, 'contained thousands of secret documents, letters, telegrams, orders, instructions and "secret command documents", which revealed the inhuman cruelty of the National Socialist regime'. Ries named them the 'secret library' of Himmler, who had been entrusted with destroying Europe's Jewry. But the ODI treasured acronyms and called them 'HFFH' or 'Himmler's Files From Hallein'.

Henry Ries was required to spend eight months all but literally chained to a desk, translating as two armed guards watched so nothing went missing. The resulting evidence would be handed over to the

Nuremberg Trials. As he told his wife, Wanda, 'It was a remarkable irony of my life to be sent to Berlin because of Himmler of all people.'

Ries's daily routine was sobering: 'I leafed through the documents with incredulous amazement, read them with horror, and translated and evaluated them with horror ... what I read and learned in these meticulous and unscrupulous experiment reports remains deeply shocking to this day.'

The contents were traumatising for the young Ries, himself chased out of Germany, returning to Berlin as if 'a thousand years had passed' in his absence. His wife tells me that he never managed, during his life, to process what he read, especially because he completed this work knowing that his grandmother and two aunts had not survived the war and had been murdered in Theresienstadt and Auschwitz. One letter from the time refers to how 'dear Himmler [is] really haunting me in my dreams'.[12]

The archive focussed on medical experiments conducted on concentration camp prisoners, including forced sterilisation, duress tests involving hypothermia and high and low air pressure, experiments with drugs. Other pages described plundered possessions, transports, and exterminations. Ries was charged too with the translation of Hitler's last will and testament, in which the leader called Jews the 'world poisoner of all peoples'. Ries later wrote, 'If the Führer knew! that one of his "world poisoners" had translated his poisonous madness for the Office of the Director of Intelligence, he would rise from his ashes.'

From his desk, littered with the bureaucracy of mass murder, Ries would then emerge in his US Army uniform into the familiar but unfamiliar bombed-out city. When he first arrived, he was unsure what to expect from Berlin: 'On the afternoon of [my first] day, I wanted to see the centre of my hometown again; I didn't yet know that this centre no longer existed.' A walk towards Brandenburg Gate led him straight to a shooting: a delivery van failed to stop at a checkpoint, guns were fired, and Ries witnessed a bleeding woman climbing out of the vehicle over a dead driver. But Ries continued to take walks around familiar but now transformed places, searching for close ones and family at old addresses. These were not just macabre pilgrimages – rather Ries hoped to deliver care packages his father, now in America, had sent him for his old friends. Most of these parcels remained stacked, unopened in his office as he discovered how many of these individuals had been murdered.

In his autobiography, Ries described how he had 'two pairs of eyes': the American ones that saw 'shattered streets and buildings' and the Berlin ones that saw the 'distraught people'. He imagined running into a former lover from before the war: 'How aged and how crippled would she look now?' Back at his US Army residence – where a warm bed and good meal waited for him – he would write to a more recent girlfriend, Dorothy Haller, still in India:

> Thrown into this boiling pot of mental stew is a gravy of emotional strain. It doesn't help to say they, the Germans, had it coming, no more than to think that things will eventually get straightened out after the necessary time of adjustment. Of course, they deserve it, at least a good part of them ... but this doesn't prevent me from feeling pains seeing hungry people, crippled people, diseased people, worried people; all framed by ruins, all smelling of filth. And there remains the special problem of the few who were left of the six million, the even fewer Jews who hid or returned to Berlin ... the past will never be blotted out by stomachs filled with all the [care] packages from the States, nor will gratitude solve the problems of the present.[13]

In his biography, Ries would later editorialise this letter, softening his position and adding the line 'Revenge doesn't help anyone'.

Ries's observing and judging soon turned inward, and he played with alternative realities. He questioned what kind of man he would be if he were not Jewish, if he had been an average Berliner who stayed and collaborated – someone 'chosen to be a superman', 'allowed' to serve the country, 'allowed' to die in Stalingrad, 'to carry out orders that violated all laws of humanity'. Soon, Ries 'became aware of this profound relief', that he had been 'able to remain a "human being" by "the grace of my Jewish birth"', knowing all the time that 'in order to experience Jewish descent as a "blessing" in this sense, one had to have survived, and not many of the European Jews managed to do that'. As he wrote to Haller at the time:

> The longer I study Himmler's secret documents, especially the translation of the descriptions of inhuman experiments on people, the more I realize how lucky I was to have left Nazi Germany in time – and not just because of the impending physical destruction, but also because I did not become a victim of moral annihilation.[14]

Ries's friend and former deputy editor-in-chief of *Die Zeit*, Werner A. Perger, would later argue against Ries's 'healthy scepticism' about himself, saying he doubted Henry would ever have made 'a real career within the system' because he had too strong a 'feeling for justice and structural opposition towards any authority ... all the gifts you needed to resist'. And yet, Ries dwelled on the counterfactual and claimed for himself the 'right to be the "mild judge"', not just of others but also of himself.[15]

Wandering into an U-Bahn station, Ries took the metro West, emerging at Zoologischer Garten next to the Tiergarten in the British zone. The enormous public park was denuded of trees for firewood. He snapped a photograph here of a man tilling the ground to plant food. From here, it was only a short walk to Budapester Straße, the address where his murdered grandmother had lived when Henry was a child, a street that fronted the south gate of the Berlin Zoo. Years before, he had watched the elephant in its enclosure beyond the fence from her high window and asked his 'Omutti' why the elephant had two trunks, the second tucked under its belly. Only a handful of the animals had survived, most found dead in their cages in pools of black blood – along with two SS officers killed in the gorillas' enclosure.[16] Now, his 'grandparents' former apartment was buried under rubble and ashes'.

From here, Ries continued his dispiriting flânerie West, past the gutted shell of the Kaiser Wilhelm Memorial Church, to the remains of Berlin's erstwhile luxurious boulevard, the Kurfürstendamm. Nearby, 'My parents' house ... where I had said goodbye to Steffi, Fräuchen [his nanny] and my father seven years ago, was also just a ruin.' Walking this once leafy, comfortable neighbourhood of his childhood, Ries finally reached the corner of Pariser and Sächsischer Straße, close to Olivaer Platz, where his sister had lived with his grandmother and Aunt Hedi in the years following Henry's emigration. This is where the women had been dragged from their homes and transported to the camps in 1942. Before him again, he found only rubble.

In his uniform, the young photographer climbed up into the destroyed lot and got down to sift through the ruins of their last address with his hands. And there, he pulled back, astonished to have found something – an object he had made himself before the war.

His widow, Wanda Ries, tells me, 'Henry was careful with symbols, but what he found made him happy.' He later wrote: 'As if by a miracle,

I discovered a photo I had taken of my then 12-year-old sister, Steffi.' It had survived the tragedies. It was not damaged, just as his sister had also survived.

Ries remembered standing there and how the light over the rubble grew dark, and he felt surrounded by the ghosts of his family, and how 'only the young face of my sister could wipe away the inferno of this shadowy world for a few moments'.

IV

ENEMY OF MY ENEMY

1

Ruth Andreas-Friedrich's friends had started disappearing.

In 1948, she was a writer for a Berlin journal, *Lilith: The Magazine for Young Girls and Women*. Although not very political on the surface, Ruth had during the Second World War been at the centre of a Berlin group called Onkel Emil, which had forged papers for Jews, sheltered them, and stored their goods, while she had distributed dissident leaflets and defaced buildings with the word '*Nein*'.

At the time of the Airlift, she was writing an advice column called '*Benimm dich, Geliebte!*', or 'Lover, Behave Yourself!', with tips for young women (she had spent the war writing similar journalism for another women's magazine, *Kamerad Frau*). Much of her advice was for tenderfoots: 'The first kiss was no promise of marriage!'; 'I have had many men tell me that they hate nothing as much as a clingy girl!'; 'No sex in the family, and not at work!' But even *Lilith*'s stock content – a serialised novel, fashion tips, and recipes – contained a glimmer of the times – how desperate life had become for Berlin women.

The patterns for clothes were simple ones for those forced to make their own from curtains or tablecloths. A chronic lack of choice was evident in recipes you might not have chosen off a menu: 'Vegetable Pudding' was a dispiriting concoction of pea pods, turnips, potatoes, parsley, sugar, vinegar, salt, pepper, and fat. The serialised novel 'Everything Will Be Better!' set a different tone than the articles about demographic issues: one about how women outnumbered men since the war – 'Anything but three-way marriages!'; another surveying whether you would still have a child today. The answers ranged from: 'No!',

'No!', 'Not now!', 'No!', 'God help me!', 'Today, that's crazy!', 'Oh god, not today', 'No and never!', 'Three times no!', 'Later', to one 'Yes' – because the child was on its way in three weeks in any case.

The magazine tended to avoid current events, but women remained in focus as independent and political agents – to set a good example for younger women, who were now emerging out of a generation of Nazi sexism. A cover showed a girl alone in a kayak charting her own course. An article read: 'When both work, he shouldn't be the king of the house!' A forum called the 'Lilith Parliament' discussed what women could contribute to the German constitution. And the magazine explored how, if men made war, why was it that women had not been able to prevent them?[1]

There were specific men the author feared. Privately, Andreas-Friedrich was worried about being absorbed into a Stalinist system that, just like the Nazis, made its intellectual enemies disappear. Because – as she wrote in her diary – her island of West Berlin was now like a 'watchtower in the Soviet surf', with 'three hundred kilometres of "Eastern ideology" separating me from the border' with the West. Living in the city was 'a dance on the edge of a volcano', but sometimes 'the crater opens up and swallows one dancer or another.'[2]

2

Dieter Friede sat at home in the British zone on a Saturday, when the telephone rang. During the week, he wrote for an American-licensed newspaper, *Der Abend*, where he was known for being an Anglophile, a liberal, Soviet-critical, and close to the Social Democratic leaders surrounding the elected Berlin mayor, Ernst Reuter.[3]

A physician he knew, Peter Dau, who lived and worked in Friedrichshagen, in the Soviet zone, was on the receiver and explained that a mutual friend had been in an automobile accident. He was lying wounded on the premises of Dau's surgery, where his residential apartment was also located. Friede should come as soon as he could to help.

It was 2 November 1947, and Dieter Friede left his home in the West and made his way East. And then he vanished.

Two days passed, and his cleaner was extremely worried about the disappearance. Then a man knocked at her door. The stranger explained to her that he was Friede's colleague from *Der Abend*. Friede had been working late in the office. He had left some papers he needed on his desk at home. The man was there to fetch those documents.

The cleaning lady eyed him, worried. Something was wrong. Was it the man's unusual accent? She said he could not come in. Her employer, after all, had not just been working late – he had been missing for two days!

Friede's friends did not know where he was. The case was in the national newspapers and even the British press within the week. The Soviets were queried, but the commander of Berlin's Soviet zone, General Alexander Georgievich Kotikov, replied that 'he was not aware of any such case, but that he would order an investigation'.

The case stayed cold until 13 March 1948, when the doctor Peter Dau fled to the West with his wife and offered a full confession about the events, recounted in *Die Welt*. He told the paper that he had been used several times by the Soviet secret police for small jobs, but then they came to him and demanded he call Friede. Dau said he resisted: 'But there is no injured mutual friend in my surgery!' The Soviet agents replied that there would be 'unpleasant consequences' if he did not make the call.

The secret police, meanwhile, set the trap. They sequestered Dau in another room. Ready for the bell to ring, they waited in the reception of his surgery. The doctor never saw Friede when he arrived. The last thing Dau saw was from his window: a limousine pulling up close to the front door on the pavement and later driving away.

The Soviets denied the arrest had occurred for almost half a year, but suspicions that they were responsible nonetheless made it a touchstone for thousands of other disappearances. The government in West Berlin collected the names of more than five thousand who had disappeared in ways like Friede: people caught in traps, people bundled into cars, people who never returned home from work. This fear of being abducted, of becoming one of the 'missing', sent a chill – as it was meant to – through life in the Western zones, where the borders felt porous. Living in the four-power city made its inhabitants vulnerable to the caprices of any one of the occupiers. The chill especially affected journalists, like Ruth.

3

Life in the Western zones was also brutal, something observed by visitors like Hans Hartmut Weil, who had been expelled in 1935 from his German school for anti-Nazi activities and eventually ended up at Cambridge University.[4] As a doctorand, he travelled to the British zone, including Hamburg, in 1948. His travel report was later published in the student newspaper, *Varsity*. Moving into a flat for a few nights with everyday Germans, he spoke of the:

> contemporary German smell of sweat, home-grown tobacco, and dust of ruins. Ramshackle furniture, almost no linen, no hot water, window broken, food mainly black bread, undefinable jam, doubtful cereals, stale brown sugar, substitute coffee, occasionally, if finances permit, a black-market treat ...

The young man even tried to live on German rations for a few days and felt 'increasingly fatigue and loss of memory. How inhabitants are still able to work after years of this diet remains a miracle.'

Many, especially young, male travellers, engaged in dark tourism. They wanted to see what it meant to push a society to the edge – to fall from the heights of Central European civilisation to somewhere closer to Mad Max. In the American zone, the future editor of New Directions press, James Laughlin, penned a series of occupation poems. Like Weil, he remarked on his first page on the stench: 'hunger's dirty smell'. Men searched through rubble for bits 'appraising worth or use', faces were so shrunk he was afraid to imagine the rest of their bodies, Germans who ate well were prostituting themselves, and a hungry man masturbating into a pan claimed spunk tasted good fried. The occupying Americans joked that the Germans should enjoy their 'hunger-punishment'.[5]

Despite such reports from the British and American zones in 1948, it was not difficult to understand why so many Germans preferred them to the Russian sector. In the Western zones, you were more likely to be hungry than afraid.

4

German rancour towards the Soviets went deep. During the thirteen years under the Nazis, Germans were educated in vociferous anti-communism. Then, 80 per cent of Germany's more than 5 million military dead died on the Eastern Front. With defeat, Germany lost a quarter of its territory to the East, absorbed by Poland and the Soviet Union, with 12 to 14 million refugees subsequently flooding into rump Germany.

Nurse Käthe Eckstein reported how, on 30 April 1945, during the Battle of Berlin, as shells bombarded Schöeneberg's Elisabeth Hospital, Russian soldiers barricaded a section of the ward to rape the sister nurses and female patients alike. In the morning, Eckstein found that section of the hospital had been bombed, and the burnt bodies of the dead women and Russian soldiers with their 'buckles, pistols and charred remains of boots' were intertwined in the iron bedsteads.[6]

As the Red Army pummelled and occupied Berlin in the war's end battle, its soldiers raped a hundred thousand women. The Soviets then spent two months in the Reich's capital before the Americans and British joined its occupation, focused on stripping economic assets to bring home as reparations. They even hauled off equipment from the Western zone, from the firms AEG, Borsig, Osram, Siemens, including the total dismantlement of the West's largest power plant. When Soviet propaganda promised the Germans 'reconstruction', the irony was not lost on the Berliners who joked: 'reconstruction begins with deconstruction'.

Many Germans, homeless in firebombed cities, saw themselves as victims, even as they had many victims of their own – the systematic murder of ethnic Slavs, Soviet prisoners of war, Roma, disabled people, sexual minorities, those who resisted occupation across Europe, and 6 million Jews. American journalist Curt Riess reported on German reactions when the Western Allies occupied their sectors on 4 July 1945, and how the West did not share this victim narrative:

> At best, they [the Western troops] did not give a damn about the Berliners. This indifference was a fearful shock to the people of Berlin. After what they had suffered from the Russians, they thought they qualified as allies of the Western Powers … [but] the Western Allies did not arrive to liberate the Germans from the Russians.

It should have been no revelation that they would be treated like humiliated pariahs by the West – for all the same reasons Ken Slaker wanted to 'give the Nazis hell'. The Allies who had firebombed their cities would give them hardly enough food to survive, and subjected them to rules of non-fraternisation with Western soldiers and the stern terms of the occupation. The relationship between the four powers was decided in Potsdam on 1 August 1945.

The Allies agreed in treaties to a programme sometimes called the 'Five Ds': denazification, decentralisation, democratisation, deindustrialisation, and demilitarisation. How each power interpreted these Ds was diverse in practice. Nazis needed to be re-educated, but the Allies had different notions of 'denazification'. The East was brutal and thorough: they hunted old Nazis relentlessly, along (conveniently) with class enemies, placing them in former concentration camps, while in the West many old Nazis eventually were seen as useful in getting the economy back on its feet, as they rose to positions of power such as in the police and government. Decentralisation was achieved through the spreading of power in Germany among many cities. 'Democratisation' also had different meanings, as the Soviets' use of the word in their 'democratic republics' suggested.

But the crucial term was demilitarisation, connected to deindustrialisation. After the horrors unleashed on Europe, the Allies did not want to see Germans in uniform again. Germany had been – to their minds – responsible for two world wars within two generations, with more than 100 million dead. Demilitarisation was connected to the German economy. Initially, the Allies agreed that a way to prevent Germany from having military means was to render it useless industrially, and the Americans floated the Morgenthau Plan to agrarianise Germany, taking it back to the Middle Ages technologically. The plan was shelved to promote new markets and trade with America through the 1948 Marshall Plan. In the Soviet zone – with the stock removal of whole factories – the focus remained on punitive reparations.

In short, the Germans were to be sorted, scattered, retrained, and castrated militarily – hardly a bedrock for friendship. These principles were codified in the directives of the Allied Control Council. But the Soviets followed these directives most severely and to the letter. It was the Soviet interpretation of these principles that most Germans would come to fear. The Soviets brought their ideas for a collectivised economy, education and property, as well as pervasive surveillance by state security. Germans understood that the USSR meant to continue stripping their country of future potential and that living under Stalinism meant many continuities with Nazism – authoritarianism and state terror.

The Germans of this still unified but occupied country were ruined. They resented the well-fed soldiers of the victors – from both West and East – who paraded in their streets. In the ashes of a cataclysmic war, to turn these Germans into the West's friends seemed hardly imaginable.

And yet, the Germans feared one of the occupiers more than the other.

5

In her 1948 diaries, Ruth returned continually, terrified – in the lead-up to the Airlift – to Dieter Friede and other sudden disappearances: 'Dieter Friede. Dieter Friede! The mystery of his disappearance has been cleared up, meanwhile, in a dreadful manner.' On 22 April, she wrote: 'Three of our acquaintances have disappeared in the past couple of days.' On 24 May, she wrote:

> The list of people we are mourning becomes longer and longer. This may be no criterion. It may be there are circles in Berlin or even in the Eastern Zone who are missing none of their friends. Under the Nazis too there were many who didn't miss anybody, who knew nothing [sic] of concentration camps and arrests, who didn't know any Jews or politically persecuted persons.

And she thought about those Friede left behind:

> Somewhere in the West lives his daughter, Christiane, a child barely 10 years old. 'I hope Papa had a chance to kill himself before they killed him,' the child said, weeping upon hearing the news. Something is very wrong when 10-year-old children talk about 'killing oneself.' The world order should not let it happen. But the world order ...

It was not that Andreas-Friedrich, in her fear of the Soviets, was uncritical of America. She knew first-hand that Americans demanded their zone's journalists conform, writing: 'America announces a comprehensive propaganda campaign against communism. All American-oriented newspapers and magazines in Germany are to take part.' And there was cause for personal resentment: on 23 August 1945, she was in the back seat of a car when her partner, the first post-war conductor of the Berlin Philharmonic orchestra, Leo Borchard, and co-conspirator of the Onkel Emil group, was shot at a US Army checkpoint when their car failed to stop. There was a whistle. Some instinct made Ruth duck as she felt the bullets exploding the rear window, scraping the back of her head. The ammunition blasted into Borchard, blowing out his face from behind.[7]

Despite its self-interest and punitive attitude towards the Germans, the West remained for Ruth the lesser evil. She summed up why Germans objected to the Soviets:

> So why do we resist? Because we are afraid. We have been afraid since 1933. First of the Gestapo, the concentration camps, and of running risks to express anti-Nazi opinions in Hitler's Germany. Then of the GPU [Soviet Secret Police], the concentration camps, and of running risks to express anti-Soviet opinions in Soviet-occupied Germany. We distrust this new call for peace because in it we discern the fatal future refrain of annexation. Intimations of lock and key. The tiny dot of Berlin locked in by the vast Soviet zone. All those countries under Soviet influence have been cut off from the Western world since 1917. And in those countries, anyone who does not conform to the will of the rulers disappears behind bars.

The story of Dieter Friede was not over and occupied the press's attention, as *Die Welt* reported: it was 'repeatedly at the centre of Berlin's political life'. And the story returned on 10 June 1948, at the height of the crisis leading to the Airlift, with *Die Zeit* reporting that Friede was in Russian custody and had signed a (presumably forced) confession that he was an American spy.[8] The Eastern newspapers for their part said that Friede was guilty: 'Dieter Friede stated directly that he had passed on espionage material about the deployment of Soviet troops, which had been collected by his party friends in the Soviet occupation zone ... defending him is no longer possible, since he himself has admitted his espionage activities.'[9]

The man was first sent to Sachsenhausen, then shipped to gulags in Russia, and would only be returned to Berlin in 1955.

V

THE REVOLUTIONARY

1

During the First World War, Ernst Reuter walked into a Berlin beer hall – the tables heaving with Pilsner, Helles and Hefeweizen beer – to commiserate with his Marxist comrades. Here, the designs for the new world were being argued, the idealists gesticulating boisterously over their tankards.

In the corner was Leo Jogiches – a revolutionary who would be assassinated in 1919. His Spartacus League group had named itself after the Roman slaves who revolted against their masters. They said they were anti-war, for social equality, economic justice, and democratic rights and freedoms.

Ernst found himself sitting stiffly between the activists and was introduced to Jogiches, who would later write of Reuter, 'He comes from a completely different background to us – a real German schoolmaster!'[1] It did not help that Ernst was teetotal. One comrade remarked they'd have got along better with him had he sometimes had a beer.

At the time of the Airlift, journalist Curt Riess would pen similarly disappointed first impressions of Reuter: 'I had expected to see a revolutionary. The man before me was a rather portly, bourgeois-looking person.' Reuter's wife explained to the journalist that her husband 'had no eccentricities, not having time for them'.[2]

Reuter's demeanour had everything to do with his upbringing. Knowing where Reuter went later in his life raises questions: is it surprising that West Berlin's leader – *the* pivotal German figure of the Berlin Airlift – became a Soviet commissar? That he later embraced the Americans?

Which was the real Reuter? The man who fell in, or out of love with communism? Can a revolutionary look like a 'schoolmaster'?

2

Ernst Reuter spoke with a North German accent. Born on 29 July 1889, he grew up in the little town of Leer. It was a river port of twelve thousand souls leading to the Ems estuary and North Sea, in Eastern Friesland close to the Dutch border. *Leer* means 'empty', just as *die Leere* means 'the void'.

But there were things in Leer – everything here was flat and canal-bound:[3] the landscape of Reuter's childhood looked a little like a Ruisdael painting, with turbulent maritime skies, reflective water-logged fields, and windmills. This is where he and his brothers would pass time, rambling or on bicycles, the young Reuter drawing medieval buildings.

This bucolic wandering was an escape because behind the wall of the family's large garden, and in the parlour of their sober red-brick house, was a world that Reuter could not wait to leave. His father was a crusty old monarchist and teacher at the nearby Prussian Naval School, who fostered a home life reduced to: King, Bible, nation, discipline – good Prussian values.

In the Ernst Reuter Archive in Berlin, there's a photograph of the family – mother, father, four sons – in about the year 1900, seated in their spacious garden. The father reads the newspaper, and a son looks over his shoulder. The mother looks immobilised in a lace collar, like a Frans Hals oil, before the white tablecloth and silver coffee set on a tray. She makes the children's clothing that looks like uniforms to save money – the young Reuter later will not be able to attend his graduation ball because he does not have the right clothes. The wooden chairs they sit on are ones that they repair instead of replacing. Only the family is present – no visitors – as they are isolated socially in the town because being social costs money, and the capital is needed for the children's education. The older brothers – nationalistic like their father – will become Nazis. Reuter meanwhile stares directly into the camera. As Reuter's own son Edzard, born in 1928 in Berlin, would later say, 'He was not bourgeois.' The family world was not his world, and he needed out.[4]

Being the best student in his class (except in physical education) didn't help Ernst win friends, as he was dubbed a *Streber* – pushy and overambitious, a swot. But his achievements earned him a ticket out of little Leer to study first in Marburg and then in Munich, where he learned about the workers' question. His studies of Kant led to practical socialism. In the city of Bielefeld, he got a job as a tutor, only to be fired when his lawyer employer found out a little too much about his emerging politics: catching him out wearing the garb of a communist ('floppy hat and Jesus sandals') at a concert and discovering Reuter was organising his domestic staff to go to political lectures.

Reuter's sudden dismissal left him homeless and destitute. When he approached his family for help, the honest, duty-bound son couldn't hold back why he had lost his job, writing:

> I cannot help the fact that I am a socialist. This a conviction that has been strengthened in me through long and difficult work and for which I have fought the hardest and fiercest battles. And you will also say to yourselves that such a conviction, which one has fought for cannot be abandoned ...[5]

Comradeship! Shared prosperity! Equality! And an end to the old order and its superstitions. The parents, however, were angry: his mother, the daughter of a Lutheran pastor, walked him around the family home in Leer pointing out the portraits of his ancestors, telling her son he should be ashamed.

Meanwhile, Ernst wrote how his father thought him 'morally half-depraved', and reacted to his (now lost) letter: 'Dear Father, I have never felt as much pain as I did in the letter I received from you this morning.' In March 1913, he penned, 'Dear Father, when I spoke to you about my innermost conviction, about my idealism, that I could not and did not want to deny ... I did not even think of denying it. I only wanted to appeal to your best side and hoped that you would understand me.'

This understanding he would not get. Reuter's parents would not support him financially or morally. So their son retreated to a North Sea island with a copy of Marx's *Das Kapital* and returned to tell them – no doubt to their shock – that he was going to Berlin to work for the socialist cause with the Social Democratic Party, or SPD. From a cheap room in Berlin-Halensee, in a city he called 'nasty', he would spearhead an anticlerical, antimilitaristic society, which would be banned before he was sent to the front during the First World War.

A revolutionary was born. Except the young Reuter didn't look much like a revolutionary. No matter how radical his politics he became, something from Reuter's family education had rubbed off. Just as he didn't have friends in his early days at school, he'd be later known for his coolness and moral rigidity, that some might confuse with, or even call, arrogance.[6]

3

On 10 August 1916, the young Ernst Reuter, 27 years old – badly wounded, shot through both thighs – was taken prisoner.[7] Lying in a hospital south of Moscow, he had time on his hands, so he learned the enemy's language. He penned a little sign and put it on his bunk: 'Reuter's Office', because he soon became the translator for the German prisoners of war. They came to him to find out what the Russian newspapers were saying about the war – and their socialist organiser eventually sent letters to the Provisional Government in Moscow arguing for better conditions. Meanwhile, Ernst's leg bone grew back crooked so that, for the rest of his life, he would have to use a cane, only adding to his schoolmasterly demeanour.

This did not prevent him from being put to work in a mine. But when the October Revolution came, Reuter joined his comrades in rising and seizing control of the facility, and – as the Russian speaker among them – he became their leader. In this way, the German prisoner-of-war-radical-Bolshevik-Prussian caught Moscow's notice.

It was convenient for Ernst Reuter that no photographs from his Russian period surfaced during the Airlift when he became the poster boy for anti-communism. In 1950, he was even on the cover of *Time* magazine. As part of the Comintern, or Communist International, Reuter rose to power alongside the Soviets' other foreign protégés, Béla Kun and Josip Broz Tito. He had joined the glitterati of the revolution. Invited by Lenin to the Kremlin in April 1918, he was appointed as the leader of a Soviet Socialist Republic and its half-million population. It was the Volga-German Autonomous SSR with a majority German ethnic community along the river, in its capital Saratov. Reuter would report directly to the Soviet Commissar for Nationality Affairs, a man named Joseph Stalin.

Ernst's industriousness now had a chance to shine, and he was a brilliant organiser, zealously meeting grain quotas set by Moscow. But Reuter also resisted some of Moscow's desires, for example to eliminate medium and large farming estates, something Lenin likely forgave because (perhaps apocryphally): 'Reuter is the only commissar who sends us bread to Moscow!'[8] Stalin would later be responsible for ethnically cleansing the German population during the Second World War.

But when the 1918 November Revolution erupted in Germany, Reuter was not about to sit on his hands in his villa in Saratov. With a letter of recommendation to the German Communist Party (KPD) from Lenin himself ('The young Reuter is brilliant and clear in the head, but a little too independent'), Reuter slipped across the border using a sledge.

In Vilnius, he picked up false papers for 20 marks and made his way to Berlin with his experience in the USSR to become the German Communist Party's, the KPD's, General Secretary. Except the 'independent' young man didn't do very well in the KPD, and its leaders thought he should be sent back to Moscow 'for a cold shower'. Reuter objected to fundamentalism, and the power and interference of Moscow surrounding the so-called March Action of 1921, when a communist splinter group staged a revolt in German regions without the KPD's authorisation. Reuter wouldn't congratulate the rebels, so he was removed in December 1921 and expelled in January 1922, with Wilhelm Pieck succeeding him, who would later become the first president of East Germany.

The break with Communist internationalism was permanent: Reuter had no truck with disobedience, fanaticism, or the long arm of Soviet meddling in German affairs. Reuter joined the SPD, becoming the head of Berlin's transport network (or BVG) and public utilities. Under his watch, the city's subway system doubled – and the job suited his personality that leaned towards logistics and planning.

Another cloud hung over Reuter in the period, and it was the question of whether he had been responsible for deaths in the Volga during the Soviet Civil War. Refugees from the Volga-Deutsch region denounced him as a butcher, and Reuter even faced trial in Germany, only to be acquitted because the court decided it had no jurisdiction in the Soviet Union.[9] Documents from the Volga show a murky picture: on one hand,

Reuter tried to maintain order in the violent atmosphere of revolution and counter-revolution to prevent robberies of grain in the countryside. He may have protected civilians by quelling unrest.[10] But, working in the little-explored documents of the Saratov city archive, researcher Victor Herdt also recently found a death warrant, dated 22 October 1918, on which is the name of the head of the committee, one Ernst Reuter.[11]

4

Ernst Reuter was skiing in Switzerland with his family in 1932.

Arosa was an unlikely meeting place for old lefties. Although the spa town – rimmed by snow-caked mountains, its seat in a deep valley – was an idyllic escape from Nazi trouble brewing in Germany.

There, Reuter met for the first time a German émigrée, Margareta (Greta) Burkill, and her husband, John Charles Burkill, an English mathematician at Peterhouse, Cambridge University. As it happens, Greta's father was a socialist newspaper editor and SPD member of the Reichstag who knew Reuter.[12]

Little did Reuter know on the slopes in Arosa that a year later, he'd be chased out of his post as the mayor of the city of Magdeburg and from his position as a Reichstag deputy for voting against Hitler's Enabling Act. One can imagine Greta's shock, back in protected Cambridge, to learn that the man she had met on her ski vacation now sat in a Nazi concentration camp and that his son and mother had watched his arrest in tears from an upstairs window. One of the earliest memories of Reuter's youngest son Edzard is when the Gestapo came and stuffed his father into a black limousine.[13]

At that time, international pressure could still get the Nazis to release high-profile prisoners.[14] From England, the Quakers – led by one Elsie Howard – first organised Reuter's rescue from the camp in 1934. The next step was to bring Reuter and his family to England. Greta became personally responsible for this operation in March 1935. When he left Germany, Reuter packed one bag, an out-of-date passport, and had 10 marks in his pocket.

Because Reuter had trouble finding work in England, when a suitable job opportunity became available in Turkey – first as advisor to the Ministry of Economics, and then of Transport – he took it. But

Britain, and specifically Cambridge, remained a fixed point in Reuter's itinerant life. For one thing, his older son Harry stayed in Cambridge for his studies, living with the Burkills, who treated him as a family member. Burkill and Howard, meanwhile, helped save two thousand children from the Nazis through the Cambridge Children's Refugee Committee, part of the Kindertransport, making the university town and nearby a sanctuary for both them and academic émigrés. And although Reuter was shocked by how terrible his son's German became – and that he eventually naturalised – he nonetheless felt 'enormous gratitude' towards Britain.[15]

Reuter spent eleven years with his wife and younger son, Edzard, in Ankara, where he learned the language, wrote several books in Turkish, and adopted his trademark fez. It was there, as the war wound down, that he caught the attention of the American Office of Strategic Services (OSS), the precursor to the CIA.[16]

Reuter had been to America from Berlin in 1929 to look at its transport and infrastructure, returning with admiration for its Fordism. The OSS started studying and meeting with Reuter in 1944 as they weighed which individuals to install in political positions in post-war Germany. Reuter passed muster as an anti-Nazi, according to his interviewer, and he ticked several boxes – the first of which was that he had been a victim of fascism.

But the Allied forces on the continent had their doubts about Reuter. In 1945, the authorities in Vienna were certain he was a Marxist and refused his entry. In Potsdam in August 1945, meanwhile, President Truman refused to meet any German democrats, and the State Department's position was not to deal with German émigrés. On top of it, they worried Reuter was 'nationalistic and anti-Russian', an 'inconvenient' personality, someone who was sure to worsen cooperation with the Soviets. Reuter, for his part, 'loved the Russian people as much as he detested the Stalin régime' – or so said his successor as Mayor of Berlin, the anti-communist Cold Warrior and future chancellor, Willy Brandt (who himself became a US intelligence informant in the period of the Berlin Airlift).[17]

Eventually, Reuter circumvented the Americans. Again, his connections in Britain came into play; he slipped into their zone instead.

5

The Reuters knew Germany was destroyed but, in the words of Reuter, 'it is one thing to know it, and another to see it', as they wandered around the wreckage of Hamburg and Hanover. Only in October 1946 was he welcomed back to Berlin, where from 5 December he resumed his old job as a city councillor for Transport and Utilities. But the former post would not satisfy a man who had already been the mayor of a major German city and ruled an SSR. Even though it shocked him, he wanted to be the leader of Germany's old capital. It's 'crazy here. Everything is crazy, the ruins of the city, the ruinousness of the people. Everything only works a half or a quarter.'[18]

But did Berliners want him? Willy Brandt recounted that 'his younger party friends could hardly remember him. The communists, on the other hand, regarded him with understandable hostility, since already in 1922, he had broken with them and had given them no quarter ever since; they described him as a "Turk"'. Reuter found himself caricatured with his fez hat prominent in the newspapers. Berliners' attitudes to Turkey he found provincial, and he even noted that he 'often had the feeling that Turks among whom I lived were more naturally democrats in their lifestyle and attitude to life than the Germans are'.[19]

Nonetheless, the Berliners did embrace him, nominating him as SPD candidate for mayor on 24 June 1947. But the Americans were correct: the Soviets did have a problem with him. Kotikov, the commander of the Soviet sector of Berlin, vetoed his election, meaning Reuter became only de facto mayor (Louise Schroeder took the reins), and he carried business cards: 'Elected but unconfirmed Mayor of Berlin'. As Reuter wrote, 'the veto was not justified, could hardly be justified, but the right of veto is independent of any justification'.[20]

The Soviets leaned on him to sign a declaration that he would work 'closely and exclusively' with them, but Reuter refused. (Hadn't the Soviets already had the experience of working 'closely and exclusively' with Reuter, and was not this precisely the reason they considered him a traitor?) For his part, the man knew the Soviet Union too well to have anything to do with their version of socialism, especially under Stalin, his old superior. He didn't hesitate to call German socialists yearning for unity with the USSR 'quislings', and he preferred the option of the Western Allies because at least there was the possibility of pluralism:

'A state in which there is only one party is not a human society, but only an ant organisation in which all true values are suffocated, killed.' He wrote in May 1948 that Stalin's 'regime had nothing more to do with socialism'. In June, he said the Soviets wanted to make them 'slaves'. 'We lived under such slavery in Adolf Hitler's empire. We have had enough of it. We're not going back!'[21]

But did the Western Allies know who he was? How far did the man, who would become the partner of the free-market West, remain a revolutionary at heart? He was not convinced of the good intentions of the Americans, writing in 1948:

> The fact that we have to wage this fight with the help of allies such as the Americans is historically determined and does not need to blind us to the fact that not everything that glitters is gold there either.

Evident too was that he wanted a socialised economy in Berlin of 'planned control and management' rather than the free market. In a 1947 interview, he called himself a 'socialist and democrat'. Social democracy promised him 'another human type', the 'creation of an alert, lively and shaken political consciousness among the people'. For this reason, he despised the right-leaning Christian Democrat establishment, focused on accumulation and wealth: 'We occasionally forget about helping others and, above all, forget that no person, no people, can live on bread alone in the long run.' Add to this a touch of nationalism: on 27 April 1947, he wrote of wanting a 'unified Germany independent of any foreign power', but this is an idea he would eventually need to sacrifice.[22]

On the eve of the Airlift, Kenneth Slaker and Henry Ries – soldier and victim – had heartfelt reasons why the West could not be friends with Germany. They had experienced crushing violence, the loss of close friends and family. Meanwhile, Ruth Andreas-Friedrich and Ernst Reuter distrusted the West who had occupied and punished the country, and feared the Soviets to the core.

Everyone was resentful. It was not a harbinger of friendship.

But the vicissitudes of Reuter's biography had convinced him of one thing: that only by working with the Americans and British could he free Germany from the most brutal terms of its defeat, the squalor of everyday life. It was the only way to avoid domination by the other power he knew best and so most dreaded.

Only an emergency could throw these peoples together. And when it came, 'red' Reuter seemed the last man to enchant the Americans – the fire of the Red Scare had already been lit at home in Washington. But he would profit from what he and the West shared: a common enemy. This put aside any other reservations in their close cooperation.

Reuter was poised to become the Americans' best buddy in Berlin, the hero of the city's resistance. He would become known as the 'father of Berlin'.[23]

WINTER–SUMMER 1948

VI

THE BREAKDOWN

1

For the first issue of *Lilith: The Magazine for Young Girls and Women* of 1948 a reporter approached a queue of women waiting to buy goods from a store. She had two questions for them: what did they expect from the year to come, and did they have any special wishes?

Fräulein Scheunenstuhl replied, 'What I expect from the New Year? Nothing new will come of it. Desires? I have none. Why should I have any when I know they won't be met?'

The reporter then turned to the next woman in line. Her name was Fräulein Ingetraut Radola, and she was an office clerk. She remarked that it had been three years since the war ended, and hardly anything had changed, 'I think everything will stay the same as it's been. *Na*, and I wish for myself that at least once in the week I could eat until I'm no longer hungry. And I'd like to be able to travel like I did before.'

Fräulein Erna Ladewig was a seamstress, and she replied glumly to the two questions, 'I see things black. Very black, and say only: it's going to get worse. *Jawohl*!'

And so, it went down the line. Everyone replied in the same vein, with the same Berliner brusqueness: 'It's all *Quatsch*. Nonsense.' 'Nothing gets better.' 'Nothing will be different in the New Year.' 'It will all go on like before.'[1]

Except, we know what they didn't – that 1948 would not be the same as other years.

2

The Soviet Military Governor Vasily Sokolovsky was great at weddings. In public, the survivor of the purges and veteran of the Battle of Berlin appeared as the archetypal soldier. Curt Riess described him 'as if poured from a mould', 'an instrument ... more accustomed to receive orders than to issue them'. But in private, the 6ft, chain-smoking farmer's son was a drinker and partier. At a wedding in 1945, President Eisenhower convinced Generals Clay, Zhukov, and Sokolovsky to compete to see who could throw themselves to the ground most often without getting hurt – vodka must have been involved. When Lucius Clay's son was married in Berlin shortly before the Airlift, he invited Sokolovsky, who was among the last guests standing at the end of the night, singing army songs with the American soldiers.[2] The Belarussian was so accommodating that even the starchy British Military Governor Brian Robertson sometimes felt 'taken in by my liking for General Sokolovsky'.[3]

The Soviets and the West at first worked well together in Berlin, a honeymoon that soured into the Cold War. The story is often told that the Soviets were the sole aggressive partner, encroaching spatially on Western interests, but the West also enraged the Soviets, breaking promises by splitting Germany into two. At the Potsdam Conference, the four powers had agreed to a united country with institutions for 'Germany as a whole'. However, on 1 January 1947, the British and Americans announced close cooperation between their zones, creating the 'Bizone'. The Soviets maintained that Germany should instead be under all four powers, as agreed in Potsdam's protocol.

As one might expect, the marriage's breakdown was also economic. The Americans wanted to invest and create markets through reconstruction: its apex was the Marshall Plan, drafted in June 1947 and in effect from 3 April 1948. Worth hundreds of billions in today's coin, the investment was meant to stabilise Europe, extend American hegemony, and push back communism by creating capital markets. The Soviets saw it as a Trojan horse and prevented their occupied territories from accepting Western investment. Instead, they insisted on dependent, contributive satellites, and on draining Germany's resources for reparations.

Ernst Reuter knew what it meant to suck a land of resources when he shipped all that grain to Moscow. But German inclusion and prosperity within the Marshall Plan would not be feasible unless there was a new, strong currency to replace the devalued Reichsmark. Lucius Clay insisted that the West could not recover without this new currency.

However, any plan to introduce a currency in the country's West and West Berlin would radically separate it from the East. Currencies bind or divide. You cannot have one financial system with two unequal currencies. The Soviets spent months negotiating against the move, resisting too because of what a powerful Deutschmark introduced in West Berlin would do to their economy. Without restrictions, it would flood their zone and make their currency worthless.

On 20 January 1948, General Clay presented the reform to his Soviet counterpart. Surviving Stalin meant anticipating the leader's reactions. So, when Sokolovsky took one look at these new currency plans, he believed they were just a prelude to a West German state. He was right. In an interview, the Soviet later summarised the currency reform as 'the direct cause of the origin of the so-called Berlin crisis ... This was the biggest step taken by the Western occupation authorities along the road of accomplishing the splitting of Germany.'[4]

These economic conflicts were closely entwined with geopolitical ones across Europe. President Truman's speech to Congress on 12 March 1947 outlined what would become known as the Truman Doctrine: the United States would not stand by to allow democratic countries to be taken over by authoritarianism. Truman was responding to the height of the Greek Civil War, as the Americans assisted the Greek government against the communists – and to intelligence that the Soviets were active in expanding their influence not just in south-east Europe but also closer to Berlin.

When Czechoslovakia was lost to a communist coup from 21 to 25 February 1948, halting a Soviet march West became urgent. As Willy Brandt described, the 'Communist coup in Czechoslovakia was a rude awakening for many "leftists and liberals" and a "tragedy"'.[5] Already on 15 March 1946, Ernst Reuter, writing in Ankara, had suspected that Germany would be the ultimate chess piece between East and West, a possible demarcation line.[6] Prague became proof of that prescience.

The creation of a separate Western German state was the subject of talks in London at the Six-Power Conference, to which the USSR was not invited. They agreed on 23 February 1948 – with events in Prague under way – to move towards creating a West Germany. This was anathema to Stalin. A diplomatic note from the Soviets on 6 March 1948 protested the bilateral meetings – they were outraged that the West was acting unilaterally – and a 12 March official memo complained that the West planned to turn Germany into a stronghold against the Soviets.[7]

On 9 March, Sokolovsky had been recalled to Moscow to discuss the matter with Stalin. He came back with orders to put the squeeze on West Berlin. A few weeks later, on 26 March 1948, the German Communist leader in the East, Wilhelm Pieck, also had a fateful conversation with Stalin: he proposed to the Soviet leader they do their best to remove the Western powers from Berlin. Stalin was recorded as replying: 'Let's do it.' It was a daring chess move.[8]

So, the dynamic emerged: maturing Western plans for their German state met with corresponding Soviet geopolitical obstruction. From now on, the Soviet response would be harsher. As Clay had written in a memo on 5 March – after Prague and London – there was already a 'subtle change in Soviet attitude which I cannot define but gives me a feeling that [war] may come with dramatic suddenness'.[9] And on 20 March 1948, communication broke down as the Soviets left the Allied Control Council in protest.

Berliners were sensitive to the West's broken promises. Ruth Andreas-Friedrich wrote that the Western powers did not have the moral high ground as they destroyed the agreements made in 1945 to keep Germany united: 'One must admit that, judging by outward appearances, the moral justification rests on the side of the Soviet Union. They demand what we should desire. Unity, joint currency reform, withdrawal of occupation forces and peace with Germany.' But she too was happy to tear up treaties if the Soviets' red sea did not come flooding her American sector of Berlin.

At the Berlin level, the Soviets were simultaneously waging the ideological battle in miniature, ridding the East's city administration of anyone who was not a loyal communist. The Berlin Kommandatura, the four-power authority that ruled the city, still forced into this grudging marriage, mirrored the international struggles as they squabbled.

At the height of the crisis that would precipitate the city's isolation, on the morning of 15 March 1948, Major Kartmazov, a Soviet delegate of a Special Investigation Committee, paid a visit to an American barracks. The Soviets were building a case against the Americans that they were violating the terms of German demilitarisation by training a secret army composed of old Nazis called the Industrial Police, or 'Black Guards'.[10]

These men in black offer, in miniature, a snapshot of the breakdown of trust and friendship between the West and the Soviets at the eleventh hour. Minutes of their meetings are the transcript of an impasse, how the final crisis felt to the former friends in the room: the mood of miscommunication, distrust, secrecy, and self-interest as they bickered about the original terms of their union, the five, agreed-upon 'Ds'. The story of the Black Guards would be the dark prelude to the Americans' pragmatic enlistment of German labour during the Berlin Airlift.

3

Andrews Barracks in Berlin-Lichterfelde was originally a centralised place of military instruction built by the Prussians in 1874. The *Hauptkadettenanstalt* was crammed with classrooms, barracks, a mess hall – everything you needed to train an army. Under the Nazis, it was taken over by the Waffen-SS, who built an Olympic pool guarded by naked statues in oversized fascist aesthetic. The Americans' legacy was more discreet, such as the poolside 'no running' signs in English. When the Kommandatura's investigative delegation arrived, the inscription *SS-Leibstandarte Adolf Hitler*, 'The SS Bodyguard of Adolf Hitler', was still inscribed over the colonnaded entrance of the brick façade.

Kartmazov was accompanied by a committee composed of all four powers who had met earlier that day in the American Club. He wanted to discover whether the United States was violating agreements by rearming Germans. He heard they had been given guns – carbines, and five rounds of ammunition for each. The British delegate, frustrated by the Soviet allegations, had suggested, 'Let's not waste time, let's go and see what these men are doing' to prove to the Soviet member that there were 'no secrets'. The Soviet member agreed, jumping at the opportunity to interrogate the force's members.

Take the Soviet perspective for a moment and imagine working with partners determined to tear up the post-war peace. The Americans appeared on the offensive. They might even be building an army – formed from the former enemy – to attack you under your nose. On a visit to the base of this secret army, what questions might trick the on-duty soldiers into divulging information? Would they be the same as those Kartmazov asked?

Two German 'Black Guards', part of a training programme, were waiting for the Soviet in a classroom.

'What are you learning at the moment?' he asked, wondering if they were training to be US soldiers.

'First Aid for accidents.'

The course being offered that day was innocuous.

'What are your duties?'

'To guard that nothing is stolen, no fire breaks out, etc., and if this happens, to report it immediately.'

'When do you use your guns?'

'Only if our lives are in danger.'

Not to use them in battle against the Soviets? No, this was not a question to be asked directly … Not getting very far, the Soviet asked to interview the German on-duty guards, also in the same classroom. But the American delegate, Major McGraw, refused a proper sit-down interview, explaining: 'We said we would check some men *on post* and see exactly what they are doing and how they are doing it.'

Kartmazov saw this as obstructionism and quipped, 'It seems very difficult to answer questions if the person is standing on post.'

'That is the only place to interview him,' replied McGraw, obstinate.

'I would like the opportunity to examine all the classes taking place', insisted the Soviet. More must be taught here than just 'First Aid' – or 'Post Regulations' and 'Personal Hygiene'. What of their military training?

'There are no other classes being held at the moment.'

'I would like to look at the empty rooms where classes take place,' he pressed.

'This is the only classroom that is used.'

Outside the building, they then stood in the enormous courtyard of the barracks, where the Soviet asked the guard on post, 'What are your functions?'

'Guard duties.'

Again, the answer was maddeningly innocuous. Kartmazov asked him about his course of study, what he had learned from the Americans in terms of using weapons – when and how to use them – and then queried slyly, 'Have your instructions always been given to you in one classroom, or have there been several classrooms?'

Now, the American's ears perked up, and he interrupted Kartmazov because he had already asked that question. The first 'statement stands', and the guard was not to answer.

Kartmazov replied again that it was difficult to hold the discussion on the spot like this. But the other committee members told him that he'd better get his questions over with, as they accompanied him to the Engineers' Depot.

There, Kartmazov asked a German guard whether he would ever salute a superior American officer? Were they expected to act like soldiers would with their superiors?

The guard replied that he would not.

He asked if there was a hierarchy of ranks, as in the Army.

The man said yes.

'Have you done any military work?'

Again, the US officer interrupted: 'Is the Soviet member trying to infer that the work of the Industrial Police is military work?'

So, Kartmazov changed tack, 'Have you been in the Army or done police work before?'

The guard replied, 'Yes, we were all German soldiers.' He had been a lieutenant in the Wehrmacht for twelve years.

Did they always wear this black uniform, with this helmet – the one that gave the guards the name the 'Black Guard'?

The German replied he always wore it because he had no other clothing.

'How many of you are there?' the Soviet asked.

Again, his US chaperone intervened and did not allow the German to answer. He told Kartmazov: 'We have already given you an answer to that question.' To ask again 'was equivalent to suggesting that Major McGraw had told an untruth'.

4

On 20 April 1948, *Neues Deutschland* reported that the Free German Trade Union, the FDGB, offices in the French zone had been destroyed. The doors had been forced, and there was 'indescribable havoc' inside. The furniture was smashed, the posters prepared for International Workers' Day had been ripped and soiled, and 'even the telephones were torn from the walls'. The trade union suspected a 'political burglary' because an election protocol was stolen while objects of value had been untouched.[11]

Over the coming weeks in late April and early May, reports flooded in of incidents involving the US Army and their police, causing fear and disturbances.[12] US soldiers fired guns, scattering German passengers waiting for the arrival of an S-Bahn train in Schöneberg. US soldiers shot from apartment windows. A uniformed US soldier dragged a 40-year-old woman to her apartment and raped her. Also in Schöneberg, 'two uniformed members of the US Army attacked 54-year-old German Arthur Engelmann from Wilmersdorf Achenbachstraße 18 and knocked out his teeth'. At a tram stop in Kreuzberg, members of a communist youth group [Freie Deutsche Jugend, or FDJ] were attacked by 'twenty ruffians armed with knives and brass knuckles'. An 81-year-old in Charlottenburg was physically assaulted by a man in an American uniform. And at Friedrichstraße station, a railwayman was kicked and punched 'for no reason at all'.

But who was really committing these crimes? On 24 April, General Kotikov – known for his amateur collection of insects and who at first denied responsibility for Dieter Friede's disappearance – embarked on a four-hour speech about the West's more significant crimes. He described police brutality in the French sector as 'pogroms'. He said the American zone was an 'asylum for spies'. He spoke of the arrest and deportation since 1945 of forty thousand communists from the US zone – a number designed to make the five thousand who disappeared in the West look insignificant. But his most serious accusation was that the Americans were building an 'independent police force for their sector, effectively independent from the authority of the joint Berlin police headquarters ... the political past of these people is quite dubious. In several cases, it has been established that they were members of the Gestapo, Hitler's police force, and the SD.'[13] As a 5 May article in *Neues Deutschland* elaborated:

> In addition to the report of the raid on the Kreuzberg office of the FDJ, we can say that [a raid in Mitte] was carried out by members of the Industrial Police set up by the American side. The accomplices were easily recognisable; they wore black uniforms, brown ties and American boots.

The article went on to explain that the 'Industrial Police are apparently recruited for the most part from mercenaries of the former SS', with a 'tradition of terror against progressive and democratically-minded people'.¹⁴ The uniforms' colour would have recalled the Italian fascists in black shirt, or *camicia nera*.

On all the front pages of these newspapers were descriptions of an unrelenting 'civil war' against trade unionists and socialist organisations.¹⁵ These newspapers also curiously shared that, in each conflict, the uniformed individual perpetrators – part of this shadowy group called the 'Black Guard' – always escaped, remaining unidentified.

The escapes might be explained because all the newspapers – such as the *Berliner Zeitung* and the Communist Party newspaper, *Neues Deutschland* – were from the Eastern zone and subject to Soviet censorship.

Goebbels wrote in 1941 about the 'principle that when one lies, one should lie big, and stick to it ... even at the risk of looking ridiculous'.¹⁶ German journalists were well-practised at propaganda: thirteen years of Nazi rule had given them ample training. Their reports became ever more vicious as the 1 May celebrations of International Workers' Day grew nearer.

Western papers responded to the East's tactics – and Kotikov's 'four hours of tirades' – often light-heartedly. As for the so-called pogroms, a French member would later say he'd never heard of such a thing, and the British joked why there wasn't a flood of refugees 'from our sector to the "Paradise of Freedom", which is the Soviet sector?' In the newspapers *Telegraf* and *Der Kurier*, the story of the man losing his teeth transformed into parodies of 'unruly American soldiers roaming Berlin and biting elderly German women, including a fifty-seven-year-old in the British sector'. (The British Commander General Herbert quipped that if such an incident had occurred in his sector, he would have to worry more about getting bitten than about the Russians.)¹⁷

However, it would be inaccurate to say that the Berliners trusted the Western media to tell them the truth. Newspapers in the US zone were not free, as only politically suitable outlets were given licences by the American censors.¹⁸ Radio entertainment was tied up with the US authorities. Celebrities such as German singer Günter Neumann worked closely with William F. Heimlich, a US spy chief in the Office of Military Government and the director of RIAS, to create what the latter called a 'think tank with humour'. But Neumann worried his show on RIAS, *Die Insulaner*, broke the first rule of his craft, which was not to produce state-desired cabaret.¹⁹ Polls taken in the American zone from

January 1947 to July 1949 showed that only one in twenty-five Germans thought their news to be more reliable than what the Nazis had provided them during the war. They understood that American officials directed the press and entertainment they consumed to exalt American democracy and its way of life.[20] American zone journalism *aimed* eventually to be free, but it wasn't quite yet – and the British also censored.

In early May, two communist newspapers were banned in the British zone, something the Eastern papers were delighted to report. *Telegraf* reminded *Neues Deutschland*, in turn, that they also could not sell their paper in the East: 'For although there is no official ban, the packages of papers have been seized, or burned, the sellers put under pressure. Together, these measures are equivalent to a ban.'[21]

5

There are pages of minutes from the meeting rooms of the Kommandatura between July 1947 and June 1948, just before the Airlift began.[22] A table was positioned in a meeting room. The delegates, dressed in the uniforms of the four powers, represented either the Public Safety Committee, Deputy Commanders, or Commanders of the Allied Berlin zones.

When asked, the Americans explained to the Soviets that General Eisenhower had authorised the Industrial Police in 1945, with funds from the US Treasury. The 590 to 650 individuals hired through the Civilian Personnel Office were solely under US control. The Americans said they guarded military sites.

The Soviets went through their list of questions, many of the same ones Kartmazov had asked at Andrews Barracks. Do you arm them? (With carbines owned by the US Army.) How do they learn to use them? (On a ten-day course.) Are they housed in barracks? (No, they live at home.) Do they have military ranks? (No, they have roles such as 'relief inspector', 'superintendent' and 'watchman'.) Do they have military discipline, such as saluting their superiors? (No.) How are they paid? (A small salary and one meal a day.)

But the question that made the Americans nervous was the next one: Who were these men? What were their names and backgrounds? Here, the Americans wavered. They did not want to disclose this information and had already asked the men to prepare anonymous questionnaires about their pasts instead. This was to prevent the Soviets from doing background checks. The Soviets were indeed annoyed that they could not 'check up on some information' since the names were blacked out. So, they asked if the men were former German soldiers.

Americans: The men are not hired on the basis of their past. The hiring office has abided by denazification rules.

[Interjection by the French]

French: It would be impossible to recruit men who had not been in the Wehrmacht!

[Interjection by the British]

British: We agree. It was disclosed that the majority of the personnel had previous military training in the Wehrmacht, but this could be said of almost all the adult male population of Germany!

Soviets: Denazification rules? Are these men former Nazis?

Americans: We are not denazification officers. Talk to Special Branch.

Soviets: According to Law 209, denazified Germans cannot be in the police.

Americans: These men are not policemen.

Soviets: Is this an armed force?

Americans: No.

Soviets: Yes.

Then the Soviet delegate stood up at the table and turned to the others in the room, aghast, and intoned, 'Do you not see the danger in rearming Germans? I do not wish to suspect the intention of the US authorities but consider that it is not possible to trust the Germans.'

6

For months, a friend had written to Ruth: 'Do what you can to get out of Berlin ... If you wait much longer it may be too late.'[23] But for many Berliners, not leaving was 'a matter of pride'. Ruth wasn't so sure. She felt like a traitor when she checked the options for a quick escape. But getting a seat on an interzonal train was difficult. And the Soviets had revoked permits for departing Berlin by car.

Would the Americans stand up for the Germans, their old enemies? General Clay, Ruth wrote, had said he would 'open fire if necessary'.

But then she asked: 'Do we really want another war?' 'If only one could penetrate the future with X-rays!'

★★★

Ruth sat on a tram going to Moabit in the British sector. Next to her was a woman with a shopping bag, which she handled as if she would spill something.

'I'm on my way to see some friends,' the woman said. 'The Russians supposedly have cut off the water supply in Moabit. I want to go over there and bring them some water. So at least they will be able to make some coffee.'

Ruth peered into the bag and saw it full of water in reused bottles, normally for seltzer and vinegar.

Ruth wrote in her diary, 'I look at the woman and think: We must stay. We must not desert people who carry water for coffee from Charlottenburg to Moabit.'

7

The US member defended himself.[24] They were dealing with 'distorted facts and falsehoods' because the Industrial Police had never been used for 'raids, to terrorize people and to make arrests', or for any purpose 'in the US Sector other than to guard US property and to protect it from theft and fire'.

He looked over at the Soviet, and suggested something else was going on, that 'the constant repetition of false charges … is simply an attempt by the Soviet delegation to hide what went on in its own sector'.

How else could he explain this all-out assault to defame the US sector in the Eastern press as 'a rubbish pit of crime, a centre of kidnappings' with former SS men in its police force? After all, the Western powers had demanded an investigation into Soviet kidnappings of political dissidents off the streets in the other sectors – something the Soviets refused.[25] The British view too was that 'most probably the Soviet action on this question is in the nature of a counterattack against … complaints that had recently been made against them'.

When confronted with the question of Soviet kidnappings, Kotikov replied: 'What is going on in the West is much more dangerous!'[26]

8

On 1 April 1948, Ernst Reuter, Berlin's 'unseated mayor', and his family moved into a 'little cottage',[27] as he wrote, deep in sedate Zehlendorf in the American sector. It was an area with broad streets, trees, lakes, and eventually the Free University he would help to establish in December that year. His house had a steep peaked roof and an austere white façade you might find in a Dutch painting. With its sobriety, traditionalism, and 'small garden with a lot of fruit trees' — where he was photographed with his wife Hanna and now university-aged son Edzard — it was a place where his parents would have felt at home. On 22 April 1948, Reuter wrote how he spent 'hours quietly enjoying the garden terrace. You wouldn't believe how peaceful and beautiful the world can be even here, if only you always got around to enjoying it.'[28]

Because Reuter was always occupied. The man joked in his letters that he had no trouble being 'active', something he shared with General Clay — but now he was particularly busy, as he wrote on 27 April: 'no period of my strange life with its ups and downs can match that of last year'. Because at the edge of the suburban calm of the bourgeois house of the former Bolshevik were the roars of the bear whose orders Reuter once followed.

There had already been a hint of the struggle to come. On 24 January 1948, a night train had left Berlin for the Western city of Bielefeld. Passing through the Soviet zone, it stopped for an inspection and was detained for eleven hours. In the morning, the bleary-eyed British passengers were allowed to continue on their journey, but the Germans were returned to Berlin 'on the grounds they carried insufficient documents', according to British Air Ministry files. Over the next three months there would be similar events. It was the beginning of using traffic as a weapon.[29]

An accelerating conflict was outside the walls of Reuter's little garden, where he'd have liked to have cultivated his private life but could not. During the first days of April, the time of Reuter's move, two British lorries and ship and barge traffic finding their way through canals and rivers to the city were told they did not have the proper papers. The next day's trains from Hamburg and Munich faced improbable bridge work. The Soviets gave a litany of excuses: problems with repairs, traffic issues, documentation. And then, it was not just supplies or civilians that were affected but also troops: the Americans attempted transporting armed soldiers from Helmstedt to Berlin, but they too were returned.

Now that the military had been rebuffed, a counter-reaction was in order. Increments were leading to the bang. The American governor, Lucius Clay, responded with an air operation, which would be known as the 'Little Lift'. Air corridors were the only transport path enjoying existing arrangements with the Soviets, and between 2 and 4 April, twenty-four aeroplanes brought in 200 tons of materials. This foreshadowed the dramatic Airlift some months later.

The Little Lift ended in a tragedy: the collision of a Soviet plane with a British one on 5 April, killing fifteen at Gatow airfield. The Soviets issued an apology for their pilot's risky aerobatics, but were meanwhile analysing how long the West could use the air corridors to feed themselves. On 17 April, a Soviet cable claimed that supplying Berlin from the air would be impossible.

Reuter's correspondence was of a man worried.[30] He met with city officials on 15 April to complain about travel restrictions, concerned that 'the Berlin economy will not survive such a regime ... every Berliner knows what it would mean if our economic life were cut off from the West.' In a private letter, he wrote that the situation in Berlin was like 'sitting in a kind of witches' cauldron'.[31] And to an English friend, he hoped the Western Allies would learn to have a relationship with the Berliners finally, 'to overcome the still existing remainders of a subaltern, purely military treatment of the population ... by replacing them by a more productive, real co-operation on the basis of which many positive results can be achieved'. He wanted to persuade them that 'Berlin is well worth a mass, and that Berlin is not a city like any other one, and an essential centre of political life in and about Germany.'[32] He needed to convince the West of the necessity of Berlin's survival outside the Soviet zone.

From the American side, the governor, Lucius Clay, realised the situation was becoming drastic enough to consider sending Allied family members home from Berlin. He eventually rejected the idea because it 'would lead to a hysterical reaction and drive the Germans in droves into the supposed safety of Communism'.[33]

Mid-June would see the crisis explode. Trains were now routinely stopped at the border, and the bridge over the River Elbe to Magdeburg was closed on 15 June, just days before the new currency was introduced.

The Soviets confirmed the political breakdown by leaving the Berlin Kommandatura on 16 June.

Ernst Reuter said that the currency reform was shorthand for everything else: 'Who has currency, has power.' It was about what political, moral, and economic system they wanted to live with, and how the German economy should be put back on its feet despite all the crimes committed.[34]

Meanwhile, each of the Soviets' steps was a calculated response to the Western monetary threat. As a US official noted: 'There will be a vast upheaval: it will be like a bomb under the economic structure.' The currency plan was not nuclear but, as far as economic warfare went, it might as well have been.

The Soviets were poised to react.

VII

CRISIS

1

In early June 1948, Ruth didn't know what to do with years of savings of Reichsmark notes. It had been announced that there would be a currency reform. But when would it happen? Would it extend to Berlin? She did not know whether her money would be worthless. Or if she would be allowed to trade her notes for new ones. And, in that case, how many? At what exchange? How much would she get?

She and her housemate Heike sat in their apartment and decided that it was better to have goods you could trade than Reichsmarks.

Heike suggested that maybe 'this pile of paper will still buy us some kind of junk, while tomorrow it might be worth no more than some scraps of paper barely worth using for wallpaper'.[1]

Junk was the right word. There wasn't much left in Berlin, and only for outrageous prices. Everyone had the same idea.

And so, the two went shopping. Or foraging. As Ruth wrote in her diary, they were

> inclined to stockpile toys, bulky kitchen utensils and ugly lamps ... six kitchen knives that do not cut, six tin spoons with edges that do, a useless soap dish, four wooden ladles full of cracks, two lamps without sockets or switches, but with nightmarishly patterned lampshades, and in spite of all, six tubes of cement toothpaste, six crumbling tubes of lipstick, and toys – enough toys to open a toy store.

These were desperate times. But soon their investment looked rather good indeed, as prices escalated precipitously. Historically, Germany had a sore spot regarding inflation – it nearly broke the Weimar Republic – and Ruth watched with alarm as 'incredible prices are paid for scarce commodities. One pound of strawberries for twenty-five marks, one pound of cherries for twelve marks', 'twelve pounds of coffee at twelve hundred marks a pound. [One man's] savings from three years of work'.

Coffee became a gradient for the day-by-day escalations. From 1,200 marks per pound on 11 June, the price increased to 2,000 marks three days later. Another two days passed, and it was 2,400 marks.

Inflation, uncertainty. Ruth wrote how 'the throng turns into panic, the fever into frenzy. To invest, to hoard, to pocket, to divest again.'

Soon, there was nothing left to buy. The two women now sat in their apartment looking at their sharp spoons and cracked ladles as if they were goods of the best quality. Storekeepers were holding onto their goods to sell for promised hard currency. Shops were all suddenly 'closed due to illness … temporarily closed due to lack of supply … "Sold out" signs posted on the glass doors of the stores are spreading like typhus.'

All this was stressful, and Ruth made her way to a bar. But here too one couldn't even get a drink: 'Beer – sold out, spirits – sold out, matches, cigarettes, tobacco – entirely out of the question!' Ruth hung off the counter and begged the barman she knew well. She had been coming to this bar for years.

Only because I know you, he obliged. And she paid 40 marks for a single cigarette.

2

Heike suggested that the two women get some fresh air on a walk, because things were getting quite tense.

They found themselves strolling along the River Havel near the beach at Kladow on a sunny June day. Enormous trees branched from the banks. The Havel ran so slowly it appeared a vast lake. It was a Sunday, and, as Billy Wilder understood in his film *People on Sunday*, going to the lakes, rivers, and forests that surround Berlin was more than just a weekend ritual. There was something primordial about the views to the waterways. The tree canopies overshadowed the news of the moment.

Ruth asked Heike if she would like to take out a boat. Ruth was 'looking longingly at the cool waves of the Havel'.

Heike nodded, and they rented a canoe that had a name: *Klein aber Mein*. Or 'Small but Mine'.

The women hesitated: the little boat looked like it would sink. But, no matter, they were soon floating in the river, looking out at the forests and beaches from this new perspective: 'rushes and pines'.

The pastoral was then interrupted. There was the sound of shots fired. Ruth turned to Heike and asked, 'Are we, properly speaking, in the English or the American sector?'

As it turned out, they were in neither of them. The bank to the right was in the British zone. To the left was the American, and just ahead was the Russian.

'And what about the Havel?' asked Ruth.

It belonged to all three. But Heike pointed to the brass letters on the boat's hull, 'When in doubt ...'

Ruth wrote in her diary:

I'm a bit overwhelmed by the symbolism of it. I see the narrow arm of the Havel. The fragile canoe in which we are floating along. Rocking pitifully between the world powers. 'Small But Mine', a nutshell in the current. If a storm came up, we would capsize. We can only hope that the weather holds.

3

On 17 June 1948, Henry Ries found himself at Helmstedt, the border between the British and Soviet zones, as a Red Army guard approached.[2]

He was sitting in his 1940 Chrysler, the car that he loved. Ries, having started in February 1946 as a photo reporter for the *OMGUS Observer* (the official weekly of the Office of the Military Government, United States), was within less than a year (from 27 January 1947) zipping around the continent as the *New York Times* photo correspondent for all of Western Europe. The 30-year-old wore his status well, with a tailored, wide-lapelled zoot suit and hair slicked back, to cover stories as diverse as the Olympics in St Moritz, the travails of Jewish refugees in Vienna, or Italy's first post-war elections. On his return to Berlin, he was acutely aware 'almost daily about tensions between the Soviet and Western Allies in Berlin ... Four victorious powers become two rival camps. Rivals become opponents. Just one wrong move and opponents can become heavily armed enemies!'

The Soviet guard approached his car window, and Ries rolled it down.

'Don't drive. The motorway's out of order,' he was told.

Ries replied to the soldier with a cool look of scepticism, and he turned his Chrysler around. Except he knew the Soviets had been blocking barges and train lines, interfering with traffic, and he wasn't about to put off his trip to Berlin. Instead, Ries drove north, found a side road and a ferry to take him across the Elbe, and made his way to the *kaputt* motorway, which was not broken, and without any trouble coasted the four hours to Berlin, throwing himself exhausted into the bed of his Berlin apartment.

The next day, on 18 June 1948, Ruth wrote how everyone was 'glued to the radio' for the announcement about the new money. Whether you could use the old marks and, if so, what the exchange would be: 'The announcer clears his throat. We hear him breathe and the rustling of paper. "The first law enacted by the military governments of the United States, Great Britain and France to reform the German currency takes effect on June 20. Devaluation ten to one. The new currency is called the Deutsche Mark."'

The new banknotes were flown in by plane, alongside grenades to destroy the secret cargo in case the Soviets downed it. Goods had been removed from the shelves in Berlin, with merchants anticipating they could soon sell them for hard currency. And then, with the arrival of the new notes, suddenly the shops were full of hoarded goods. The currency reform was the 'starting gun of *Wirtschaftswunder*' – the Economic Miracle in the West. That was if you had money. Many people stood before the full stores and gaped.

Each West Berliner could exchange only 60 old Hitler Reichsmarks for 60 new Deutschmarks (DM) – those circulating in Berlin were marked with a 'B' that was known as the 'Bear' mark. And as soon as the currency was introduced, 90 million unconverted Reichsmarks flowed into the East and threatened its economic collapse.

The Soviets scrambled to respond. On 23 June, they introduced their own currency. They did not have time to produce new bills, so they stuck 'wallpaper marks' on the old ones. Three currencies were now circulating: Bear-marks, Wallpaper-marks, and Reichsmarks. The Soviets forbade the use of the Western currency in all the zones, a move not accepted by the Western allies. The Western currency gained in value, as the Soviets foresaw, while the Eastern currency and the old bills plummeted.

The USSR's response could not be just monetary. In this situation – Soviet accords with the West broken, the East's economy in a tailspin – there needed to be a robust response to the West's unilateral moves.

Ruth and Heike were now back in their apartment, observing the currency chaos outside their door. And Heike predicted a blockade.

She said, 'If they're clever, they will close the border. Otherwise, they'll be up to their necks in Western currency and old Reichsmarks.'

On 23 June, the Soviets announced: '*Infolge einer technischen Störung an der Eisenbahnstrecke ...*' 'Due to a technical fault on the railway line ...' traffic would stop.

Everyone knew there was no technical fault and that the USSR authorities always preferred a false excuse. Perhaps they were thinking too about Lenin's words: he who rules Berlin, rules Germany; and he who rules Germany, rules Europe.

4

On 23 June, shortly before midnight, lights extinguished when half of the city disconnected from the Golpa-Zschornewitz power plant, located in the East. In the early hours of 24 June, road and rail traffic between West and East halted, and then also ship traffic. Berlin's isolation had begun, although its duration was unclear. There had been many interruptions throughout the spring. The Berlin newspapers wrote headlines about currency, not about a blockade. Only with hindsight would the public look back and say: yes, that's when it all began.

Ruth wrote in her diary:

The reprisals have begun. In diplomatic language they call them sanctions. 'Sanctions' sounds nicer and less brutal. As of this morning, the Soviets have cut the supply of electricity to the Western sectors. No radio, no light, no electricity for cooking, which means – like so many times before – no way of heating up a little water for coffee. Our brick stove, from 1945, has been dismantled. Heike prepares a breakfast of bread and soaked prunes. By tonight we definitely have to find some candles. But with what are we to pay for the candles?

In their executive ether, the Soviets were not thinking about two middle-aged women's kitchen candles. They felt justified and exalted in their reaction, as Sokolovsky would later tell *Soviet News*:

> The Soviet occupation authorities were compelled to introduce restrictive measures on communications with the Western zones in order to protect the economy of the Soviet zone and Berlin from the influx of the valueless old currency from the Western zones.[3]

Apparently, his staff rejoiced when these restrictions began, thinking they might finally force out the West, with a landlord's stratagem of starving them of fuel and electricity. They took it for granted that it would work and were startled when the Airlift began.[4]

On 24 June, Reuter addressed 80,000 Berliners at an SPD rally in the Hertha stadium in working-class Wedding. The unseated mayor had never relied on written notes.[5] This allowed him to speak directly to the audience. Reuter's oratory was clearly enunciated. But it also had a hypnotic, sing-song quality – syllabic and full of internal rhyme – that blended the sermons of his Lutheran upbringing with the fervour of the October Revolution. At this rally, he made clear that the Berliners wouldn't become the Soviets' 'helots' as they had been under the Nazis.

Reuter began gravely: 'We all know that today here in Berlin, on this 24 June of the year 1948, we find ourselves in a crisis in our city, which will ultimately decide our future fate.' Speaking of how 'Russian imperialism' took Prague, he insisted, 'Berlin will not be next!'

Reuter told his audience they must 'raise their voices before the whole world' and 'state clearly what is at stake'. He defended the new currency because 'without good, clean money, no country can have a proper economy. No one is as dependent on clean money for better or worse as the workers and employees, the working masses of the people.' Meanwhile, in the East, the Soviets had stripped Germany of its wealth. Reuter was too much of a nationalist to accept plunder.

The elected mayor's project was a social democratic Germany, not an appendage to an empire. He compared the Nazi concentration camps to Soviet ones and said, 'We know the connection between Communism and National Socialism.' Like in Nazi times, 'Berlin can only live, Germany can only live, if it learns to fight for its freedom, for its rights and for its self-assertion and not to sell its birthright. People of Berlin!'

But not everyone wanted to stay in Berlin. The French agitated against the idea. The Brits worried the Americans would make unilateral decisions. But General Clay believed that a pack of dominos would topple across Europe if they gave up.

The view was not shared unanimously back in Washington, with General Omar N. Bradley wondering if they shouldn't bring them home, and Secretary of Defense James Forrestal stating the decision to leave must be made before winter. The CIA was also pessimistic. The Germans too were not optimistic, with Willy Brandt writing on 14 June 1948 that the Communist leader Walter Ulbricht 'has said privately that the Western powers will be forced to leave Berlin before July 15'.[6]

How could an occupying force remain in the city without access to fuel, personnel, electricity, and other operational necessities? There was no clear way to stand their ground forever: they would run out of these resources. Would holding out until then be only a show of pride and futile when capitulation was almost certain? Even Reuter wasn't sure how long Berlin could resist. Later, he decided that enduring for fourteen days could be a useful symbol.[7]

But a plan was being hatched in Fehrbelliner Platz, in the British zone. A British idea – that the West could supply Berlin from the air – would change the game.

5

RAF Commodore Reginald 'Rex' Waite, Head of Air Branch of the Control Commission, was sitting in his office on Fehrbelliner Platz, in what was now called Lancaster House. Previously the 1943-completed Nazi building, with its grand Tuscan-columned rotunda, was used by the German Labour Front. Only the roofs were damaged during the war, so the offices were repurposed as the British headquarters.[8]

A usual morning buzz filled the halls, everyone running around. Then the group captain appeared at the door with the most serious of expressions, 'Any tea this morning?' Never mind about the blockade! 'If the morning tea was OK, then it was all under control', or so David Edwards told me, who worked in this office in 1948 as a teleprinter operator, listening to signals, breaking codes, and monitoring the Soviets' interceptions.[9]

Edwards was the junior colleague of Waite and described him as a quiet man, the kind who got on with his work and did not expect recognition. He told me, 'Waite didn't have that boorish voice typical of an Air Commodore; rather he was softly spoken and more concerned about that morning tea.'

On 24 June, when the Soviets closed the borders, Waite was not in Berlin but stuck on a train in Helmstedt. In those many hours when the train could not move, he thought about how to supply the city by air.

Not much had been transported during the Little Lift. Andreas-Friedrich wrote on 5 April 1948:

> it has been reported that already twenty-five tons of food have been flown into the city. Twenty-five tons is twenty-five thousand kilograms. Since the population of the Western sectors is about two million people, that means twelve and a half grams per person. Not including members of the occupying forces. May Heaven preserve us from having to depend permanently on this means of supply.

But Waite had watched the Little Lift closely, worried that Soviet intentions would make a repeat necessary, on a grander scale. Waite had been involved in the investigation when the British and Soviet planes crashed on 5 April and became convinced that more significant conflict was around the corner.[10] On that Helmstedt train, he identified eight potential air bases in West Germany and two airstrips in Berlin that could handle mass cargo.

Waite had a knack for logistics. He was from Duffield in Derbyshire, chose to join the RAF and was accepted on their course. During the Second World War, he was group captain at RAF St Eval in Cornwall, and helped plan the Normandy landings. His daughter, Romilly Waite, explained to me how her mother never knew where he worked during the war because his work was so secret.

In 1945, he was charged with disarming the Luftwaffe in the British zone. He was then appointed head of the Air Branch for the Control Commission in Berlin – in short, he oversaw anything that flew in the British sector – and relocated to the city with his wife and young family in December 1946.

In Berlin, he was aware of how little Berliners ate. In a letter, he wrote exasperatedly about the food situation, how they were allowed one thousand calories a day. Only the black market kept them alive. He would share his sweets ration with the children, noticing their poor clothes and bare feet in the cold mud, 'the saddest thing of all'.

Even with such meagre rations, to feed all West Berlin would be a tremendous undertaking. There were 2 million Berliners in West Berlin, and their daily needs amounted to 4,500 tons (rising to 5,000 in the autumn). On top of that, there were 30,000 soldiers and administrators (including 9,000 Americans, 7,600 Brits, and 6,100 French), which meant another 500 tons daily. This did not count the resources needed to sustain Berlin's industry. Food reserves in Berlin, meanwhile, would only last one month; medical reserves six months; motor oil and petrol three to five months; and coal one month.[11]

Where would the food come from? In the UK, individuals lived on 1,800 calories daily after the war, as did their pilots abroad. As the RAF engineer David Lawrence said, 'The butter and margarine we took to Berlin were all produced back home in England ... We had candy rationing in England.'[12] How could they justify feeding it to their old enemies?

Despite these odds, Waite was undaunted and put his plan to paper. Perhaps he was so concerned about his morning tea because, once back in Berlin from his stationary train, he worked through the night, calculating cargo and lift capacities with a slide rule. He could predict where planes were, and how many, because of his experience on the Normandy landings. He imagined a 'complete rearrangement for life for siege conditions', as he wrote in a letter to a RAF office. In this way, he devised the baseline plan for the Airlift. Operation Plainfare (yes, a pun) would later be called his 'logistical masterpiece'.[13] They wouldn't be flying in gourmet.

Edwards, Waite's junior colleague, told me that he was not terribly surprised when he heard about the plan. Waite was a man who knew what he was doing:

When we were all assembled there, he gave a brief view of the situation; 'We are blockaded here; negotiations had failed' – there was no movement in that direction. We didn't know if there would be an evacuation or there might be a third world war ... I remember him saying, 'What we are going to do is try to supply the Western section.'[14]

Waite, however, first had to convince his superiors. He was rebuffed by a senior officer who, taking one look at the plan, said: it's impossible! Out of the question!

Waite pleaded for just ten minutes with Governor Brian Robertson to give the idea a fair hearing. Those ten minutes changed history. Robertson agreed to send the plan to Lucius Clay, who would in turn propose it to one Ernst Reuter.

6

Reuter was invited to Harnack House Officers' club to meet Clay on 25 July, the day after the enormous rally of Berliners at the Hertha stadium. The house was set in a garden with red peaked roofs, built in the 1920s for academic events. Where Albert Einstein had once visited was now a US officers' mess.

Clay was a cantankerous fellow. He was only two years older than Reuter but from a different world. Born to a Georgia senator in 1897, he came from power. Both men had spent the Second World War on the sidelines: Clay was known as the four-star general who had never seen any combat. But, like Reuter, he did know something about organisation. And, like Rex Waite, that experience in procurement and moving men came from work on the D-Day landings. From 15 March 1947, he was the military governor of the US zone. Reports on his personality ranged from the suave – always photographed with a Camel in his hand – to hyperactive, as he apparently drank twenty cups of coffee a day. A joke went around that Clay was a really nice guy when he relaxed, except he never relaxed.[15]

The Americans prepared an upbeat meeting for the Germans. Willy Brandt remembered going to the talk with Reuter: 'They tried to "encourage" us – perhaps it would yet be possible to supply Berlin. Reuter smiled sceptically. He couldn't quite believe it.' But he listened politely to the American general.[16]

Other things stood in the way between Reuter and Clay, apart from Reuter's disbelief in the possibility of the Airlift's success. Clay didn't have much nuance in the difference between democratic socialists and communists. Willy Brandt remembered how:

> At first, the general had clearly given him the cold shoulder. By the way, this was mutual. Reuter, too, had at first a rather critical attitude towards Clay. The Southerner, grown up in the ideas of American federalism, thought Reuter too authoritarian, too centralistic; it may not have been easy for Clay to free himself from the prejudice to see a 'Red' in every Social Democrat.

President Truman had issued his executive 'Loyalty Order' the previous year, checking federal employees for their affiliation with 'anti-American' sentiments – a milestone of the Red Scare. It was a test that Reuter, had he been subject to the same scrutiny, would have failed. Later, in his memoirs, Clay would skirt his association with Reuter, mentioning him only as an 'experienced administrative expert'.

Reuter also didn't like Clay. He said his conversations at first with Clay 'inevitably hardly went beyond the formalities' – they worked together because it was necessary. As Brandt again recounted:

> Reuter, on the other hand, believed that an American general could hardly understand the European conditions, and the position of German democrats in particular. He definitely refused to be considered an instrument of American policy, or of any other foreign government.

Indeed, Reuter was no one's lapdog in a meeting of strong wills. Brandt opined that Reuter – just as Lenin had intuited decades before – was 'a little too independent and self-confident'. And there was another reason Reuter never liked Clay: he felt the Americans had sold him out when he was first elected mayor and had done little to protest about the Soviet veto. In some ways, Reuter had the upper hand. He spoke English, while Clay could not put a sentence together in German.[17]

Diffidence hung in the room. Mutual interest, however, bound them: Berlin must not give up. Clay, for his part, needed the city, saying: 'If Berlin falls, West Germany will follow next ... If we intend to hold Europe against Communism, we must not move one inch.'[18] Clay's attitude to the Germans was ultimately pragmatic, as he believed they – already trained in virulent anti-Communism by the Nazis – were the best buffer Americans could have against the Soviets.

But his methods were brash and hawkish and may well have frightened Reuter. The American did not shy away from an enormous response to the Soviets' restrictions. Often discussed is Clay's idea to plough an armed convoy through the Soviet sector to open Berlin. This idea didn't get very far. Brian Robertson told Clay that, if he used a military convoy, it would mean war with the Soviets, while President Truman weighed in along the same lines, saying that there was a line they would not cross.[19] Nonetheless, as a pre-emptive safety measure, which indicated just how much was at stake, the Americans moved B-29 bombers, known for carrying atomic weapons, to Britain on 28 June, bringing the Soviets within range of a nuclear attack. How, then, to support and defend Berlin without engaging directly with Russia would become a major theme of the Cold War and after.

Reuter also knew he risked everything. In the words of Robertson, if the Western allies were forced from Berlin, Reuter's 'would be one of the first heads to fall'.[20] Reuter also had a 'magnet theory' – which he expanded on in the *Saturday Evening Post* – that by working cooperatively, despite their differences, with the occupying powers of West Germany, he could draw West Berlin fully and permanently into their orbit and thus gain sovereignty within a two-state solution.[21] Even if the Airlift failed, as he expected it would, the gesture of resistance would be a symbol to the West. Meanwhile, by aligning themselves with the West, the Germans could change their victim, defeated status into something vastly more attractive: partners. As Reuter would say later: 'In Berlin, something was washed away from Germany that needed to be washed away.'[22]

Clay was in a bind: the man in front of him was a socialist, and the American needed his support. He had a plan from Rex Waite on his desk arguing that the city could be supplied from the air with an airbridge for a maximum of forty-five days. Reuter, meanwhile, did not believe him. But what they shared made it happen.

It was Reuter who extended his hand, as Brandt remembered:

> He spoke without any sharpness – 'We shall, in any case, continue on our way. Do what you are able to do; we shall do what we feel to be our duty. Berlin will make all necessary sacrifices and offer resistance – come what may.' The gentlemen were visibly impressed. They had perhaps expected to hear complaints, reproaches, conditions – instead, they heard quite another sound ... Reuter's frankness and his firm, unshakeable attitude won Clay's sympathy ... In the course of this crucial year, the two men formed a close partnership which secured the victory in the struggle for Berlin.

7

Fred V. McAfee was relaxing in Hawaii at a tropical band party when his colonel took the microphone at midnight and told his officers they were leaving for Germany in two hours. About the same time, in Nebraska, one Ken Slaker abandoned his new car near an airport. Another pilot in Anchorage, Alaska, put down his beer as the phone rang: it was 'Germany callin''.[23]

What Waite, Clay, and Reuter had set into motion on 28 June rippled worldwide. The West needed planes and pilots, wherever they might be. The aircraft began arriving from Hawaii, Nebraska, Alaska, Tokyo, Panama, the Caribbean, Bermuda, the Azores, and all over the States and Britain.[24]

Connecting from airfield to airfield, these airmen arrived at Rhein-Main, Faßberg, Wiesbaden, and the other airfields designated by Waite. They stepped off their planes in clothes from various climates – be it a parka or a pair of tiny shorts – to find themselves housed in rough conditions.

The sudden and improvised nature of the Airlift meant the authorities could not prepare adequately for overcrowding. A post-operation evaluation of medical conditions at the Airlift airfields in the *US Armed Forces Medical Journal* lamented the inadequate housing, heat, lighting, hot water, latrines, and hospitalisation facilities. Non-chlorinated water at some bases contributed to sanitation problems. The pilots were 'compromised by maladjustment, fatigue, and illness', especially respiratory and venereal disease. The slapdash arrangements had the investigator Harry Moseley calling working conditions at RAF Faßberg 'similar to working in Nazi concentration camps'.[25]

Most men had hardly time to put down their bags at these airfields. Regardless of their garb, within hours they were flying cargo to Berlin. Some planes, like Ken Slaker's old rust bucket, had trouble taking off. Freddie Laker remembered having to go around his Halifax bomber with a screwdriver after every landing. But most, like our Hawaii pilot McAfee, were quickly on their way. McAfee became a flour and dehydrated potato man who was 'not above hauling macaroni',[26] while some British pilots found themselves flying salt. Unlike conventional aircraft, their Sunderland flying boats were sealed against salt's corrosive effects with control wires in the plane roof. They landed on the Havel until the water froze over in winter.[27]

If the conditions at the airfield bases and the state of the aircraft could be primitive, the masterwork of radio technology was not. Back at the Pentagon, mathematicians developed algorithms as they attempted to compute the best time to deploy materials and people with their punch card calculators. The algorithms were too complex for what they could compute, but the demands of the Airlift set in motion a generation's computational work. As the planes took off in their orderly formations to Berlin through the air corridors from the airfields in the US and British zones, they were guided by the most sophisticated interplay of signals ever experienced – and all before the age of modern computers. It brought modern air traffic control forward decades.[28]

Pilot Jack O. Bennett remembers the beautiful pattern of green dots on his radar and how its precision was metronomic. There was not only poetry but also some humour in the timed departures and landings. Pilots were known for rhyming to Control to break the monotony of repetitive work: 'I'm a Yankee with a blackened soul, bound for Gatow with a load of coal.' The controllers had to listen too, however, to the Soviets, who did their best to interfere with the channels with strange vacuum-like noises.[29]

Despite the sophistication of the radio and radar operation, this did not prevent crashes. On 25 July 1948, a DC-3 ploughed into the Berlin neighbourhood of Friedenau, in Handjerystraße, killing both pilots. The fiftieth day of the Airlift, 13 August, would be known as 'Black Friday', when a C-54 burst into flames at the end of the runway, bringing another

C-54 down. Then, on 24 August, another four Americans were killed in a midair collision. The Soviets, meanwhile, were known for buzzing the Allied craft – flying alongside to unnerve, shining bright lights into cockpits, or playing polka music on the airwaves.[30]

Seventy-eight Brits, Americans, and Germans lost their lives in aircraft crashes. Because more severe incidents could risk war, reasons other than Soviet interference accounted for most of these tragedies. The pilots were exhausted, flying blind in almost every weather, working overtime around the clock in poorly maintained vehicles. Bennett remembered sleeping under a desk in an office at Tempelhof between flights, although many pilots slept during the flights themselves, with the pilot and co-pilot taking turns and making sport of being able to land so softly you wouldn't wake up the other.

Slowly, these men, who came from everywhere at short notice, began to feed a city. Ruth Andreas-Friedrich looked to the sky as these planes started to descend on Berlin, overwhelmed by the sound: the roar. She wrote:

> Blockade, as another airlift plane drones by overhead every eight minutes. Blockade, we are reminded by the hours without electricity, the RIAS vans, the deserted highway to Helmstedt, the rusty railroad tracks of the interzonal line, the cancelled streetcars, the idle factories, and the streets and houses without light in the Western sector of the fortress of Berlin.[31]

From the ground, the sight was spectacular. However, the *New York Times* reported, that 'the Berlin airlift – magnificent achievement in logistics though it is – is a losing proposition'.[32] Compare the daily needed tonnage of between 4,500 and 5,000 to the first week's deliveries of only 1,273 tons daily on five hundred flights. At this rate, the city would run out of power in ten days and food in a month. Only 2,500 tons a day was carried at the end of July, proving the *New York Times*'s point.[33]

All this would change with the arrival in Germany on 28 July of a demanding boss: Lieutenant General William H. Tunner. He was made the head of the US operation and in October the supreme commander of the US-UK Airlift. Tunner had commanded the 'Hump' airlift operation over the Himalayas in the Second World War and emerged as respected, if not much loved as he was known to dress down officers in front of their fellow men. He was an artist of high-altitude logistics and was shocked by the low volumes: on the day of his arrival, only 1,550 tons had reached the city. His job was to turn the US operation, called Operation Vittles, around.

Not everything he tried worked: dropping coal from the air on a US firing range meant it crumbled into dust, leaving watching dignitaries covered in black.[34] Efficiencies needed to happen other ways. With a wall of graphs behind him, Tunner improved deliveries, increased the number of crews, jostled for faster loading and unloading times in the airfields, and quicker turnarounds for aircraft servicing.

Turn it around Tunner would: already on 7 August, 3,800 tons were lifted in one day. On the 12th the tonnage went over 4,500 for the first time. One of Tunner's most effective methods was to set off a competition for speed of loading and unloading. From 22 August, the *Task Force Times* began to report on the tonnage, creating a 'Kentucky Derby' among planes over figures. The lieutenant general wanted to show that the mass transport of cargo by air was actually feasible. And he would hold up his success as 'more than just an airlift. It's a propaganda weapon held up before the whole world.'[35]

8

Western propaganda about the Airlift presented it as a humanitarian mission to save Berliners from hunger because the city was blockaded. In his memoir, Brandt described a sealed city: 'Even the supply of medicine for sick persons and milk for little babies was stopped. Two million West Berliners were to be starved into capitulation.'[36] Lucius Clay spoke of 'one of the most ruthless efforts in modern times to use mass starvation for political coercion'.[37]

The trope of a city saved from famine reappears not just in histories of the operation but predictably when the Airlift is commemorated on official anniversaries or mentioned on the websites of NATO, the British government or the German Bundestag. Berlin was 'completely cut off' and there was 'no way in, no way out'![38] Even Berlin's official Airlift monument inaugurated in 1951 is popularly called the *Hungerharke* ('Hunger rake'). According to the city's description, it 'symbolises the

Airlift that ensured the survival of the West Berliners'. In popular culture, the most famous German television series on the operation, from 2005, is called: *The Airlift: Only the Sky Was Free*.[39]

This story of 'hunger' and 'survival' in a blockaded city is a Cold War legend questioned in mainstream German historical debate – by historians such as Jörg Echternkamp, Volker Koop, Michael Lemke – but rarely abroad.[40] As these researchers observed in the everyday history of black market exchanges between Berlin and its hinterland in the East, the 'sealed city' narrative did not match reality. Instead, Lemke refers to a 'relative blockade'. But if one adheres to a formal definition – of a place that is sealed off – then one can no longer speak of a blockade at all. This is not just a matter of splitting hairs over a dictionary definition: permeable is not the same as blocked, and Western actors publicly claimed that Berlin was inaccessible by land routes.

Initially, the extent of the Soviet restrictions was unclear, and the Allies prepared for the worst using Waite's plan. They counted remaining reserves, and on the Airlift to replenish them. However, although barge and lorry traffic to the Western zones stopped, passengers continued to travel between the zones in Berlin and the surrounding area using functioning public transportation and walking easily between sectors. While passenger train travel to, say, Munich in the Western zone, was no longer possible, travel to points in the Soviet East continued to run.

Although there were (insufficient) checks to prevent it, there was a flourishing cross-border black market, smuggling, and hoarding expeditions. This is because there was more food in the East: rationing ended in the Soviet Union in December 1947 and was abolished in neighbouring Poland in 1948, while in Britain it lasted until 1954. In the words of the Soviet-zone head for Trade and Supply – 'if the [Western allies] should leave Berlin, we would take over [supplying the city] at once, and there would be no hitches'. From 1 August 1948, there was even access to Eastern rations.[41] Berliners in the West, who could easily travel across the border, obtained at least a third of their food from the East and could have obtained much more,[42] an aspect expounded on later in this book.

The Soviets fêted their allowance of civilian access to the East to diminish attention to their restrictions on military traffic. Governor Sokolovsky's public assessment of the situation was:

> There neither was nor is a blockade of Berlin. If there had been a blockade the Berlin population would have been deprived of the possibility of receiving supplies of foodstuffs, fuel and other essentials. In fact, however, the entire population of Berlin has the full possibility of receiving all supplies due to it, including coal for the winter, from the Soviet sector of Berlin ... The costly transportation of food and coal to Berlin from the Western zones by the so-called air lift is thus an unnecessary and purely propagandist measure ... Is it not clear, in view of what has been said, that the talk about a 'starvation blockade' of Berlin is a premeditated slander and a provocative invention?[43]

This position is also misleading. The restrictions might not have been imposed to starve civilians, as the West claimed (they had been hungry since the end of the war). Nonetheless, the Soviets made Berliners dependent on a trickle of electricity from a few outmoded relief stations, so subways shut by dusk and teeth had to be drilled by hand. Even Willy Brandt's child was born by candlelight. Meanwhile, schools were heated in shifts and some essentials, such as medical supplies, were limited. The Soviets were starving the Western Allies of military goods – heavy equipment, land access for movement of personnel, bulk shipments – necessary to occupy the city. The restrictions would have also eventually destroyed West Berlin's economy.

Even though they knew Berlin would not starve, the US and British authorities leveraged the illusion of a sealed city for propaganda. The British control in its instructions for publicity about the Airlift articulated matters internally:

> The blockade of Berlin is NOT a siege, but it is not far removed from it, with certain marked differences. It is not a siege because movement in and out of Germans is possible all the time and because of the airbridge: this is a help to us ... We might be aware of this but it is clear that many outside authorities are NOT clear, and certainly not the general public.[44]

Since the public was not well informed, they could be manipulated. British publicity instructions urged that the 'repeated theme' should be that 'Berlin is a city blockaded', 'a massive and sensational story of air power applied to humanitarian ends', to debunk Soviet claims that there is 'no blockade of Berlin'. The focus of the press should instead be on signs of a sealed city, such as vehicle checks on the East–West border and spot checks on trains. The campaign depended too on cultural stereotypes, 'the superiority of "Western" to "Eastern" civilisation'.[45]

The US Department of State articulated that one reason 'to remain in Berlin [was] to utilize to the utmost the present propaganda advantage of our position to supply the city by air and, if the restrictions continued, to protest to the Soviets and keep the Berlin situation before world attention'.[46] This also happened in the United Nations Security Council, where the Soviets used their veto on the Berlin Crisis. The home press, meanwhile, was crucial because of the shocking price tag of $224 million, or $3 billion in today's coin. Such an ambitious operation in a US election year required steadfast public backing. The blockade of an outpost of freedom, cut off by a brutal enemy – where 'only the sky was free' – causing a humanitarian crisis involving starving women and children, better justified an expensive and logistically complicated operation. It created a script of benevolence that could win the hearts and minds not only of Americans and the British, but also Germans.

Without starving mouths to feed, the Airlift as a humanitarian venture lost its moral force. But with it, it became a winning ticket in an election year. The Airlift's popularity proved decisive in Truman's upset re-election in November 1948 – 'his greatest asset' as historians have argued, because he met US public demand to be tough on Russia (69 per cent wanted a firmer stand in the summer of 1948) without causing another world war.[47]

Starving Berliners would only pull at the heartstrings of the Western public, however, if they were worth saving. After all, the Berliners had been, until recently, the West's enemies portrayed as heartless, sadistic, humourless, rule-following Nazis. Now, they would need to be converted for the Western public into amiable victims of Communism, meriting forgiveness. The emergency had arrived that would transform former enemies into friends.

9

The reader now might ask why Clay depended so much on Reuter's support. After all, weren't the Berliners just a defeated people, and surely the

Allies did not need their permission to pierce the Soviets' isolation from the air? Were not international relations independent of how everyday Berliners acted?

At the heart of the matter was the peril that Berliners would turn to the Soviets as saviours. In the East there was food, and they could travel there for it. How could Berliners be convinced to accept the limitations brought on by an airlift instead of buying from the contiguous East? Would the Berliners go hungry for democracy when the Soviets offered food? This is what Brandt meant when he wrote in his memoir:

> Could one subject the Berliners to such a severe test? Would they be willing to take upon themselves still greater privations? The decision of the Western occupation powers depended in the last resort on the answer to this question.[48]

Feeding Berliners, then, was, paradoxically, not about feeding Berliners. It was window dressing, but with an important propaganda task that justified the Western presence in Berlin to halt Soviet encroachment. Who fed Berlin controlled it. The British Foreign Office knew this perfectly well and explained it clearly to their Intelligence units in Berlin:

> We are not in Berlin in order to feed the Berliners. We feed them because we are in Berlin. We intend to stay in Berlin and we shall continue feeding them ... the presence of the Western Powers in Berlin is the only real safe guard of the political liberties and personal freedom of those Berliners who have expressed their belief in Western democracy. Berliners who have openly supported the Western Allies are not unaware of the implications of that part of the Soviet announcement which says that they will have to enter the Russian Sector to collect the offered rations.[49]

The 'implications' are spelt out in a separate report. Turning to the Soviets for food would mean that 'the presence of the Western Allies in Berlin' would be seen as 'not any longer necessary'.[50] If they had to depend on the East, Berliners would have to bend to any condition the Soviets imposed on access, including the use of their currency. Such a defection would be a very public propaganda victory for the Soviets.

Declassified British intelligence reports from the crisis's first days are extremely sensitive to public opinion in Berlin. The Soviets threatened the Berlin public with predictions that the Western powers would be unable to supply their presence. *Neues Deutschland* blamed the transport chaos on the West, telling Berliners that 'it can only be remedied if those who are responsible for it disappear'.[51] These were not so subtle calls for insurrection. With the world watching, Clay could not risk this betrayal.

This is why the American had turned to the elected Mayor for his help – the man with the charismatic power over the population to keep the Berliners from turning to official sources of provisions in the East. Clay told Reuter in no uncertain terms that depending on the Airlift would be tough. But Reuter replied: 'Let me take care of the Berliners.'

The conversation between Clay and Reuter resonated at the highest levels. On 28 June, a few days later, President Truman made his policy clear: 'We are in Berlin, and we're staying. Period.' Two days later, Reuter addressed his Berliners on the radio, RIAS: 'These days will decide our fate in Berlin. Each of us knows that … That is why we Berliners are turning to the whole world.'[52] Except he did not mean the 'whole world' – he meant the West. In this way, the most ordinary, everyday Berliner had a role to play in what would become a brilliant performance.

VIII

CHAMPAGNE

1

Alec Chambers sits in the front row in the former British headquarters on Fehrbelliner Platz. It is the seventy-fifth anniversary of the Airlift. The veterans wait for the unveiling of the plaque for Rex Waite. They are almost all in wheelchairs, although Alec normally does not need his conveyance. He's 99 years old, plays golf, has his wits about him, and is in the chair only because he's broken a toe. Smiling and laughing, the old servicemen are dapper, dressed in uniform. Many remember standing in this hall almost eight decades ago, on their two feet, in the rush of the Airlift's operations.

Alec is recognisable from a picture of him in his twenties: high cheekbones and something mischievous in his thin smile, something just withheld. But it's hard to get a word out of him during the busy event, where he grins and shakes my hand. Perhaps it is too loud, but I get slightly worried that he won't speak to me during our interview at his hotel. But his son-in-law David puts his head to one side and says jokingly, 'A lot of what he tells you, you might not be able to print!'

Alec is lodged in the old British sector at a high-rise near Wittenbergplatz. The next evening, I alight at the subway station and walk the airy spring streets buoyant with pollen. There's been another day of Airlift anniversary celebrations, and I've been warned Alec might be tired by all the events at Tempelhof.

David picks me up in the lobby, and we chat in the lift to fill the uncomfortable space between people who don't know each other that I'm used to from such interviews. I'm reasonably adept at polite talk about the hot weather.

With a keycard through one of the hotel's anonymous doors, I find Alec in his wheelchair, still grinning. Again, I see – how should I put it? – something contained, not yet said in his smile. As if he is waiting to tell me something, as if it's on the tip of his tongue. When we get past the shaking of hands, I realise there will be no problem with stamina. Alec will speak for almost two hours about his experiences as a flight engineer during the Airlift.

Alec chats softly but with unvarnished description. His was the 'Liquid Lift', the most dangerous aspect of the Airlift. Chambers transported fuel by plane from the British zone to Berlin, from Wunstorf and Fuhlsbüttel/Hamburg airfields to Gatow and Tegel. 'Liquid fuel was either petrol or diesel. We transported fewer containers of diesel because it was heavier than petrol,' Alec says. By the beginning of 1949, 'every motor vehicle in West Berlin was running on fuel flown in by British civilian pilots'. The British even brought petrol cars to Berlin to be used by the police. The American Tempelhof did not have tanks to store the fuel, so the Liquid Lift became a British job.[1]

I get the feeling that he must have been a crackerjack as a young man: is it that Alec is almost boyish in his enthusiasm and laughter, that his smile remains a little naughty, as if the really good stories are yet to come?

I'm in a chair that belongs to a desk in the hotel room, and he sits in a wheelchair opposite; his daughter and son-in-law take turns overseeing the conversation: who knows what he might say! And from the upper floor of the hotel room, there is a sweep of Berlin below us – towards the West, over Schöneberg, Kreuzberg, and Tempelhof – as if we are flying.

2

The story can begin near the Cotswolds, in Shrivenham. The little town, once part of Berkshire, had a population of less than a thousand before the war. A bucolic place of thatched roofs and box hedges, nestled in a landscape thick with ash and willow trees, the community had two churches, four butchers, and four public houses. These grouped around the High Street leading to Oxford some 20 miles in one direction, and Swindon 7 miles in the other. Most of the land was owned by the Barrington family, seated nearby in Beckett House, in whose 'Stew' the village children would swim and catch fish.

Shrivenham was an isolated place, turned in on itself, an unlikely home for a young man who moved here when he was only a few months old – Alec was born on 2 June 1925, not far away in Long Wittenham near Abingdon – and would follow the linden trees of High Street to those of Unter den Linden, Berlin.

Alec Chambers's father Ted came out of the navy and ran what was known as the best pub in town in the 1930s, called the Barrington Arms. He was respected but the type who 'broached no argument'. Local children knew this, and they would hide in a hollow tree out front to tease the farmers who tied up their horses. Alec was undoubtedly one of the naughty ones about town and remembers going into the well-stocked village shop, Dike's Store, where the pub had an account. He once took all his friends and told them to take what they wanted – perhaps he thought everything was for free.

Conversations in his father's pub would change young Alec's life. At the village school, he feared the headmaster, Mr Dance (whom they called Dicky-Dance), who regularly used his cane on the students. Once, Alec heard his father in conversation when he was hidden at the top of the staircase. Alec recounts that 'listeners rarely hear anything good about themselves, and I was no exception. When asked how he rated me as a pupil, Mr Dance said that I was gifted in the hands rather than the head.'

Alec was already drawn to flying. A flying school was established near Shrivenham in 1940. Alec said of RAF Watchfield, 'Blind flying was practised with what was called the Beam Approach. This was an exciting new development and enabled pilots to fly and land safely at night.' The war brought soldiers evacuated from Dunkirk, American soldiers who preferred whisky to beer, and German prisoners of war who were allowed into the local pubs before 9 p.m. Shrivenham's exposure to the war opened him to the world. Alec, meanwhile, was 'making models of different planes with my school friend', watching the Tiger Moths, and Avro Ansons at Watchfield Aerodrome, and was delighted by pictures of the flying boat, the Short Sunderland, and the Supermarine Spitfire.

He remembers, 'Pre-war, there was a little hangar there [at Watchfield], and a chap used to fly a yellow Piper Cub, and we used to go there and watch him, and I eventually saved up, I think it cost me quite a lot of money, but I did get a flight in the damn thing.' But the 1942 Lancaster bomber inspired him the most and, seeing it, 'I knew my future lay with aircraft, and I firmly rejected any idea of university.'

Another conversation in the pub would again change Alec's life. John Cave was a regular guest and even lodged there temporarily. As the Chief Ground Engineer at Watchfield, Cave suggested to Alec that he apply for a job. So, as a 16-year-old, he became a spare hand in engine overhaul, working on 'the Ansons and Oxfords, on the old cheetah engines, to take them out and take the pots off and de-coke them'. It was a key moment, and Alec decided to join the RAF. He was called up only towards the end of the war, got bottlenecked in Britain, and did not see active service.

After he was demobbed, Alec received a grant to complete his flight training, got busy with courses, and went to work for de Havilland's up the road at Witney. Alec remembers the excellent toolbox he got from an ironmonger in town. Learning to be a flight engineer meant working in audio, deciphering dots and dashes, listening in on enemy transmissions, studying navigation and learning to approach different kinds of airfields. He completed courses in airframes and engines, and converting Mosquitos into fire bombers.

After twelve months, Alec had his civilian licence as a flight engineer and a job near Blandford in Dorset, joining Alan Cobham's Flight Refuelling Ltd, first as a ground engineer and then in North Atlantic trials of inflight refuelling. Cobham was famous in the UK in the early 1930s for his 'flying circus', which toured the UK with aircraft to allow ordinary people to fly.[2] 'Great bloke', says Alec, 'Certainly on the lift, Sir Alan was always with us; he came out to Germany quite frequently to see if we were OK and everything shipshape and Bristol fashion, or any complaints.' When the company became the first civilian contractor to offer its crews and heavy bombers – Avro Lancasters and Lancastrians – to the Berlin Airlift, Alec would find himself on his way to a defeated Germany.

3

'Initially, we thought it was a bit of a joke, and it wouldn't last long,' Alec tells me of how they arrived in late July, bringing nothing with them, not even formal clothes. During the expected three-week wonder – or one hundred hours of servicing – they thought they'd borrow what they needed from the Air Force. Alec tells me how the crews that went out first got 'spelly [sic] with stinking underwear'. They were also a little naïve about what was required of them: for night flying, they believed, 'Only owls do that!'

Their Lancaster and Lancastrian operation started on 8 August 1948. And, during that time, they thought 'they'd make a mess'. What does that mean? Alec recounts, 'We were young men and spoke of how we should make the best of it, with as much flying as we could wish for, cheap alcohol, supplemented with affrays in the local nightclubs and bars. What was not to like!'

Here we come to a little point of debate in the Berlin Airlift story: the civvies versus the RAF. Because the crews of the private contractors, as civilians, were not subject to many of the rules of the RAF, they were known as the 'rebels' of the lift. Perhaps this is a euphemism, but I also imagine this dichotomy provided a convenient opportunity to blame any bad behaviour on the civvies.

The civilian contractors weren't put in the barracks but in a hotel organised by the Control Commission Germany (CCG). They were housed in Bad Nenndorf, a spa town 10 miles from the base at Wunstorf. This hotel had two bars run by wartime German servicemen – one who regularly opined that the British should have joined the Nazis against the Russians.[3] Since the civvies were not subject to military discipline, they could go out into the town as they wished, giving them opportunities to cause trouble. But Alec – as a long-standing company man – reflects that there were also differences within the civilian crews. Alan Cobham's memoirist put it down to some bad apples: ex-RAF war veterans added to Flight Refuelling Ltd as aircrew for the Lift, who were not concerned about the company's reputation. Alec says, 'We had one or two characters, you can imagine. The initial hard-core crews had to be supplemented.'

They remained in Bad Nenndorf from July 1948 to March 1949 before the RAF happily dispatched them north to Hamburg. Wunstorf was at first chaotic, and the civvies and RAF weren't well coordinated and had differences. But it soon became 'highly organised', with tankers running twenty-four hours and three crews of four per aircraft: flight engineer, navigator, radio operator, and pilot. When the original five tankers increased to ten, thirty crews of young British men were foisted on the sleepy spa town.

Chambers remembers their camaraderie fondly, but also the mishaps, such as when the hotel kitchen caught on fire. One flight lieutenant remembered seeing flames bursting from one side of the building, and Chambers recounts: 'There we were in the small hours fleeing to safety wearing almost next to nothing. Being youngsters, we regarded it as an adventure.'[4] The civilian crews tried to save the furniture, which, when placed on the pavement, was immediately stolen by the impoverished local Germans.

The men also risked fire in the air. Part of the adventure was the cargo: highly inflammable. In one case at Wunstorf, a worker was burned when a lantern affixed to his chest ignited a petrol tanker containing 8,000 litres. The Lancasters could hold 10½ tons of fuel, just as they had once dropped 10-ton bombs. Many planes were converted after the Second World War to new uses, mainly civilian, only to be overhauled again for the Berlin Airlift. They were now fitted with Rebecca transponding radar, set to the same frequencies as military aeroplanes. Unlike many planes hauled into service for the RAF, these were no clanky, unreliable conveyances. As Alec told me, 'They were the best.'

He explains: 'We used Lancaster bombers, which had been all stripped of their original fittings. We likened this stripping to turning aircraft back into saucepans! The huge bomb bay could hold two tanks of liquid fuel, one of 600 gallons, the other 400, a total of 1,000 gallons.'

The liquid was in various-sized drums, 'difficult to secure and left many "voids"'. They were so full that the men had trouble moving around the cabin and had to climb over tanks.[5] The British were alert to how dangerous liquid fuel could be, so the civilian crews were paid a higher rate to transport it.

'Danger pay,' Alec tells me with a grin. 'And did you know we smoked on board? With all that fuel … At that age, we felt invincible.'

4

Today, computers do much of the flight engineer's work. But in the day, their on-board station was an enormous panel of switches behind the pilots. These controlled power to the engines on take-off and landing, cooling and hydraulics, electrical systems, and the pressurisation of the cabin. Apart from monitoring the aircraft's systems in the air, the flight engineer specialised in fuelling, keeping an eye on weight, and inspections on the ground before take-off and after landing. In short, the pilots would fly, but the engineer would take care of the plane and take the lead should something go wrong. In the Second World War, the flight engineer often doubled as the gunner. During the Liquid Lift, the role rose to a pinnacle of importance as the aeroplanes were in constant use and so subject to extraordinary stresses as heavy loads constantly ran down the tyres. Kenneth Slaker's gooney bird could have used a good flight engineer.

I imagine the crews waking at the hotel in Bad Nenndorf, hungover and starved for sleep, then picking themselves up with a good breakfast: 'We were well fed – twenty-four-hour meals were available. Meat and two vegetables. Breakfasts with eggs and bacon. English breakfasts with beans and toast.' Then the men packed into a bus to the RAF base at Wunstorf, where in the ops room for an hour the rest of the crew were briefed on take-off time, weather, and the flights ahead – three returns during the block – as well as any Russian interference that could come their way. But Alec was consulting with the ground staff, looking at the aircraft, doing his own inspection, kicking the tyres, and checking, especially on the fuel.

The men at Flight Refuelling Ltd were careful about the fuel because of a little mishap. You could do the trip one and a half times without refuelling again, but if you forgot to top up, all the engines would stop halfway through the return: 'It's good the North German plain is fairly flat for a belly flop.' This had already happened to one of their planes because someone forgot to check. The Russians kindly let them go but stripped the plane.

Alec told me, 'Wunstorf had been one of Göring's crack fighter stations. This was where we collected the fuel for Berlin and had a coffee break while the drums were being loaded.' It was convenient that there was a rail spur in old Luftwaffe bases, so the fuel could arrive by railway tankers.

Alec tells me they had to be careful because, before pumps improved, it was easy to flood the aircraft with fuel, and then they weren't dry enough to go out. German workers sometimes mistook the word 'off' for *auf* ('up') and would give the aircraft an inflammable bath. One of the advantages of liquid cargo, though, was they had none of the dust of coal and flour. They didn't need to caulk their aircraft floors with plasticine, like in the RAF, to prevent the coal from getting everywhere. It meant 'ventilation, and breathing was also good'.

Now, the planes were lining up, ten in a row, to take off at three-minute intervals. Even in the air, Alec says, 'You could see the chap in front of you and, if you looked behind, you could see the chap behind you.'[6] Alec was there starting up all the engines – the plane was heavy to lift from the runway, all four motors hurtling you into the air. Once in the sky, it was tail heavy to steer. They needed to behave themselves, at least on the way out. Even so, 'spirits were high. It was great fun.' And then they'd play some games on the way back.

But not yet. The air corridors were tight at only 20 miles wide over the Soviet zone, with a 10,000ft ceiling. If you exceeded these limits, you could be a target. The destination was Gatow, nearly two hours away – 110 minutes. They climbed to 3,300ft and navigated towards a series of beacons at 180mph. Alec called this 'beacon-hopping'.

The first beacon was near Hamburg, at Egestorf. These beacons kept the planes flying close and in check, the navigator coordinating the time with Control to know how many seconds, plus or minus, they were early or late. You could learn a lot – about changes in weather, about how late you were – by communicating with the other pilots: 'We were always listening to the bloke in front.' The next beacons followed the River Elbe, on the Western side along the Soviet zone, in Dannenberg (they called it 'Danny-berg') and Restorf. They needed to coordinate with the other pilots and command to get it just right because there wouldn't be another beacon until Frohnau when they arrived out of enemy territory into West Berlin, where they had to land within a twenty-second window. For a while, they were allowed to orbit the beacon to find a slot, but the risks of a collision with another aircraft were so great that it became policy to turn planes that weren't on time back home. 'If you were late or early, you had to bugger off back. It was a cock-up at Gatow if you were early.' Alec remembers the intense shudder when passing close to another plane.

But it was a masterpiece of timing and coordination: they were usually on time, and there were very few accidents. Now they approached. If Tempelhof was a difficult landing, Gatow was easy. But the Russian airfield at Staaken wasn't far away, and the enemy could send up interfering searchlights at night for the approach. And if the cloud was thick at night, it was a relief to be told, 'Look ahead and land!' and find oneself coasting down the runway towards Gatow's ten hangars. Except, their loads were so heavy they tended to 'hoppety-hop' rather than land cleanly. The Lancasters were built to take off with bombs but not land with them – they were used to dropping their cargo over Germany.

Once, they had to make a single-engine landing and found fire engines and an ambulance waiting for them, with Alec thinking, as he managed the failing systems, 'We shouldn't be doing this!'

5

'Gatow was … a wide and good airport,' Alec remembers his twenty-minute fuel drop-offs there.[7] The place was always busy and dangerous at night, 'the bloody noise, the roaring engines, and the bloody propellers', all from thirty to forty aircraft on the ground at any one time.

They taxied to defuel their cargo into one of the eighteen fuel discharging points. He speaks about the elliptical shape of the airport, the oval discharging station, where they would feed the liquid fuel into huge underground storage tanks by gravity. The fuel would later be pumped through a pipeline to tanks floating on barges in the nearby River Havel. Whatever was left in the hoses would be surreptitiously drained into thermoses by the German ground crew. But the twenty minutes was time for coffee. Coffee served by beautiful girls! But also an opportunity to sell black market coffee to the German landing crew.

Sometimes, the weather turned bad. One night, they spent the night in newly built Tegel (without the girls), with a 'hangar there with a storm shed, and a concrete floor. We were told that if you fly out tonight, you won't come back! So, we were stranded on that bloody cold stone floor.' But in the middle of the night, the British crews were rescued and offered a tour of midnight Berlin. All he remembers of the Brandenburg Gate was: 'It was dark.'

'Did you ever get into Berlin proper otherwise?' I asked.

'We usually never went into Berlin and never got off the airfield,' he told me, 'But we'd put chocolates through the fence for the kids at the airfield's periphery. They were always waiting there. On the other side of the Gatow wire, it was Russian territory, so those kids were Russian zone kids. Russian patrols were there too, and we'd tell those through the fence to exaggerate our load to get the word out how much we were flying in. The kids never ate their chocolate – they traded it.'

Another coffee, another load – 'now and then we took passengers, but we were not to inquire' about the 166,000 flown out of Berlin, mostly from Gatow – and they'd call the tower for permission to join the queue, and off they'd go, back to Wunstorf. A poetic image: 'Towards sunset, the Germans called us "pearls in the sky" because of the polished fuselages lined up in rows.'

6

Now, up in the sky, the return trip was always relaxed: no beacons, no strict times, and the planes were light without their loads. They'd drink and play cards and smoke.[8] The landscape was tranquil: they were amazed by the corridor as they followed the broad expanse of the River Elbe: 'It was bloody great, but nobody there: no fishing, no one on the beaches, nobody. It was always dead.' No boats, no barges, just a half-dismantled railway by the lines of towns between Berlin and Hamburg.

They could fly balletic over northern Germany, catching up with the plane in front of them and riding close and together like buddies. And they could coast low, at not even 1,000ft, which would provoke the Soviets. They would 'resume [their] best behaviour' only when they reached the border.

The Soviets were especially a temptation for the young crew because their airbase at Perleberg, a Soviet garrison town for the 2nd Guards Tank Army, was only 30 miles north of the corridor. It was known to pilots as a tricky place at night when, out of the shadows, the enemy became night 'stalkers'. But the British reciprocated 'depending on our moods', sometimes approaching the Soviet planes close, 'blowing them on their back', or buzzing the roofs of their buildings. Alec tells me of their so-called 'navigation error' at 4.30 a.m. when they decided to give Perleberg with its 4,600ft runway a little 'wake-up call'.

The base was in a pine forest, and generations of its Soviet conscripts would remember the smell of the needles, the pine sawdust on the floors, the wild mushrooms in the forest, and the sound of an organ moaning from the nearby Gothic church.[9] But no doubt those present that night also remembered what happened next.

Usually, when they were buzzed by one or two Soviet planes, Yak-9s, 'if they were rude, we'd give them the finger!' but they never shot at each other. But Alec's pilot, Mariusz Kuzubski, was Polish and 'absolutely detested the Soviets', even more than the Germans. 'He and I hit it off straight away, and we did everything together from that time on.' He was a 'two-tour bomber commander who could work a Lancastrian with a little finger' and had guts.

At dawn, he aimed their plane straight at the old Luftwaffe airfield, where the Russians were now installed – at the ranks of aeroplanes and the tank destroyers. At the rows of Yaks, the Russian equivalent of the Spitfire. The enemy aircraft were all menacingly visible below as they zoomed down to that airfield, as if to land or to attack at 300 knots. The shallow dive levelled to 50ft as they hovered above the runway: 'We had a radio altimeter, so we knew where we were.' Below, they saw the Russians in panic, 'all rushing about in all directions'.

The boys had been drinking champagne on the way back, so the back of their plane was full of empty bottles. It was the navigator who gave the word: When? Now! And they threw open the back door. And then, boom, down went those champagne bottles, bombing the runway, dispersing it with broken glass: 'Ping, ping, ping!' 'That will puncture a few tyres!'

Alec recounts, 'The captain grinned, saying "I loved that", as we watched the startled guards running for their AA guns and running around the rows of Yaks and Sturmovik tank destroyers before we hi-tailed it back to Wunstorf ... We were badly behaved when we came back from Berlin. We'd dive at those Russians if we could.'

'How often would you do this?' I ask.

'Not very often. Maybe three times during the whole lift!' he replies. Three times!

Back in the air, rising into the corridor at night, once there was a Yak plane. The crew suspected it was there: right behind the Lancaster. They had the navigator stand up and look up through the trap door above the cockpit. There, he confirmed the shadowy aircraft behind them, stealthy with no light on. All he could see was the exhaust.

Alec tells me: 'Mariusz had an idea: the escape hatch! The escape hatch? Release it, send it flying. He won't know what hit him!'

And so, he did.

'How did you explain it back in Wunstorf?'

'Later, we said it came undone. We had a hole in the top of the plane. We could have started World War Three!'

SUMMER–AUTUMN 1948

IX

CULTURE WAR

1

By the end of August 1948, with tonnages up, it looked increasingly like the Allies could feed Berlin from the air, and the front shifted to the ground. It became a competition. Who could win Germans' hearts — even minds — the Russians or the British? And could they do it by presenting the 'best' of their culture?

The Russians invited the Red Army Choir, also called the Alexandrov Ensemble. Four hundred military performers — singers, dancers, and orchestral musicians — in their dark uniforms sang not only in the public squares of East Berlin but also in the State Opera housed in the Admiralspalast. At enormous expense and effort, outdoor stages for thousands were erected in numerous bombed-out cities of the Soviet zone.

The Soviets did not know how the Germans would react to their singing soldiers.[1] But the 1948 film *Botschafter des Friedens* (Ambassador of Freedom), produced by the state-owned film company of the East, DEFA, showed that the spectacle electrified the audience. It recorded Berlin's most handsome but tattered square, the Gendarmenmarkt, cleared of rubble. Two eighteenth-century temples — the French and the German churches, built in an act of tolerance and mutual understanding — stood with their domes smashed. Crowds climbed into these skeletons to perch on the pediment of the Concert House like swallows among the blackened statues. Below them, banners and slogans in Russian and German — 'Germany's capital', 'Soviet Culture — Peace and Friendship' — hung over the balalaika orchestra and brass band.

Cossacks, lithe and muscular, leaped. Their kick dance was legendary, and they roamed the stage, soaring from squat to jump — each lower, then higher than the next. Women weaved in circles of white dresses, pansied sleeves, and flowers braided in their hair. Soldiers clashed swords, and clapped and egged on one another: a display of solidarity, power, and exactitude, with only one army hat accidentally tumbling to the floor. Victor Nikitin, the virtuosic, heroic tenor – a mechanical engineer in civilian life – gave three encores of 'Kalinka' to the gathered crowd of fifty thousand. Singing their folk music in the ruins of defeated cities, the Red Army Choir's 1948 tour was their event of the century.[2]

Famished Berliners gaped at the display of energy and at the well-fed, muscular bodies of the occupiers. The East Berlin newspapers reported dithyrambically, with the *Berliner Zeitung* intoxicated by the 'unique group of singers and dancers, which erupted in storms of applause of unprecedented force'. The evening paper, *Nacht-Express*, described the 'masses of people before the Admiralspalast. Masses of people in the square. Masses of people in the corridors and stairwells of the State Opera. Masses of people in the hall', and how the gymnastic stunts left the public 'breathless'. On 20 August 1948, even the British authorities noted bluntly in diplomatic correspondence that 'this choir has, according to all reports, had great success in the Russian Sector of Berlin'.

What especially penetrated the audience's reserve, according to the Eastern papers (beholden to their Soviet benefactors) was that the ensemble sang two songs in German. As the *Tägliche Rundschau* radiated, the inclusion of 'Heidenröslein' and 'Träumerei' for choir was 'more than a friendly gesture. It is ... a document of the unifying mission of culture.' The *Berliner Zeitung* on 27 August echoed:

> It was as if, on the stage, the German song was sung with no different emotion than the Russian one; the enthusiasm in the auditorium was no different, whether it came from a Russian or a German heart ... No, a better international pact than here, between stage and auditorium, could not have been concluded ... What the Alexandrov ensemble has brought to Berlin remains a reflection of the inexhaustible power and fertility of the Russian national genius.

The Soviet cultural authorities knew how to earn dividends from the event. Not only did DEFA produce their widely distributed film, but the East German radio station stamped an album of the event, newly released and still popular in the 1980s. The Soviets now wanted what the Western Allies did. At the edge of their empire, it was better to have a bulwark of comrades than enemies.

The album's title was *Auf gutem Weg mit guten Freunden* or 'On the right path with good friends'.

2

In the crowd, watching the Alexandrov Ensemble on that 18 August, stood a familiar man of 30 years with blond-brown hair and blue eyes with his Leica snapping pictures of the spectacle, accompanied by his girlfriend. Henry Ries was a tall man, but he could not see over the Soviet officer blocking his view to the furious music and leaping on stage.

Ries wrote that day in his pocket diary: '18 August, 6:00 to Alexandrow Soviet Army Choir – Sov. major threatens Ann and me with arrest if not leaving in three minutes.'³ The nature of the confrontation was made clearer in his 2001 biography: the officer 'grabbed my Leica and threatened in a sharp tone that he would arrest me if I did not leave within three minutes. By now, I had learned from experience that arguments had no effect on Soviet officers, especially since the blockade had been in place.'

Ries may have realised that argument was futile, but he got into one anyhow. He tried to explain to the officer that there were no military secrets at stake here: in Gendarmenmarkt, only country dances were on display for everyone to see.

The Soviet officer was not interested in Ries's explanations and was insistent: 'Three minutes out!' Although Ries had only been able to take a dozen photos, he stopped trying to explain himself, quickly realising that any former friendliness had vanished. He was no longer even among begrudging allies. And he certainly did not want his camera confiscated.

As Ries later wrote about the shifting relationship with the Soviets: 'It was only a small incident, but one that sheds light on the already very tense and suspicious atmosphere. What a difference to the courteous treatment in the Soviet zone a year earlier!'

The event entertained the masses while Ries felt an edge sharpening of intimidation and control.

3

Well before the arrival of the Cossack dancers, the British felt that the rug was being pulled out from under them when it came to the propaganda war. They were under increasing criticism for being a lightweight in Berlin's cultural arena, and other occupying powers felt they had neither the money, the will, nor the institutional organisation to promote themselves.[4] The Americans had cultural centres throughout their zone. The French had cinemas. The Soviets had opened a stately House of Soviet Culture on Unter den Linden in the old Prussian Ministry of Finance, Palais am Festungsgraben. On 12 March 1948, Robert Birley, the British education officer in Berlin, wrote a brief that the Americans were attracting people because of their courses and the Russians because of their library.[5] Although the British had finally opened a large Information Centre on Lehniner Platz, in the complex of today's Schaubühne Theatre, it was no buzzing hive of visits and lectures. As Félix Lusset, head of the French cultural mission, penned, British efforts were 'sporadic and insecure in character'. Not one British theatre company had visited the former Reich capital. Not a single important speaker, bar the poet Stephen Spender, had been invited.[6]

In April 1948, Britain's Foreign Secretary Ernest Bevin called an urgent meeting in London to rectify the situation, telegraphing Birley. An ambitious, inaugural event displaying British cultural prowess must happen that summer. Birley was a Shakespeare specialist, and his Berlin political intelligence advisor, Tom Creighton, a Cambridge man. Together, they devised a festival of Britain's golden era of literature and music, the Elizabethan age.[7] It would be the West's biggest cultural event of the Airlift. It was also to be the only such event the British ever attempted.

Their choices would illustrate something about the occupying powers and their relations with Berliners. How the British countered the Russian spectacle, the same week as the Alexandrov Ensemble's departure, was later reported on 4 September 1948 by the Western weekly *Der Spiegel*: 'The change from the Russians to the British was like a lesson in international psychology.' In penniless, ravaged Berlin, these were among the only shows in town. The spotlight was on. The Russians' strengths were the British's weaknesses, and vice-versa – a test of cultural and political alternatives.

4

The minutes of a 10 May 1948 meeting at York House in Berlin proposed the Cambridge University Marlowe Society as a guest for the festival.[8] Professional theatres were booked months in advance, and students, frankly, were cheap – with only transport, room, and possibly board to be paid. The University's Madrigal Society was quickly added to the programme.

Fourteen days of guest performances were planned, including two plays (Shakespeare's *Measure for Measure* and John Webster's *The White Devil*) at Berlin's Renaissance Theatre, along with concerts of English Renaissance Madrigals and the composer Henry Purcell. That much of the programme came from periods later than the Elizabethan – the Jacobean and that of William III – attracted no criticism. Two large exhibits at the British Information Centre – of jewellery, furniture, urban planning photographs, and heraldic paintings – refocused the event on the Age of Shakespeare.[9] Opportunely, in this golden age, the enemy was Spain, not Germany. Lectures by the era's specialists would happen in the British Information Centre. Most of these overseas visitors came from Cambridge, particularly King's College.

The University and its rows of colleges along the River Cam, rounded by walls and gates, conjured the adjectives ancient, elitist, intellectual, protected, handsome, and unbombed. In August 1947, Ernst Reuter made a short visit to England on an official invitation from the House of Commons.[10] He went to Cambridge on his days off on a 'visit to my old friends' and his son Harry. He wrote of the 'magic of this untouched university town' and later described the remarkable contrast to Berlin in a letter to an English friend:

> Cambridge was unchanged, with the lovely green ornament of its old trees, its ancient colleges. Well, its bookshop [Heffers] was a bit emptier than in former times. But on the whole, I thought this Cambridge is a place of peaceful and quiet life, just a paradise for us, who have to live and work among dreadful ruins in Berlin.

King's fifteenth-century College Chapel peeked over the manicured lawns rolling down to the stone bridges, where each June crowds sat on the riverbanks listening to choristers warbling Renaissance madrigals from shallow punts. At the end of the evening, their voices floated downstream to John Wilbye's 'Draw on, Sweet Night'. Optically, Cambridge could not be farther removed from the ruins of the isolated city.

But behind this old-world, even dainty, appearance, Cambridge was a pivot of political muscle. King's John Maynard Keynes had fundamentally changed international macroeconomics before he died in 1946. The UN summoned the college's Professor Nicholas Kaldor in the winter of 1948–49 to help solve Berlin's currency impasse.[11] Many students had already experienced war, as they had been drafted.

They returned to King's after active service to complete their degrees, meaning that, by the end of the war, 90 per cent were ex-servicemen and, among the undergrads, there were three colonels. Nor were conditions as luxurious as the architecture suggested. Rationing was applied in the college dining hall. During the especially cold winter of 1946–47, the servicemen who had before been in the tropics now huddled in shared rooms. By 1948, as younger students – in terms of experience and age – began to fill the lower years, a disconnect grew between those who had seen horrors in Europe and those just out of school who had not roamed much farther than their college's gates.[12]

However, there may have been another reason for the Foreign Office to choose Cambridge. It was a hive of spies central to Cold War intrigues. Infamously, the Cambridge Five defected to the Soviets. Of them, Anthony Blunt was consulted for the Berlin festival's exhibits.[13] Noel Annan, a history fellow of King's College, was also part of the secret society, the Apostles, before the war, which included three of the Cambridge Five. He was recruited to military intelligence in 1942, later working in occupied Germany for the Control Commission. He was charged with leading the Marlowe Society visit, along with the King's Provost, Donald Beves, later named and then cleared as the fourth man in the Cambridge spy ring.[14] Elizabeth Wyndham, appointed the liaison officer for the entire trip, was not only regarded as an expert on Elizabethan drama and music; she worked for MI6.[15]

Students on the Berlin trip also were deep in British intelligence. In 1944, Bernard Keeffe from Clare College, at 19, was asked to learn Japanese in six months to work secretly as a language specialist at Bletchley Park. When interviewed for the Royal College of Music in July 2014 about his intelligence work, he hesitated to provide too many details, saying he was still very 'careful about talking about it'.

Soon after the atomic explosions in Hiroshima, he was dispatched to the destroyed Japanese city, where he went between singing Schubert's 'Winterreise' to burn victims and spying on a group of German-Jewish émigré musicians.[16] Back in Cambridge in 1947, his voice was good enough to join the Madrigal Society under the direction of King's College's choirmaster, Boris Ord. When he went to Berlin, the fresh-faced, innocent-looking 23-year-old, singing Purcell, already had four years of spy work behind him.

King's College Choir is famous for its Christmas service of lessons and carols and has a long choral tradition. Ord had been the choir's organist since 1929 and music fellow from 1936. By all reports, it was a joyous community – minutes from the Madrigal Society's meetings noted how they would end gatherings by 'bursting into song'.[17] But bringing music to Germany was no easy task. How could these madrigals – delicate part-songs for different voices in counterpoint – stand up against the giants of the German tradition: Bach, Beethoven, Brahms? And how would audiences receive them, fed a nationally narrow repertoire prescribed by Goebbels's Propaganda Ministry for thirteen years?

The Madrigal Society had its academic side: it specialised in reviving little-known corners of the repertoire. They did not arrive in Berlin with a more familiar Purcell classic such as *Dido and Aeneas*, but rather the rebarbative *Circe* and *Ye Tuneful Muses*, of which only a few recordings exist today. The music they brought was ungrateful and not up to the task of defeating stereotypes. As a special issue of the western German paper *Die Welt* noted in September 1948, Germans considered Britain *Das Land ohne Musik*, or 'the land without music'.

5

Likewise, the Marlowe Society had their work cut out for them. German audiences had naturalised Shakespeare through the popular, and prudish, Schlegel/Tieck translation. The Nazis did their best to claim him as their own, adoring *A Merchant of Venice* and canonising the Romantics' translation.[18] When the Marlowe Society played *Measure for Measure* in Berlin, they faced resistance. That Shakespeare was English was an irritation. As the *Berliner Zeitung* put it on 27 August, when reviewing the play: 'Shakespeare has become so strong on the German stage through an ingenious translation that one almost inwardly resists hearing him in a "foreign" language.'

The Marlowe Society was founded in 1912,[19] with the poet Rupert Brooke among its first members. Like the Madrigal Society, it was on the edge between a professional and an amateur student group, whose actors would go on to careers on the stage and in broadcasting. One disarming — and perhaps foreseen — effect of bringing amateur singers and actors to Berlin was that it protected them from disparagement. Germans call it *Welpenschutz*, or 'puppy protection', when the young, shielded by their elders, are subject to milder critique. Indeed, the German reviews were kind.

The director of the Marlowe Society was a 'bright young thing': the celebrated Cambridge dandy, George Humphrey Wolferstan 'Dadie' Rylands, born in 1902. The wealthy son of a Liberal MP (he gave most of his money away), he was a student and actor at King's from 1921. As Noel Annan described his fellow Apostle:[20]

> He became a Cambridge celebrity almost as soon as he arrived. His looks were remarkable: fair wavy hair, slim, feline in manner, he was a fascinator ... for the next twenty years and more the old and the young, men and women, fell in love with him, and suffered disappointment and despair when he was unable to return their passion.[21]

Rylands worked at the Hogarth Press for Leonard and Virginia Woolf, applying stock labels to *The Waste Land*. Virginia depicted him, when she saw him in his baby blue suit with his blue eyes, as a 'cornflower'. She wrote:

> He is a semi-Neo Pagan perhaps ... a very charming spoilt boy ... but at heart he is uncorrupted (so I think — others disagree) and all young and oldish men ... fall in love with him.[22]

He remained at King's after his graduation as a Junior Fellow, his rooms adorned with nudes. He had engaged a decorator who later complained that her interior design 'resembled that of a diseased mouse and attributed her failure to too many cocktails'.

And yet, Rylands hated arrogance and pomposity in the people he met and had no trouble telling them so. His friend Arthur Marshall said,

'Friendship with Dadie was like being on an ocean liner from which one was hurled into the sea for a misdemeanour. As one surfaced, one saw the heads of a dozen old friends bobbing in the waves. But a life belt was soon thrown out.'

His exacting eye for human behaviour and assurance in criticism delivered results on the stage. Rylands had an illustrious position in the professional world as the governor of London's Old Vic Theatre, where he produced plays starring John Gielgud. Rylands once startled the actor when he interrupted a soliloquy, cuttingly, to say: 'John, have you any idea of the meaning of what you've been saying?'

The last time the Marlowe Society had performed *Measure for Measure* was in 1941. Both productions, including John Webster's 1612 work *The White Devil*, were tailor-made for the Foreign Office Tour, with pre-performances in Cambridge early in August with the same cast. *Measure for Measure* was an intriguing choice for Berlin. Considered one of Shakespeare's 'problem plays', it is not quite a comedy (although it ends with marriage) nor a tragedy (although the play revolves around characters who face imminent death at the hand of Vienna's despotic ruler).

A play set in a Germanic capital ruled by authoritarian leaders who survey and cruelly manipulate their subjects, enforcing rules in the most draconian manner possible, was familiar territory for Berliners. *The White Devil*, on the other hand, was one of the bloodiest plays in the repertoire. As the western *Telegraf* newspaper wrote about the choice: 'All murder variations are performed with the most gruesome mastery: poisoning, daggers, strangling, shooting, madness, and falling off a horse. It's death as a dramatic state-of-being!' Or, as the *Manchester Guardian* remarked on 26 August:

> It may be that the violence and amorality of the age are not a very good diet for contemporary Germany. Webster's plays are too much like life as it was lived under the Nazis. But the results are always interesting when one age discovers another age for the first time. Nothing but good can come from acquainting Germany with Byrd and Purcell. It will be odder if the knowledge of them is brought by the Airlift.

The selection was likely purposeful. The Cambridge programme from 2 August makes clear the society's political mission: 'The poison of power ... when wisdom and goodness fail [is] alike in the Rome of Sixtus or of Mussolini, at Berchtesgaden or in the Kremlin.'

6

In August 1948, Berlin awaited the arrival of both the Soviet choir and the Cambridge students. The British authorities took their plans seriously and tried to impress on their military staff that the festival was not just an expensive form of entertainment, a mere 'Berlin affair', but 'a definite cultural/propaganda move and should be treated accordingly'. Governor Brian Robertson even spoke of a 'battle for the German soul'.[23]

On 21 July, Brigadier E.R. Benson wrote of a 'cultural offensive ... and [was] especially anxious that our publicity should appear in the Russian Sector'. The British would infuriate the Russians, as Birley later penned to Annan, when two thousand posters – a significant expense – were printed and posted in all the city's zones, including the Soviets'.[24] The British made contingency plans to soften the blow:

> [We] took the step now of notifying the Russians of our plan for the Festival and of inviting their participation to the extent of sending a lecturer to lecture on Russian ideas on Shakespeare. Mr Birley feels that nothing would really be lost by such an invitation, and there is just a chance it might prevent the Russians trying to spoil the show.[25]

But the Russians were not interested in participating, having already complained about performances of Tchaikovsky and Mussorgsky on RIAS as 'falsified'.[26] Instead, they took the opportunity to position the invitation of the Alexandrov Ensemble as competition for the planned British events. They saucily requested that their Soviet choir sing in Berlin's Olympic Stadium in the British zone on 22 August, the second day of the Elizabethan Festival. In diplomatic correspondence, the British noted bluntly that the Soviets were turned down 'on the grounds the stadium is booked up'. The Soviets retaliated with film footage of empty stands.[27]

Meanwhile, the students were still practising lines and counterpoint before packing their belongings. Costumes were put in boxes. Calls were made to the Foreign Office. Then, from their medieval colleges, dozens went to stand on Cambridge's long station platform before boarding a train. From Harwich, they crossed the Channel to perform their plays and songs on the ravaged continent.

7

Patrick Magee, a young tenor at King's, remembered in his unpublished journal how the group travelled inland from the Hook of Holland.[28] Entering Germany, he encountered in Essen the 'biggest mass of destruction' he had ever seen. Framing this aesthetically, he observed how 'the masses of tangled steel at the side of the [train]line were an artist's paradise'. The actors and singers had a good meal in the restaurant carriage, feeling acute embarrassment as starving Germans passed by on the platforms.

Arriving in Bückeburg, an airfield town in the British zone not far from Hanover, Magee remembered how they 'packed us secretly into an aircraft and smuggled us to Berlin, much to the fury of officials who were unable to get their families in or out because of the heavy restrictions on air space'.

The students packed the empty hull of the plane like cargo and took off East. As their aircraft cruised to Berlin, one of the engines failed, and the plane sank low over the city as it approached Tempelhof. The pressure changed quickly, nauseating the passengers. Noel Annan wrote later in his memoirs how 'for the last two miles, the aircraft seemed to be level with the top storey of the houses on either side'. Finally, they reached Tempelhof and its steep landing, the impact so abrupt that all the vinyl albums of James ('Jimmy') Beament – a future insectologist – brought for the incidental music of the theatrical productions smashed, forcing him to compose music for live performance instead.[29]

Rattled, the student thespians and musicians emerged one by one from the cargo plane. They made for a veritable 'Who's Who' of the post-war British Broadcasting Corporation, likely due to Dadie Rylands's emphasis on enunciation. Richard Baker, 23 years old at Peterhouse, thick with dark hair and playing Lucio in the Shakespeare, would become BBC television's first-ever news bulletin announcer. Michael Ashbee, 24, playing the Provost, would work for the World Service. The chorister Bernard Keeffe, 23, already mentioned, became the BBC's opera producer. And Charles Parker was the mind behind the BBC's '50s radio ballads.[30]

Traditionally, all roles in the Marlowe Society had been played by men, which only changed in Cambridge in 1929. Rylands first famous role at King's was as Electra in *The Oresteia*. But now women also joined the production, including Gillian Webb – tabby-like, with a mane of ribboned hair – from Girton College, who played Isabella, the Shakespeare lead across from Rylands in his role of Angelo. She was the only professional actor among the students, having just toured in America with Michael Redgrave in a production of *Macbeth*.

But the person whose face was perhaps most intriguing to observe when it emerged from that aircraft, her feet touching the tarmac of Berlin, was a young Jewish-German woman of 26, Gabriele Ullstein. She was to play Zanche, a Moorish servant to Vittoria, in *The White Devil*. Her Berlin family had owned the largest publishing firm in Europe, subject to a forced sale in 1934 by the Nazis. At 11, she fled the country and was educated at a British boarding school before reading Modern Languages at Newnham College, Cambridge. Margareta 'Greta' Burkill, who had also been at Newnham – and who had sponsored Ernst Reuter's son, Harry – remembered how many well-to-do Berliners threatened by the Nazis sent their children to Cambridge for reasons of education at the time, as Cambridge was so tightly connected to the German émigré experience. Gabriele would later become a literary critic, writing hundreds of essays for *The New York Review of Books*. Apart from her brilliance, she was universally known as a snappy dresser. Ullstein now returned to the country that had exiled her and her family.[31]

What the Cambridge cast saw of Berlin shocked them. King's Provost, Donald Beves, 52, who played the clownish Pompey in the Shakespeare, gave his impressions to *Die Welt*:

> The destruction seemed so complete, and so endless: impossible to imagine that any human being could still live amidst these ruins, or that anyone could survive such destruction. And for a while, the horror of the senselessness and the feeling of being in the midst of this decay gave rise to a sense of depression that could not be alleviated. Everything seemed like an endless desert, formless and shapeless.

Only with time did Beves begin to distinguish the city plan, particular trees, and the ability of Berliners to trudge on. In the same vein, one of the invited lecturers, the Shakespeare expert H.B. Charlton, who had lived in Berlin thirty-seven years before, wrote in the *Manchester Guardian* on 20 September how he had:

> never returned to Berlin until [that] week ... Rubble, the grim skeletons of street after street after street, for mile upon mile – that is the pictorial impression of Berlin to-day ... A stab to the memory of the returning visitor who recollects that the popular song of the city he formerly knew was 'Du hast ja keine Ahnung/Wie schön du bist, Berlin [You have no idea/ How beautiful you are, Berlin]'.

When the cast arrived from the airport to their hotel in the erstwhile wealthy neighbourhood of Grunewald, Annan remembered just one flower, Loves-Lies-Bleeding, parched in the garden. Patrick Magee, when he wandered about the hot city, again felt embarrassed among the 'tired, shoddy, and hungry' locals scouring the streets for a cigarette butt or piece of food. He thought that the Germans he met were happy with their gifts of tea and coffee. They 'longed to get rid of the occupying powers, but greater still was their terror of us walking out and leaving them to the Russians'. The contrast between British power and Germany's defeat was all the stronger when the students frequented the British Embassy Club, where Magee jotted that some British acted as if they were the 'master race': 'One man in the Embassy Club could think of nothing better to say than shriek at the German waiter for not mixing his cocktail correctly.'

8

The festival's opening concert was initially planned at a villa on the River Havel to imitate a 'water party' of the kind favoured by Elizabeth I. Robert Birley then offered his residence, a mansion in Grunewald, instead. Imagine the young Gabriele Ullstein – the Jewish Berliner studying at Newnham – walking up the drive and entering the mansion. By sheer chance, this place was not only familiar but meant a great deal to her. Her family had lived here until they were expelled by the Nazis. As Noel Annan wrote later, the house had:

in fact, been built by Gabriele's father Louis Ullstein, the businessman and most prestigious of the five brothers who owned the publishing house Ullstein Verlag. She had lived there only a short time: her father died a few months after Hitler became Chancellor. Mother and daughter later came as refugees to London. During the Occupation, the house became the residence of our ambassadors, and years later, two of them, with characteristic solicitude, invited us to stay there and sleep in the room that was Gabriele's as a child. Now it looked strange, filled with economy furniture, the bookshelves boarded up to stop theft.[31]

The manor is still the British Ambassador's residence and hosted the Queen on her Berlin visits. Perhaps, already in 1948, Gabriele walked through the interior reminded of childhood and exile at every turn.

The Elizabethan Festival finally settled on a rambling estate, located at Bismarckallee 46, approached by a drive through the 86,000 sq ft property. The big event was scheduled for 21 August, 7 p.m. for 7.15 p.m. No crowds of thousands, as in the Gendarmenmarkt, were permitted through the gates, but rather five hundred carefully selected guests.[32] There, thirty rows of seats were arranged in the garden. The house's balustrade was strewn with banners of St George and St Andrew.[33] *Der Spiegel* reported they were lucky it did not rain. The weather was 'lukewarm', cloudy and humid 'like in England'.

At 7.15 p.m. – with punctuality that impressed the German press – halberd-carrying Beefeaters appeared and stood motionless in their red and black. The yeomen were, in reality, occupation soldiers commanded to stand still for two hours. The *Manchester Guardian* reported:

> What has especially caught the imagination of the Berliners has been the Beefeaters who have lined the stage at concerts. The Russians produced their singing Cossacks. What reply could be better than the Beefeaters?

According to the Foreign Office, they were in hired garb from a costumier,[34] something the Berliners did not notice. At least one journalist confused what they wore for Renaissance costume. In any case, what the Berlin press did detect was the intended 'sense of tradition', a Britain not rooted in revolution but in stability and continuity. Even the beverage plans had a tint of anachronism: Rylands was consulted on serving mead.

The German public also heard something familiar as twenty singers emerged onto the terrace in black evening dress and gowns. As *Der Morgen* reported, the choir did not just recall Leipzig's 'Thomas Choir, or Dresden's Kreuzchor, Regensburg's Domspatzen, or the Vienna Boys' Choir, but madrigal choirs all over Germany'. When the conductor Boris Ord spoke to the audience in German, 'it made things feel close. It was less foreign than an Italian or French evening.' And more than anything, it was the refreshing intimacy of the experience rather than any mass spectacle that impressed. The music critic of the East's *Neue Zeit* wrote:

> A full, beautiful sound is coming to us from the musical silence of England these days ... This intimacy corresponds to the numerically small size of the choir, its style and its original intention of scoring with amateur singers ... The result is a fresh, unforced naturalness of interpretation, which is borne by personal experience, by an inner involvement with the music; one can sense the organising hand of conductor Boris Ord. He is not interested in creating virtuoso artistry but, above all, in a spiritual grasp of the style. The singers find the way to this from their connection with a music, which is an expression of their highly developed culture.

There was the disparaging reminder of England's 'musical silence' – the 'land without music' – yet this is quickly morphed into 'music in which one soon feels at home', something the Germans could naturalise. Thomas Morley, Orlando Gibbons, William Byrd, Thomas Bateson, Thomas Tomkins, John Bartlet, and John Dowland, and, of course, John Wilbye's madrigal sung from the back of a departing punt, 'Draw on Sweet Night', all appeared on the programme.

Patrick Magee, the tenor from King's, wrote how 'our own contributions were received with much enthusiasm; after all, we were the only entertainment the citizens had'. But it was more than that. German observers repeatedly noticed a 'freshness' in the sound. By offering a choir mostly of undergraduates marked by 'natural voices ... great clarity and freshness', or so wrote the *Berliner Zeitung*, or, as another reporter put it, 'expertise combined with love', an atmosphere of youth reigned over the gathering.

More concerts followed in the British Information Centre, where they were marred by the roar of the Airlift overhead. There the Madrigal Society played the choral programme of Henry Purcell, with an entr'acte of his Chacony in G minor. They were accompanied by a pick-up chamber ensemble composed of members from the Berlin Philharmonic.[35] Fritz Peppermüller – who wrote the receipt for their involvement – was a second violin of the famous Berlin orchestra. He was well used to gig jobs, having financed his studies in the Roaring Twenties by playing violin in Berlin coffeehouses.[36] Patrick Magee later wrote about the cross-cultural musical exchange – invoking a stereotype of German rule following – and how the Germans at first 'played with usual German accuracy and precision, but also with inflexibility. Skilfully, Boris Ord brought them to understand Purcell. They were much impressed by this Englishman who was gifted enough to teach them in their own language how to interpret a composer with whom they were not acquainted.'

Only the most doctrinaire of the Soviet-zone newspapers did their best to detest what they heard and saw. *Neues Deutschland* argued the sound was 'brittle and sober' and that Purcell was 'actually the only creative musician of European standing in England'. The performance of *Circe* was 'inadequate', and the conductor couldn't 'bring this old music to life'. According to the reporter, the so-called 'festival' required much more than a few modest performances. The contrast with the Alexandrov Ensemble was clear: in the next column of the newspaper was a glowing ode to the Soviet concerts as 'the artistic experience of the summer', with the ominous wish not only that they come back soon but that they 'play in every sector'.

X

THROUGH THE IRON CURTAIN

1

Meanwhile, Kenneth Slaker shook all over and vomited.[1]

He saw the geography from above, from the map he had studied. And he knew he had parachuted from the failing aircraft twenty minutes after they passed into the Soviet zone, which he estimated as approximately 50 miles from the West's border. In that direction, there were more potato fields, and then higher, in the mountains, were the thick woods. That is where he needed to go. He calculated the considerable risks of being caught: 'The Russians said that we pilots would be held as spies. Which means that you could end up at a work camp in Siberia, never to be seen again or be shot.' Whatever happened, it couldn't be that.

But Slaker was also badly hurt: his back roiled with pain from where he had landed. It took everything in him to keep walking. The thought of giving up came, went, and never returned. He turned his leather flight jacket inside out to hide his name and wings.

In terrifying flashes, he imagined how he would be captured – with the shimmer of a distant ox cart or the roar of a truck – but he followed one lane to another, along a ridge with a weed-clogged ditch. He could hide there if needed. When a bus approached ahead, he crouched down in 4in of water.

High above were the trees. Closer, at the intersection of a paved road, was an old directional sign. He approached and it was wooden, its western spur pointing to Eisenach, '35km away'. Again, it was a name he knew from the map, and it comforted him to position himself. The town hugged the fortified and mined border of the West.

The more Slaker walked, the more his body was in pain. He continued on the paved road instead of cutting through more mucky potato fields, even though he wanted to reach higher ground quickly.

Then, up ahead, he saw something that set his heart racing: a bicycle approaching just yards from that forest, gaining momentum, and pointing straight at him. On it was a Soviet soldier, hoping to force him from the road. Slaker moved off the lane and caught the icy stare of the enemy. After he passed, he turned his head. But the soldier did not look back.

Slaker remembered, 'Little did he know that he had just ignored an American Air Force captain.'

2

Lieutenant Clarence Steber saw his co-pilot Ken Slaker escape out the back of the falling plane. But, just then, the engines started up again and, with sudden optimism, Steber returned to the cockpit to regain control of the failing aircraft.

The sounds of rain thudding dully on the fuselage were drowned out by the sudden roar of the reviving engines, which lasted only four minutes before they came again to a windmilling stop.

'MAYDAY,' Steber radioed on the emergency channel and then gave up, standing before the cargo door in his parachute, to plummet to a seeming abyss.

Except the plane was already too low.

'My parachute opened, and I hit the ground at nearly the same time,' the US Air Force man said later.

He fell unconscious. It was only when he woke that there was the smell of coffee. They'd given him gallons of it. Most likely forced it down his throat. He was covered in manure from where he'd fallen.

The Soviet soldiers who had captured him pelted him with questions, but they did not need to ask his name. They knew who he was. The lost aeroplane had been reported, but they had been lucky enough to find him. Bleeding and bruised, Steber was squeezed for information, treated as an enemy agent by a country that was, until recently, his ally. For three days, he was 'roughed up' and interrogated as an American spy, except he had no information to share. All he could do was repeat his name, rank, and serial number repeatedly. Because he had not been sent East to spy on the Soviets.[2]

Steber remembered, 'I was a young American, and I gave them a hard time. Everywhere I went, they had a bust of Stalin on the desk and a picture of Stalin on the wall. One day, I got tired of their questions, so I reached over, grabbed the bust of Stalin, and pulled it toward me. "Who's this?" I asked the interpreter. "Napoleon?"' His interrogators were unamused and replied by beating him.

Steber was eventually taken to an East German hospital, where his injuries were treated. Guards stood at the door of his ground-floor solitary room. There was the smell of alcohol, the scrape of bandages, and the feeling of being far from home.

From the yard, though, came the sound of car doors opening and closing, the bass of American voices: a staff car, with diplomatic plates. In plain clothes, the visitors were two representatives from Berlin's Potsdam Liaison Committee. Steber stared at them, a prisoner in his hospital bed, as the Soviet guards pulled the door closed, allowing the Americans to be alone for their brief authorised audience.

One of the Americans brought his voice to a hush, 'Do you think you can make it out of this here window?'

Steber replied, 'I sure can.'

But Steber was hurt and struggled as they helped him out to the waiting car.

The guards were still standing at the door. It took some minutes for them to realise the hospital bed was empty. Steber was now in the diplomatic vehicle's boot, the car rushing back to Berlin through the Soviet zone.

The men cruised up ravaged Friedrichstraße, approaching Checkpoint Charlie and the West. Steber was still in the boot when the Soviet guards advanced for the inspection. The two Americans showed their diplomatic passes and played nonchalant. The guard circled the vehicle and then got down on his hands and knees. He looked under the car but not in the boot. Everything appeared in order, so he waved them through.

When the boot was finally opened to reveal the battered, travel-worn man inside, they had already passed through the armed gate, with Tempelhof airport looming above him.

Steber was put on a C-47 and flown like a sack of flour to Wiesbaden.

3

To Ken Slaker's surprise, deep in the trees he observed a man coming towards him. He thought he had been more careful than that, that he had scanned the woods for anything that moved, but now he was face to face with a German. Slaker was not partial to Germans. He had spent the war giving them hell from his bomber.

To defend himself, Slaker only had a 3ft-long piece of wood that he had used as a walking stick. He was buckled over in pain and had not slept for more than twenty-eight hours, but the stick could double as a club.

'*Guten Morgen*,' Ken said, moving to pass the other.

Slaker continued a few paces, then turned to look. A suspicious man would turn back. One who thought nothing was amiss would keep walking. In the first case, Slaker would need to confront the other to stop him from reporting to the Russians.

The man had not kept walking. He was standing there, looking. Slaker's accented '*Guten Morgen*' had given him away, and he didn't look like a German peasant foraging in the forest.

Slaker remembered: 'I gripped my club tightly and started to walk towards him. It is amazing how strong you can become when your life is threatened … I had killed before, and now I would be able to do it again to save my life.'

But he first spoke to him tensely, in English. 'I am an American pilot. Which way to Fulda?'

The man was dark haired with a broad face and inquisitive eyes. He replied that Fulda was in West Germany and not a good place to go.

Slaker replied in his German, pointing to himself, 'Fulda *gut*.'

Another moment passed, and Slaker gripped his club.

The German knew he was in danger. He raised his hands as if to surrender. Then he explained, pulling some papers from his pocket: *Schau mal! Schau mal!* Look! Look! I was an American prisoner of war in Nebraska. Here are my discharge papers. The Americans were good to me. I am only here looking for food for my wife and for my baby.

Between Slaker's German and the other's English, they began to communicate. Slaker pulled at the lapels of his jacket, turning it inside out to show his hidden wings and name, and he said, 'I am a pilot.'

Rudolf Schnabel, or so his name was, said that his family was starving. If Ken could help him get milk and shoes for his baby in the West, he would help the pilot through the border. 'I'll get you anything you want.'

Kenneth shook his head. It was too risky.

But Rudolf approached the American, brought one hand to his forehead, and tapped it, saying, 'I'm not afraid: Soviet dumb.'

The pilot stared at the other, looking for sincerity in his eyes.

'Kenneth no trust Rudolf?' the other asked.

'*Ja und nein,*' Kenneth replied.

Rudolf shrugged. 'It doesn't matter. Come.'

And one followed the other through the woods.

4

Kenneth's tongue was swollen; he could hardly speak. From his shoulders to his lower back, he gnawed with pain. They walked and walked, continuing until they found a cart pulled by oxen that carried them several miles through the potato fields, now cultivated by pensioners in cloth-wrapped feet because the young had died in battle or were taken by the Soviets to work factories and mines. Along the way, Rudolf stopped at a farmhouse of someone he knew and got potatoes, and civilian clothes for Slaker.

There was a train stop within striking distance. Rudolf insisted they take the railway to Eisenach.

Kenneth was worried: If the Russians saw him at the *Bahnhof*, would they not be suspicious since he was a young man?

'I will tell them you are mute,' said Rudolf. He would do all the talking.

Slaker stared, thinking the plan sounded like suicide.

'You are a brave man, much braver than I; therefore, I am leaving you now and will make my own way through the woods to the border,' was Ken's reply.

But Rudolf turned to him seriously and said, 'Let's talk. If we get to Eisenach this afternoon, my friends will get you through the border tonight. But the longer it takes you to get to the border, the greater chance you have of being caught.' They would be looking for him.

Kenneth met his eyes and thought for a long time about what to do. Finally, he said, 'We do it your way, Rudolf, let's go.'

Rudolf led him towards the Soviet encampments – places where the Soviets had concealed gun emplacements, where their military vehicles milled, and the sound of gunfire echoed in the background. A Red Army training camp was visible up ahead, a mile away. Kenneth looked nervously at his guide but followed him down the roadway towards the enemy.

Then, a Russian vehicle roared past at top speed. The road had a bend, but the truck did not slow down.

Ken remembered:

I watched in amazement as the driver started into the turn without easing up on the gas, and just as the truck started to turn over on its side, the driver straightened his front wheels and drove into the muddy potato field. As the truck ploughed to a stop, several Soviet soldiers jumped off the truck, all of them laughing and enjoying the thrill. They pushed the truck back onto the road, climbed aboard, and away it went again at high speed. Rudolf looked at me, tapped his forehead, and said, 'Soviet dumb'.

The sun came out over the railway station in the small village, with a dozen people waiting on the platform. Three Soviet soldiers with sidearms guarded it, and Slaker barely restrained himself from bolting into the woods.

Rudolf put one arm under the pilot's and led him to sit on the grass opposite the station.

He would be back in a moment. He went to buy the tickets, leaving Slaker alone.

Kenneth noticed his brown Oxford shoes as he sat down in the sun. They were conspicuous, so he crossed his legs to conceal them. Everyone seemed to be looking at him. Was it his imagination?

Across were Soviet soldiers. One was gawking – he felt the 'full stare' of a Russian major. Now he was very nervous. But where could he go? The village? The hills? Otherwise, he would be asked to identify himself, and then it would be arrest, interrogation, torture, Siberia …

Then another realisation came to him: the soldier across the street was not looking at his face. No! He was looking at his arm. At his bright gold Bulova wristwatch shining in the sun.

Ken pulled it from view, but it was too late. The officers were now conversing with each other, and now all three were peering across at him. Slaker stood up. It was time to turn and escape, perhaps into the village –

But just then, the passenger train pulled into the station for a quick stop. The Russians turned quickly from the road to their designated wagons while Rudolf, with the tickets, grabbed the American by the arm and raced to the front car for the Germans, which stank of crushed bodies.

It was a lucky escape.

When they reached Eisenach, Rudolf woke Slaker. They were not yet in the clear.

There, Rudolf pointed at the terminal gate where the Soviets were checking tickets. Slaker would need to summon his acting skills. He had to say nothing, keep walking, and remember he was mute and deaf. 'Do not run, walk only' were Rudolf's instructions.

Slaker felt his back in intense pain: 'It was a very tense situation for me, and I was sure the guard would hear my heart pounding.'

Up ahead, the soldier was inspecting papers. A crowd pushed forward, with Slaker buoyed in the middle, pointing his thumb at his friend as the guard shouted. But the man could not leave his post. Slaker heard Rudolf speaking to the guard. So, Slaker turned his back and walked silently – past the checkpoint, out the terminal door, and with a right turn, out of sight.

'I never looked back but expected to feel a heavy Russian hand on my shoulder at any second,' he remembered, but it was Rudolf who caught up with him, 'giving me the V for victory sign.'

5

They took a tram to Rudolf's apartment, just one room with a wood stove in the back and his welcoming wife and their baby girl by the door. They invited Slaker in to sleep on the couch, but every sound from the street made the pilot panic. He thought of Steber, perhaps falling to his death. But he was not there long: there were preparations to be made.

Down a narrow street, in a dimly lit space, three men sat at a table telling Slaker they could whisk him into the West for money. How much did he have on him? There was an East German border guard who would take a bribe. Slaker had 700 Western marks. He gave them 500 because he was in no position to bargain.

That night, there was a tight time window to cross the bridge over the River Werra. At 8 p.m., during the changing of the Russian guard, the bribed East German policeman would be left alone. The river was not yet the border. Once over it, they would still need to follow the bank through the weeds to a clearing. Kenneth wouldn't be alone: two others escaping that day would meet them there and, together, they would cross at midnight the mined, guarded, armed border to the West.

It was a mad plan. A bridge, Russian guards, strangers, mines, guns. 'I thought to myself that at least I didn't have to swim across the cold river.'

That evening, Rudolf's family shared with Slaker the little food they had: potatoes and onions, which he ate despite his bruised tongue. There was a tender moment between Schnabel, his wife, and their child. When would they next see each other? Slaker took the man's wife by the hand to thank her.

A streetcar took them to the edge of Eisenach, tucked in the Thuringian hills with the Wartburg castle looming over. It was another 3 miles to the river and the bridge. They were early.

Rudolf turned to the pilot and explained how he planned to cross with him, buy the things he needed, and then return. It was difficult to leave the Russian zone, but no one minded if you came back. Ken shook his head and told Rudolf he shouldn't risk his life over shoes and milk. But the German was adamant; perhaps he never intended to return to the East.

It was just before eight, and they hid near the head of the bridge, over the River Werra tucked between the green hills and flowing lazily. They watched as a Soviet squad assembled on the far side of the bridge, taking the sentry stationed there with them. Soon, only a lone East German policeman was left standing at the crossing.

Rudolf and Kenneth stepped onto the bridge from their hiding place and began to cross toward the policeman, who had now seen them. The pilot's heart tried to 'escape his chest'. 'I got the feeling that he was going to challenge us and that I had been suckered out of 500 West German marks.'

They grew closer, within 6ft. The policeman made a move.

The guard turned his back to the men, and they walked right past him!

Walk, keep walking!

When on the opposite side, they quietly dropped off the bridge into the brush.

They waited in the clearing, hidden from the bridge, until there was a sound. It was the others: a young man and a girl. Kenneth remembered that he was a German veteran while she was an 18-year-old whose wealthy family wanted her out.

The border was at the top of the hill – the West German police station was a shining light above.

The route up led through a cabbage field between two Russian sentry boxes. The way was strewn with barbed wire and mines. The goal was so close, but Kenneth suspected that many people had been shot in the undergrowth trying to reach it.

6

It approached midnight. Rudolf went first, followed by Slaker, the girl, and the former soldier. The gibbous moon shone too brightly, casting silver over the cabbage fields, and the searchlights blinded them before the sentries. They suspected the guards would shoot before investigating. As for the mines, it would be a matter of luck.

Kenneth thought to himself: What will you do if they start shooting? Run back to the river clearing? Make a break for the hill? What if Rudolf is blown up? Is it every man for himself?

He wondered if he would hold back to help the others. He shook his head. No, no matter what, he would escape. He wouldn't stop to help these Germans. They weren't his friends. Now was the time to survive.

Only when the sky clouded over did they crawl single file over a bur into the cabbage patch. It was a slow, methodical, and painful process of advancing and stopping, listening, tapping each other's feet to signal they were still together for what seemed like hours.

> We were flat on our stomachs, and my heart was pounding so loudly that I knew it could be heard several feet away. The cabbage plants did give us cover, but it was difficult not to make any noise because of the crackling of the stiff leaves. We dared not raise our heads above the cabbage heads because the sentries would see us.

Then they left the field, and they could now see the Russian in his box, cradling his machine gun. All four of them were together, whispering, deciding what came next. It was Rudolf who gave the signal: *Jetzt! Now!*

And they ran.

At that moment, Slaker's tired body seized up on him. His legs weighed like lead, folding in the cabbage field. Through the darkness, he saw nothing – he only felt the pricks of barbed wire tearing all over his body, leaving scars he would carry for the rest of his life. But he didn't feel pain: 'Everything disappears in those moments.' He trampled through the mined border strip, breaking through one fence after another.

Then the shouting began, and the bright red tracers from the Soviets' automatic weapons lit up the sky. 'For every tracer, there were three to five unseen metal bullets.' They danced around them, and he couldn't believe he hadn't been shot yet. The firing intensified.[3] He collided with Rudolf at the bottom of the hill, the final ascent to the West.

Jetzt! Now!

But now the pain in Kenneth's back was 'agonising', and he had sharp pains in his legs from the barbed wire's cuts. His philosophy during the border crossing was 'every man for himself' – that the Germans did not feel the same would trouble him for the rest of his life.

As Kenneth braved the hillside, with the others all up ahead, racing toward the border as shots rained down on them, his back finally gave out. In a dead roll, Slaker tumbled all the way back down the bank.

Then he heard the German girl's voice from above: 'The Captain has fallen!'

Despite the rain of machine gun fire, the Germans turned around to get him. They formed a chain to hoist him back up the hill. He felt hands pulling him. The red tracers intensified. 'It is a miracle that not one of us was injured,' as they catapulted over the ridge and onto a paved road leading to the West German crossing.

Now, he was invigorated. Kenneth found his legs. With his military ID in one hand, he ran, 'the fastest I had ever run in my life … '

7

Kenneth Slaker began to fall asleep in a hot bath. That afternoon, an Army doctor had examined his back – damaged but not broken. His

German peasant clothes were now crumpled in a pile on the floor. He didn't remember being helped into bed or the maid dressing his cuts. He blacked out.

He was woken early, his body 'stiff as concrete'. A uniform was folded and waiting for him. He appeared at breakfast in the house of the American colonel in Bad Hersfeld. It was 'absolutely the best breakfast of my life'. He would be flown that morning from an airstrip to Wiesbaden. General Tunner was waiting to meet him.

So many things had happened: the two young Germans who had crossed with them disappeared before American counterintelligence arrived twenty minutes later. Slaker had given them each 50 marks. Rudolf stayed but had lost his papers somewhere in no-man's-land, and this was a big problem. As Rudolf rode in the front seat to Hersfeld, Slaker explained how the man had saved his life. Slaker recounted, 'The Colonel said he would see that Rudolf received his new shoes and milk for his child if he still wanted to return to the Russian Zone. He instructed the driver to take Rudolf to the compound. That was the last time I was to see Rudolf for almost a month.'

Journalists had meanwhile bribed a guard at the border for any good stories. The Associated Press had been on the phone. The story was already exploding. Slaker was told to say nothing until they decided on 'an official version of events'. When he unloaded from the plane at Wiesbaden, Slaker was met by a brigade of press people and photographers, who tailed them all the way to the command post.

In the moving car, Slaker asked his driver what had happened to Steber.

The driver only replied that the Russians had informed them that one of the pilots had survived the crash and the other was dead.

Steber was dead?

No, Slaker was supposed to be the dead one.

The precarity of his situation in the Eastern zone became blindingly apparent at that moment: 'This fact made my escape from the Soviet zone absolutely necessary, for if they had seized me after reporting me dead, I would never have been released.'

The briefing with General Tunner was supposed to be short, twenty minutes, but it lasted twice as long, followed by a one-and-a-half-hour debriefing, another visit to the Army hospital, and then being escorted to a press room where he saw ... Steber!

The official story was that Slaker had unproblematically walked through the Iron Curtain without help and without being shot at.[4] In order to protect the East Germans who had helped him, 'The true story was classified and not released for forty years for security reasons.'

8

Clarence Steber returned to constant Airlift flights and became known as the owner of Vittles, one of the Airlift's mascots. He would go on to fly 131 flights with the dog he loved, a 1-year-old boxer from Germany.

Caring for the animal at the base was a problem because Steber was flying so often. He explained in an interview, 'I couldn't leave him in the bachelor officers' quarters all by himself because sometimes I would be gone for two or three days at a time. So, I started taking him in the plane with me.'

But Vittles had a life of his own. Steber said, 'In Berlin, as soon as we were unloaded, we had to take off again. Sometimes, Vittles would be nosing around other aircraft, and I had to take off without him.'

But the world of the US Air Force was small: Vittles would show up either in Berlin or one of the bases in the American sector, catching rides back and forth but always finding his way back to his master. That was unless Vittles was drunk, as the pilots who took him to the officers' club had a penchant for filling his bowl with beer, in which case the dog would be carried back to Steber.

Vittles became a celebrity, with photographers taking every opportunity to put him on magazine covers back home. He was also in the comics section. In one cartoon, Vittles sat at a table in the officers' club with a knife and fork. The chief cook threatened to banish him from the dining room table despite all the missions he'd accomplished.

News about Vittles soon reached the top brass, and General Curtis LeMay called in Steber.

'Are you the pilot who owns the dog who is flying in our airplanes?'

Steber was sure there was a problem.

'Yes, sir,' Steber said.

'Vittles doesn't have a parachute. He is one of the best morale builders that I've had over here. I want that dog to have a parachute!'

Vittles was given a parachute he had to wear when flying. It was specially designed with a dog harness and tethered to Steber's parachute, so if the pilot opened his, Vittles's would follow automatically.

Except Vittles never needed to use that parachute. Steber never again went down as he had with Ken Slaker. And the story of Vittles remained uncomplicated and easily told to the press, unlike the continuing and complicated drama of Ken Slaker and Rudolf Schnabel.

XI

STUDENTS IN THE RUINS

1

Berlin summers are known for late sun. Emerging from the performances, the Cambridge students found the streets still bright. They did not hesitate, in those off-hours, to wander into the Eastern zone. Some were sent on forays by British intelligence. Antony Vachell – playing only a bit part of an armourer in *The White Devil* – had a more significant role in a separate operation, euphemistically described in his obituary for King's:

> As a budding economist, Tony had somehow been persuaded to take part in a highly unofficial research project which involved him and his partner straying into the Soviet sector to see how much people there would pay for the newly introduced Deutschmark. The pair were soon approached by a Soviet officer who saw them off with the threat of Siberian exile, and Tony's brief career in espionage was over.[1]

That Vachell was given a specific task to complete suggests the instructions were not exactly unofficial.

Patrick Magee also strayed, as he put it, 'by mistake' into the Soviet sector, 'which was *verboten*'. In his unpublished diary, he presented a remarkable, Ozymandian scene. On Voßstraße were the gargantuan ruins of Hitler's chancellery building, designed by his chief architect Albert Speer and completed in 1939. The edifice had mostly survived the war. The cathedral of crimson stone was then quarried for a nearby metro station, the university's foyer, and memorials to Soviet dead.[2]

The Soviets stripped away the memory of the Führer's legitimacy, and Magee wandered into the innards with a friend:

> We entered the wreck of the *Reichchacellery* [sic], now bereft of all fittings, and the Russians had stripped the place of all marble. The vast corridor outside Hitler's study, 100ft long, was once covered by a single strip of carpet. Here ambassadors would be kept waiting. Opposite the building lies the broken bunker in which Hitler and Eva Braun finally had their swan song.³

The weight of the history impressed the young tenor as he imagined Hitler cowering in his palace as the Red Army battled through the Tiergarten, some 300 yards away. Now, the space was deserted and silent. The momentous events were only three years in the past.

A guard suddenly appeared and confronted the young men.

Who were they? 'Russian?'

No.

Then the guard vanished and returned ten minutes later to ask: were they Czech?

No. The Cambridge undergraduates grew nervous.

Magee wrote, 'After a further lapse of time in answer to his query as to whether we spoke English I replied we spoke just a little, but we were Italian-speaking Swiss: time to go ...'

They quickly slipped out of the erstwhile chambers of power back to the West.

2

The undergraduate actors found their way to the aptly named Renaissance Theatre in the British quarter, ready to perform to the assembled crowd. The art deco venue was a snug proscenium arch affair, with a rounded upper gallery of seats. It was also a mirror of the miserable living conditions of everyday Berliners – so hot inside that the staff kept fainting from hunger, and so penurious that the visiting Brits had to provide essentials such as light bulbs, even as the theatre worried about overrunning their power quota. Meanwhile, the stage was too small for the action.

Yet, the atmosphere was electric, the *Manchester Guardian* comparing the buzz to 'the Berlin of Weimar times'. There was a hunger for theatre because so little had been performed since the capitulation.[4] Shakespearean scholar H.B. Charlton observed how 'each night the theatre was packed, predominantly with Germans. Attendance was so great that many had to stand.' They attended even though 'most would have to walk home, sometimes as far as five miles, through dark and debris-piled streets'.[5]

These Berliners came even though the play was in English. Dressed in period garb, British wives of the Control Commission Germany distributed programmes with drawings of an Elizabethan gate, the Globe Theatre, and King's College Chapel. But the only words in German on these programmes were: *Die Aufführungen finden in englischer Sprache statt. Eintrittskarten sind an der Theaterkasse erhältlich.* 'The performance is in English. Tickets are available at the theatre's box office'.[6] No plot summary in German was offered. As *Der Spiegel* reported, the play being in Early Modern English produced a certain 'coolness between stage and audience'.

Shakespeare had never felt so foreign, at least to the Eastern paper *Der Morgen*, which took a nationalistic stand: 'it's clear the Germans have found more in Shakespeare than his compatriots looked for'. With some relief, the *Berliner Zeitung* reviewed a German production a month later: after the 'immensely English performance', it was a pleasure to enjoy finally 'a thoroughly German Shakespeare, one that belongs to us as if it were a piece of our own poetry'. But Hilde Spiel, in *Die Welt*, chided the audience to remember that 'authentic Shakespeare is in English'.

Director Dadie Rylands's rooms in King's may have been ornate, but his productions were not. One scholar quipped this meant there was 'a certain absence of semen',[7] but Annan wrote more chastely that Dadie 'used no scenery, never cut the text, and attended to the words'. The austerity, wrote Ivor Brown in the *Manchester Guardian,* suited a city under siege. The Berliners were 'quite ready for a sober statement instead of a fantastic scream'. The *Guardian* opined that minimalism was also not very Elizabethan – 'An unkind critic might say it is less a festival of the Elizabethan age than of how the Elizabethan age appears to Cambridge' – however, this is probably not true, as Shakespeare's stages were likely almost bare.[8]

The critics of Germany's largest theatre city knew precisely what they were seeing. As *Berliner Zeitung* noted, there was nothing in the way of external scenery. With two sets and an intermediate curtain, they achieved a pace of play that has never been seen before in Germany. Monologues, spoken into the space in front of the dimly lit intermediate curtain, gained an incomparable unparalleled intensity – and once again it should be said that this so magnificently spoken Shakespearean English conveyed a convincing legitimacy.

They contrasted the production to their handling of the Bard. As *Telegraf* noticed, 'The English take the verse very seriously, every movement comes from it ... The fact that we Germans find this view somewhat unintelligible and cannot connect it with our Shakespeare productions reveals the glaring difference.' For these reasons, the Shakespeare was mostly celebrated in the press, as was the Jewish actor Gabriele Ullstein, now performing in what the press called her *neue Heimatzunge*, or 'new native language'.

Rather, what upset the German audience was the Webster, with its series of on-stage murders. Ivor Brown noted: 'it may well be asked whether Webster ... is a suitable export ... he may be said to have strangled his plots in the entrails of the murdered'. Perhaps the Webster was intended to depict the disease and Shakespeare the cure. *Measure for Measure*, after all, ends with a timely moral lesson as the Berlin programme of the Shakespeare advocated: 'Forgiveness fits the human situation better than justice.'

But the Eastern press, which had not hesitated to write generally positive reviews of the Madrigal Society and the Shakespeare, had words for his contemporary. *Nacht-Express* found the play's structure 'primitive and unmotivated'. But it was the *Tägliche Rundschau* that went for the kill, so to speak:

> Did the Marlowe Society want to pollinate the brains of German poets when it made this play the subject of a festive performance at the Renaissance Theater? Perhaps it is only the lack of paper that prevents so many West German publishers from giving space to 'animal religious pornographers' of the calibre of Henry Miller or to the 'witches' sabbath of the irrational forces of our animal nature'.

H.B. Charlton, writing on 20 September for the *Manchester Guardian*, thought the festival's purpose was to remind the German of 'his roots in Western culture'. But the *Tägliche Rundschau* flipped this observation on its head. With the experience of a destroyed city under their belts, Berliners were inured to the theatrical bloodletting. It was 'a good omen', said the newspaper, when Germans expressed their 'insensitivity to the horribly grotesque through delighted laughter'. The home audience became the civilised ones, watching corrupt theatre makers import 'English neuroses' on stage.

3

The students moved freely around the Reich's capital. The musicians attended a full Berlin Philharmonic rehearsal with Sergiu Celibidache conducting. Magee remembered the maestro cursing and stopping the orchestra every three bars. The Cambridge actors were meanwhile reprimanded by the German director, Jürgen Fehling, for coughing during a dress rehearsal of *Egmont* at the Hebbel am Ufer theatre.[9] But they were impressed by German dramatics – by what Annan noted was the 'attention to detail, dedication to theatre as an art', just as the Germans had been captivated by the British attention to verse.

Naturally, not all the explorations were high culture. Annan recounted that one of the British actors managed to have an affair with the male lead of the production of *Egmont* within forty-eight hours. At a political cabaret called *Die Stachelschweine* (the 'Porcupines'), the students watched a group of performers act out black marketeering, banging their hands on a long table to imitate the sound of an S-Bahn train smuggling food in from the Soviet zone, as they shouted: '*Kartoffeln, Kartoffeln, Kartoffeln!*' The lights would go off, and they pretended they were in a tunnel, their chant turning to: '*Polizei, Polizei, Polizei!*'

After the last event on 4 September 1948, the students themselves were whisked back to Britain for the start of their academic year a few weeks later. They left behind a conversation.

The British brought these plays to Berlin with a purpose: to show that they would stay in Berlin. This would require living and working with the Germans, becoming closer to them as human beings, and recognising their humanity. The French officials called the Elizabethan Festival the British 'chess move'.[10]

But had quaint madrigals, obscure Purcell, and student productions of Shakespeare and Webster delivered? There was something comical about serving up so many cultural stereotypes. The *Sunday Dispatch* wryly compared the staid events in the Grunewald garden to the bread and circuses of the Russian performances for readers at home:

> The Russians attacked, using searchlights, balalaikas, trumpets, and harmonicas in close support. An audience of 2,500 Germans are believed to have been almost entirely captured. The British Cultural Forces counter-attack was opened by six British soldiers dressed as Beefeaters, who took up positions on the first-floor balcony armed with home-made halberds. The main fighting was borne by the crack troops of the Cambridge Madrigal Society, commanded by Boris Ord. Their Elizabethan songs are understood to have made some impression on 150 already cultured Germans. British casualties were two Beefeaters who fainted while on active duty outside Mr Birley's bedroom. During the following days the British forces gained valuable ground with performances of 'Measure for Measure' by the Marlowe Society.[11]

Doubt underlay the parody: what was the point of culture in the Cold War effort? This lingering suspicion would put an end to British cultural missions to Berlin. An audit of the visit did not see all the receipts add up, and military administrators in London were perplexed that culture should cost money instead of make money,[12] despite the fervent belief of educators on the ground that it was crucial in the Airlift operation's effort to battle Stalin. After 1949, West and East Germany would not learn the same lesson. They would treat each other's Berlin zones instead as *Schaufenster* or 'shop windows' to show off each other's cultural and architectural achievements, and so the superiority of their systems.[13]

4

Der Spiegel on 4 September compared the British performers to the boisterous Alexandrov Ensemble:

> The Elizabethan Festival of the British military government followed on the Berlin cultural battleground. Despite its considerable

size, it was the most measured, closed-minded and buttoned-up event in the world ... There, intoxicating brotherhood, here, stiff elegance.

There, casts of thousands, acrobatics, and open-air performances in publicly accessible spaces. Here, small group performances, rarefied repertoire, and concerts with tickets or invitations to chosen dignitaries. *Der Spiegel* continued to describe the two approaches: 'Broad effect there – peak effect [*Spitzenwirkung*] here.'

The British tactic was not only about putting an elite over the collective. Other glaring cultural differences were at play, remarked Félix Lusset. Why had British propaganda efforts before the festival been so half-hearted? The French official blamed the Brits' 'peculiar characteristic', a 'British temperament ... averse to bluff and exaggeration'. He reckoned the Britons found propaganda distasteful and argued one could learn from an understated festival because it respected the intelligence of the German audience:

> All in all, there is no doubt that the British solution is a good one. There is a lesson for everyone who believes that in an occupied country, and especially in Germany, one must avoid everything that is reminiscent of propaganda and advertising. Despite their consideration and restraint, the cultural-political activities of the British in Germany appear to be suitable for effectively preparing the future.[14]

British understatement was also a result of impecuniousness and the constraints of the Airlift. The Russians could bring hundreds overland but, for the British, every person imported was at the expense, as *Der Spiegel* observed, of 'the corresponding weight of flour or hard coal. This is how the gaunt Brigadier Benson, deputy city commander, put it with a smile on the opening evening, with a serious look at the seventy kilograms of the first speaker'. Rylands's aesthetic of spare sets was admired by destitute Berliners, but it also suited the British Office financially and logistically. Aesthetics followed the capacity.

Understatement was not the only virtue of a high-culture approach. Soft power could plant seeds in the minds of the young. Charlton later wrote in the *Manchester Guardian* that young people in Berlin 'are already in serious danger of drifting intellectually'. Through critical engagement with works of art and culture, they could undercut 'the frustrations of life in a deliberately disorganised society [where] these young people may ... even march into Stalinism'.

German observers also noticed how non-hierarchical and focused on student development rather than the professor's authority British pedagogy could be. The *Kurier* praised the lectures, referring to Charlton: 'Hardly any other German professor is so Socratic, so confident in his approach, so affable and relaxed'; West Berlin's new Free University should ban 'the preceptor type of German professor'.

In the end, it was also about the Bard's role in times of conflict. Should we always forgive? Does rancour lead to more bloodletting? Was this not also the future question for the new enemies – East and West – in the Atomic Age? Herman Kamps, writing in *Die Welt*, asked pointedly if historical theatre pieces 'could still interest us today in our constant crisis situation?', and replied that Shakespeare in 'the summer of our discontent, 1948' returned one to the most basic of existential questions laid bare by conflict: 'What is man?' Kamps recognised 'the role that the great English playwright has always played for our *Volk*: to be a mover and deepener of purely human relationships'. Theatre was to bring people together. To make friends of a hungry occupied city with those who had bombarded it. To befriend a population implicated in a murderous regime that had trampled Europe in a frenzy that made the villains in a Webster play pale in comparison.

5

Hilde Spiel, the Viennese cultural critic and journalist, wrote of the festival in her 1990 memoir. Like Annan, who began his memoir contrasting the Soviet and the British efforts of that summer, she could not resist the juxtaposition. At first, she was bowled over by the Soviet visit. The song 'Kalinka', she wrote, sung by Nikitin,

> had such an incomprehensible effect on friend and foe as only 'Lili Marlen' had before. Thousands of people fill the square, we stand in the middle of it and listen to the orchestra and its singer until we are completely exhausted.

Spiel invoked the 'fantastic picture' of ruins, the beauty of the melody, and then the marring effect of the British or American planes drowning out the Russians' songs from above. The Soviets might be the Germans' oppressors but somehow the Alexandrov Ensemble made everyday Berliners 'surrender to the Slavic melancholy'.[15]

The British approach had a distinct, lasting effect on this critic. Not just the intellectualism of the Elizabethan choice struck Spiel, but a touch of romance. Having met Rylands, Ullstein, and Annan, she was impressed at the former's connections with the Bloomsbury Group and Virginia Woolf. Of the performances, she said:

> the most beloved England swells up around us, Cambridge, to which I have been addicted all my life ... All these heartfelt, wistfully quiet or even passionate testimonies to the early fertile era under Elizabeth I – no, 'Kalinka', the rousing Russian girl, does not come up and sinks into the darkness of a nostalgia that has been lived out and outlived.

Precisely, the words 'wistfully quiet' come to the heart of the difference. One performance flooded the audience, while the other invited it in.

6

Return to the closing night of Shakespeare at the Renaissance Theatre, with its borrowed lightbulbs, its hot, stuffy interior, and the now familiar faces of Annan, Rylands, Webb, Ullstein, and the other Cambridge dons and 'fresh' students as they stood on the stage. They were uplit before the Berlin audience, the defeated of a tired, isolated city, who had spent hours in their seats observing young people from the occupier's country. Nonetheless, the audience erupted in applause.

One detail of this final moment on stage, as *Measure for Measure* concluded, charmed even the most severe Eastern journalists. The Marlowe Society advised the Berlin press corps that they usually did not include actors' names in the programme, only when they toured abroad. And they explained they did not normally take endless curtain calls.

Looking at the Cambridge programmes, we know that the former, at least, was a lie. But the clever fabrication worked on several levels. Not only did it suggest that the actors were not private persons but part of a group British effort, but the note of collectivism appealed to the socialist newspapers and their audiences, happy to efface individuality. As Walter Lennig noted in the *Berliner Zeitung*: the ensemble that 'spurns all "curtains" in its homeland, bowed three times in unison, and one would have liked to bow once more before such a strict, uncompromising, and devoted zeal, which snubs all applause'.

With the smallest of gestures, as opposed to a big one, something more had been said.

7

Shortly after the departure of the Cambridge students, on 6 September 1948, Henry Ries was hiding in the toilet of the New Town Hall, a sober Nazi-era building in the Soviet sector. A mob of communist workers had interrupted the convening city council and was doing its best to destroy the edifice with the officials inside – the united municipal house of representatives still met despite the Soviet restrictions. The last thing the photographer wanted was for his camera to be broken.

To his relief, Ries saw his driver through the frosted window, and the man helped him escape through it. As he left, he saw 'the camera of Hank Burroughs, United Press, being smashed by demonstrators at the entrance'. The 1946-elected city council was practically dissolved by the events, completing the governmental division of the city. The Soviets would later blame the chaos on the Americans and their Black Guards.[16]

Two weeks earlier, Stalin had invited Western officials to the Kremlin with an offer: withdraw the new Western 'Bear' Mark, let there be a single currency in Berlin, return Berlin to being a four-power city, and the restrictions would immediately cease. Reverting to the pre-currency reform status quo was not a good offer. With tonnage increasing, the propaganda battle under way, and the promise of a Western buffer to Stalin's long arm, the West felt they were well ahead of the Soviet game. A single currency in one country would bind the West to a socialist economy and not the capitalist model favourable to American markets.

The Airlift would go on. And the Berliners would go along with it. The armed disturbances as the city council convened were a signal that the Soviets would not let West Berlin go easily.

Berliners took the aggression against their democratic assembly seriously, treating it as a coup. On 9 September, they came out en masse to protest. Ruth Andreas-Friedrich described how 'housewives ran away from their stoves, the hairdresser abandoned his customer under the drying hood, the news vendor closed his newsstand. Everybody came running, thinking we must demonstrate.'[17] Half a million Berliners became an ocean of bodies in the Platz der Republik, the enormous lawn fronting the burnt-out Reichstag, the former seat of government. Berliners spilt out into the denuded Tiergarten. It would be the largest public assembly since the war.

Henry Ries now stood in the crowd facing the man they came to listen to: Ernst Reuter. The *New York Times* photographer remembered: 'I have seen and been moved by many crowds. But none, not even the people of London bidding goodbye to Winston Churchill, has moved me as much as that vast throng.'

It would be the first of many great Berlin Cold War speeches. Kennedy's 'I am a Berliner' and Reagan's 'Tear Down this Wall' orations – both also given before monumental buildings of the divided city – were born from Reuter's. The Reichstag speech would make Reuter the best-known German leader of the time.

8

As usual, Reuter worked with just a few words jotted on a little piece of paper. But his characteristic incantation – staccato, deliberate, eloquent – made the speech feel like a continuous sentence, with something for everyone. It showed how far Reuter had come from his days as Bolshevik commissar. The internationalism of the Comintern had evaporated, as he pointed nationalistically to the 'proud inscription' on the Reichstag, 'Dem deutschen Volke' ('To the German People'), and even promised German trains would run again to Breslau and Stettin, cities Germany had lost to Poland.[18] Berlin would not be traded to the Soviets: 'We Berliners do not want to be an object of exchange'. Their common identity would not be broken, with Berliners tricked into opposing each other as 'White Guards and Black Guards'. The crowd answered with rousing cheers. Here, finally, was a speech addressed directly to them, not the occupying Allies.

But the culminating words that were addressed to the whole world sparked the powerful electricity in the crowd – a voice of resistance with the cameras rolling:

> You peoples of the world, you peoples in America, in England, in France, in Italy! Look at this city and realise that you must not and cannot abandon this city and this people! Peoples of the world, look at Berlin!

The crowd was stirred to a frenzied pitch. Reuter became the man of the moment. His talent for logistics and oratory and his convictions from a life spent between East and West seemed purpose-made for this moment of crisis. His rhetoric of Berlin as the 'outpost of freedom' against the 'forces of darkness' was also music to many Americans' ears,[19] becoming stock phrases of the Cold War. Self-interest reigned here, too: Reuter pitched his message over the heads of the 'diplomats and generals' to reach public opinion in the States. He wanted the whole world to rescue Berlin, not just crusty military governors like Clay.[20]

More than ten thousand from the Eastern zone had come to the rally. Elated, they flowed back home through the Brandenburg Gate and Pariser Platz, joined by demonstrators from the West. But there a chain of militiamen was waiting for them.

A loudspeaker announced that the square was closed, and the Eastern zone's police gripped their rifles against a crowd that threatened to overwhelm them. Then, Berliners were climbing up the Brandenburg Gate. One shimmied up the flagpole and tore down the Soviet flag. The crowd's applause was deafening.[21]

Ruth wrote in her diary: 'After the demonstration was over, dangerous incidents took place at the Brandenburg Gate. They tore the Soviet flag off the gate and started shouting and making threats. The Russian police interfered.' First, there were warning shots, then shots into the crowd.

Wolfgang Scheunemann, 15 years old, tried to escape the scuffle through a gap in the ruins of the Adlon Hotel, located on the square. He was not supposed to be at the demonstration. With four or five other friends, he had skived off from a three-week summer camp on Berlin's edge just to hear Reuter speak. As the bullets cut through the crowd, Wolfgang found himself at the wrong place at the wrong time. Twelve others were injured, as Wolfgang buckled over, hit in the stomach. The demonstrators hauled the teenager's body through the Brandenburg Gate, back to the Western side, throwing it on top of a truck that rushed to a hospital. He arrived dead. The bullet came from the gun of the Soviet zone's German People's Police, or *Volkspolizei*. Wolfgang was counted as their first Cold War victim.

The East made arrests. As Ruth wrote: 'Five demonstrators were arrested. Yesterday, the Soviet military court sentenced each of them to twenty-five years in a labour camp. That means death. Sooner or later, in a concentration camp or a uranium mine.'

The day ended violently. But these struggles with the Soviets at the Brandenburg Gate clarified something else. As Ruth wrote of Reuter's speech: 'We belong to the West. We are Berliners. We are a community of fate. It is a great thing to feel a part of a community of fate.'

For many years, before the Wall fell, two enormous photographs by Henry Ries hung in the West Berlin city hall, of that sea of humanity in front of the Reichstag – a half million, angry and defiant.[22]

XII

SWEET VICTORIES

1

Mercedes Simon never liked chocolate. She had an aunt living in Switzerland who, in 1945 – when Mercedes was only 4 – sent a chocolate bar to her relatives living in the ruins of Berlin.

The package arrived from Basel to the neighbourhood of Friedenau and its five-storey residential blocks, with stuccoed classical flourishes, built at the turn of the twentieth century. Today, riots of wisteria, a boulevard of maples, and old gas lights sleeping under their domes give the place a secure feel. They are also signs that the street, hidden behind Bundesplatz, mostly escaped war bombing. Except for those marks on the façades or dents in the ironwork, telling of bombs dropped nearby, down the street on Stierstraße. Or that the oldest trees are from the 1950s.

Up in the house, with its bay windows and loggias, whose façade was once taupe blue but now appears through a veil of coal, Mercedes Wild, née Simon, is 83 years old.[1] She still lives where she did as a child. Her flat is expansive, with six rooms, and we sit in a living room full of books, photographs, and fragile Delft dishes, the door open to the sunny balcony. She points to the salon's ceiling, still cracked and bare from the bombs that fell over adjacent streets. The whole house jumped, and the ceiling mouldings came down.

The sound of the aeroplanes stays with her – the *Brummen*. The bombers flew low, and she remembers sitting in the basement as a toddler and how the lights flickered. It still bothers her when lights flicker. And she remembers emerging from the cellar into the street, seeing an abandoned baby carriage or a streetcar on fire, memories seared into her.

When the United States started flying in goods for the Airlift, it was difficult for Mercedes to adapt to the sound. The situation was worse than elsewhere in Berlin because their home was located directly under the flight path, 2 miles west of the runway of Tempelhof Airport. The planes soared low there, on their way out to the middle corridor, returning to Frankfurt or Wiesbaden, and the boom of their ascents frightened the 7-year-old. Mercedes remembers how her teacher explained in school that they no longer needed to fear the sound. It was a different *Brummen*.

Mercedes calls herself 'mouse-like, but resourceful'. Her childhood friends would go out together through the ruins, looking for old metal, bits of paper, and bottles. They would trade potato peels for a piece of coal, to contribute to the stove at school. From remains of wax, they learned to make candles. From bits of cotton, they twisted wicks. Mercedes says she preferred to go around with little boys rather than girls. They made a good clique, working together and sharing everything.

What else imprints her and dominates any conversation about the period is hunger. In 1948, 7-year-old Mercedes was so malnourished that she was put on a list to leave on a rescue flight out of Berlin to her aunt in Switzerland. There, she would be fed. But one day, she was in the kitchen, telling her mother she didn't want to go, and her grandmother overheard from the next room. Speaking solemnly in the third person, her grandma decided: '*The child* will not go.'

Seventy-five years later, Mercedes explains how even the next generation inherited memories of the hunger or 'wolf' times. The *Wolfszeit*. 'I still always stock reserves. And I always clean my plate,' she tells me, 'My children do too. It's the grandchildren who don't understand why.' They still ask her, 'Why must you taste everything?' Everything still goes into her mouth.

The starvation occurred directly after the war but, even in 1947, US Commander Lucius Clay estimated that Berliners were 'living' on 900 calories a day. In the *Telegraph,* Anthony Mann observed a typical diet consisting of a breakfast of one slice of black bread, lemon blossom herbal tea and acorn coffee. Lunch was 'two thin slices of bread and a potato'. Dinner was one bowl of 'watery soup made from carrots or barley'. To this, you could add scraps of fat. One year later, during the Airlift, most Berliners only (officially) had 400g of bread, 40g of meat, 30g of fat, 40g of sugar, 400g of dried potatoes, and 5g of cheese per day.[2]

Families were forced to supplement. In the courtyard of Hähnelstraße, the Simon family grew potatoes, apples, and even flowers to cut and sell. They had animals, too: rabbits and white chickens. But the constant sound of low aircraft over their courtyard terrified the animals, preventing the chickens from laying eggs. The young Mercedes would scold her birds, saying: we need food, and you'd better lay some. Because these eggs were valuably exchanged at the bakery on the corner for bread. Or at the butcher for some beef. 'Everyone bartered', she told me, 'Even the children.' As a child, she watched through the mail slot of their apartment building as her mother sold the last of her jewellery on the street. Mercedes's shoes came from the black market. You could tell: they realised they were different sizes when they got them home.

Berlin children born just before or during the war had never tried many foods. When they first encountered oranges during the Airlift, some tried to bounce them. Chocolate was an untested treat until it surprisingly fell from the sky.

It was only because of Mercedes's aunt in Basel that the girl knew what it tasted like. And, when she had tried it, opening that care package, she didn't like it, deciding at a young age that it was altogether too sweet. But Mercedes still wanted chocolate. Not for the taste but because it could be used for something else.

'Still, when I see a chocolate bar,' she tells me, 'I don't think of it as something to eat. It's something with value. You could trade it.'

This is why, one evening in October 1948, Mercedes took particular interest in a newspaper article that her mother read her. An American pilot named Gail Halvorsen was dropping chocolate and candy from his plane as he landed and took off from Tempelhof Airport. He would wiggle his wings to indicate a drop of his sweet cargo, to which he affixed little white parachutes so the mobs of waiting kids wouldn't get injured. This 'chocolate bomber' was by now famous and had been receiving piles of thank you letters written in crayon by Berlin children. Mercedes made her mother promise they would go to the airport and get their hands on one of those chocolate bars.

2

For years, the US government worked with chocolate companies to produce bars with military applications.[3] The Tropical Bar, created by Hershey, withstood heat. The D-Ration Bar, developed in 1937, was cut with oat flour for survivalist use. So thick that it gummed up the factory machines, the D-Ration Bar had to be moulded by hand into 4oz blocks. US soldiers, finding it in their kits, dubbed it 'Hitler's Secret Weapon', an observation about the taste. The bitterness – which Mercedes might have appreciated – was deliberate so that it would be eaten slowly in an emergency (the military's only requirement was it 'should taste better than a potato'). M&Ms were also developed for the military and sold exclusively to the US Army in the Second World War because they resisted heat and did not melt in soldiers' hands, mucking up military hardware.

The chocolate business made a wartime fortune, making it a close government partner. Hershey alone produced 3 billion bars exclusively for the US military after lobbying Congress not to shut down their candy industry as superfluous in times of war. Hershey had a point: chocolate was good for US Army rations for two reasons: it contained caffeine and a lot of calories. A D-Ration Bar alone had 600.

By war's end, the D-Ration Bar may have been thankfully discontinued for sweeter, more familiar varieties of the Hershey bar, with milk or dark chocolate, or almonds. But the military's connections to the chocolate business had not ended. Chocolate and candy continued to be part of every US soldier's ration. The Airlift pilots were given Mounds, with shredded coconut in dark chocolate, or Butterfinger, peanut butter in chocolate. Life Savers, Bazooka bubble gum, and Wrigley's Doublemint were all supplied in the take-off bases of the Western sectors. The persistence of these sweets in US rations would allow history to take a surprising turn in Berlin in 1948. A Soviet diplomatic note would, in turn, call their role in the Airlift an 'outrageous capitalist trick'.

3

Gail Halvorsen, born in 1920, was an unlikely hero.[4] The prematurely bald farm boy was no Hollywood poster boy. His life tilling sugar beet and feeding the pigs apples in Utah, near the Idaho border, was an incentive to fly far away, despite his mother's huckleberry pie. They were Mormons who drank milk, not alcohol, and were used to discomfort, living in a farmhouse without electricity or running water. They brought hot bricks to bed in winter to keep warm before waking early to work the beet fields. Gail was a man who knew poverty when he encountered it in Berlin. But in 1939, he wasn't too fond of Germans. In high school, he'd learned that the Germans had developed the sugar beet.

Like Ken Slaker, Halvorsen became a pilot because of his childhood. When tilling his family's fields, he heard a staccato roar from the west. A crop duster descended rapidly and lunged over the field. The boy found the experience exhilarating: 'I just had to learn to fly!' When he finally became a pilot, he pulled the same act on his farm folk: 'the nose plunged almost straight down; mountains, sky, fields, Mom, Dad, spun around crazily in a characteristic blur.' But he almost gave his mother a heart attack, and — dutiful as he was — Gail promised never to pull such a stunt again. Instead, he would always wiggle his plane wings to let them know, if they were looking up, that it was him.

Halvorsen becoming a pilot was something of a miracle. He never thought he would fly because, for that, you needed a university degree. He worked too long hours on the farm to have those kinds of opportunities. But then the war began, and pilots were in sudden demand. Halvorsen was able to get the training he always wanted. But his position in the US forces from March 1943 was not illustrious. He was posted to work in transport, rather than bombing missions, doing runs from Brazil to Atlantic and Pacific islands. Air folk said the Air Transport Command's ATC acronym meant 'Allergic to Combat'.

When Gail was finally demobbed, the last thing he wanted was to return to 10 acres of sugar beets in Garland, Utah. Instead, after some deliberation (Halvorsen was known for indecision) he ended up with a regular commission with the peacetime Army Air Force. Like other pilots, he was taken off guard when, on 10 July 1948, he was ordered to leave his base in Mobile, Alabama, and join the Airlift effort. He quickly ditched his new red car — a 'beautiful new, red, four-door Chevrolet' — in a grove of pine trees to fly via the Azores to Rhein-Main where, an hour later, his crew boarded yet another plane to haul cargo deep through the Soviet sector, to Tempelhof.

Conditions at Rhein-Main – or Rhein-Mud, as they called it – were even worse than his childhood farmhouse in Utah. The pilots were to sleep in a barbed wire compound in a tar paper shack previously occupied by displaced people. Two to three pilots could take turns sharing the same bed. Halvorsen later wrote that the whole place smelled. Instead, he and his buddies found a nearby barn whose loft was full of cobwebs, but it was reasonably clean. Halvorsen put himself to bed there, his nose running from a head cold, for which he'd packed extra handkerchiefs.

That night, Gail quickly met other pilots, including one from Travis Air Force Base in California who explained that he was at first 'downright resentful' when he started flying for the Airlift, but soon he figured: 'When defenceless women and children are involved it cancels out a lot of the past. I didn't feel too good about dropping the bombs. Now maybe I can do something about the food.'

The next morning, 27-year-old Gail got ready to fly East on a C-54 Skymaster with a cargo of flour. The radio directed them: 'Big Easy 548 cleared to runway 07, altimeter 29.98, time is 12:50 hours, wind East at 15 gusts to 20, call when ready for take-off.' Gail replied, 'Easy', feeling the heavy load weighing them down, but soon they broke from the earth – a bracing feeling he never got used to. 'Gear up!' Halvorsen commanded. He quickly learned to remain within the 20-mile air corridor or risk intersection by a Russian fighter. With good weather, the three-man crew could see in every direction, including the planes intervalled ahead and behind, the distant ones just specks. 'For the first time, the enormity of the operation began to sink in,' he later wrote.

As his plane descended over Berlin's lakes and forests, he neared the Dolomitic crags of the rubble, stretching in all directions. Halvorsen was stunned by what he saw. He had never seen so much urban poverty. It was a frieze of misery flitting under the rushing plane. It both repelled and fascinated him: brute evidence of the war he had only seen from the sidelines and the defeat of millions somehow existing within. In his memoir, he writes:

> As we looked down, it just about took our breath away. Nothing I had read, heard, or seen prepared me for the desolate, ravaged sight below. The gaunt, broken outlines of once-majestic buildings, struggling toward the sky, supported by piles of rubble at their base, irregularly

stretched from one end of the city to the other – a mottled mass of total destruction.

On the steep dive into Tempelhof, something else caught his attention: dozens of children standing and waving on a grass strip before the airport fence. With its planes landing in succession, the Airlift had become a spectators' sport. But Halvorsen saw only glimpses of all this: he had only thirty minutes after landing to 'Follow Me' to the refreshments, for the refuelling and the reloading, before they took off back to Rhein-Main.

From that first landing, he remembered best the Germans working as crew at Tempelhof and the moment one asked him for a handshake. He thought about how he hesitated before taking the former enemy's hand. He then realised that the Berliners looked at the American pilots 'as though we were angels from heaven delivering the news of the resurrection ... We were friends, working for a common goal: to be free.' With that handshake, as he descended from his Skymaster, Gail understood that, before, he had taken the Germans as an 'impersonal mass of humanity'. Now, he had to recognise them as individuals, with faces and fears.

Meanwhile, the image of kids staring up at the departing planes was a momentary snapshot of a hard life most pilots would never engage directly.

4

Only about a week after Halvorsen arrived in Germany, on 19 July 1948, his buddy Lieutenant Bill Christian, a roommate in the barn loft, offered to take him to Berlin with a load of potatoes. Not on a cargo run, but to see the city and take pictures. Halvorsen had already flown through the night and was very tired, but he was also determined to dip into the city that he had only experienced in glimpses from the air and the tarmac.

As soon as the plane landed and pulled up under the overhang of Tempelhof, he walked over a mile to the perimeter fence, where he had seen the children from the air. Thirty were there that day, both girls and boys, children and teenagers, all clean but worn, watching him in uniform. Halvorsen was waiting for a jeep to take him around the city, so he had only a little time to chat once he realised they spoke some school English. But he noticed a few other things about these kids.

The first is that they were timing the planes. They were also interested in how much the aircraft could carry, especially food such as flour. But Halvorsen remarked, 'They said they could get along on very little food.' They also told him – perhaps words taken from their parents – that they understood that the planes stood for things like freedom and their ability to read what they wanted or live under good government. 'Freedom' was not something abstract: it meant living without intense state surveillance and the cult of Stalin's personality. That children understood this 'got to him' more than even the handshake with the German mechanic on the tarmac.

Knowing he needed to get to the jeep, because an hour had already passed, Halvorsen turned to leave. But what he expected did not happen. Children in other poor places where he had landed his plane had always come running, asking for something, food or money. But these Berlin kids did not ask him for anything. They refused the 'beggar's role'. It was Halvorsen who hesitated and turned back to the children to offer them whatever he had, which happened to be two sticks of Wrigley's Doublemint gum in his pocket.

There was not enough to go around. Splitting the two gum sticks in half was only enough for four lucky children. Gail was worried there would be a fight. But he noticed how the other children reacted to the unfamiliar packaging. They handled the foil that protects the gum and the paper slips. They smelled it – the slightly industrial, bitter but sweet tang – and passed it around. Halvorsen observed that these children had not had sweets for a long time – or ever – and, without thinking, he promised to drop enough candy from his plane for all of them the next day. They would know it was his C-54 descending because he would wiggle his wings as a signal. The children were confused. 'Vhat is viggle?' one asked. So Halvorsen awkwardly acted out the gesture.

Late for his jeep ride, Halvorsen spent the rest of the day rolling through the Reich capital. They passed through the deforested Tiergarten, now a muddy vegetable garden with statues randomly studding the landscape, robbed of their symmetrical clearings and rose beds. Even though it was against the rules, it was easy for their jeep to pass near the blasted Brandenburg Gate into the Soviet sector, where they were angrily chased out by Russian soldiers wielding guns. Halvorsen wrote in his memoir that the visit had been a 'scene of man's inhumanity to man'.

On returning, exhausted, to Rhein-Main, he gathered his buddies in the barn loft and explained what he had in mind. He asked for a favour: to donate their gum, candy, and chocolate rations of Hershey's and Mounds. Worried about hitting some kid on the head with a heavy rations bar, he took three handkerchiefs he had brought and tied them to the piles of sweets.

The first drop happened, as promised, the next day, on 20 July. His co-pilot and engineer on the plane sat in silence, unhappy with his task, worried it was against the rules, that they would get caught, their tail number recorded. Halvorsen was only concerned they wouldn't hit the right place. But as their plane descended, just past the seven-storey apartment block with skid marks on the roof, they used a chute for emergency flares next to the wing and hoped for the best. Their wheels churned down on the metal runway, and there was no way to know whether Halvorsen's promise had been fulfilled.

Only when they were flying back did he see proof of their success through the fence. The children were there, 'waving three handkerchiefs through the barbed wire. Kids were jumping up and down and waving like mad.' Later, he would recall that 'I wished they wouldn't do that' because what the pilots had done was against the rules, and the children were drawing attention.

This did not prevent them from dropping candy over the next two weeks. Halvorsen and his buddies were now exhilarated, enthusiastic – on board with their mission. It distracted them from their mundane and tiresome return flights from a barn in Rhein-Main. They were doing something worthwhile for the kids. But their drops caused headaches: the crowd of children outside the fence grew. Base operations were alarmed and confused by the piles of thank you letters that began arriving, addressed to *Onkel Wackelflügel* (Uncle Wiggle-Wings) and *Schokoladenflieger* (Chocolate Pilot). The men grew nervous. They stopped dropping candy entirely for two weeks, which only meant they had a pile of two weeks' rations when they finally decided to try again.

Just one more time. It would be their final drop.

One drop too many. The next day, Halvorsen's plane was met by an officer, and the pilot was ordered to report immediately to his base commander. As he waited, his blood pressure rose. What if he were summoned to Tunner, the stern, chart-obsessed commander of the Airlift, more concerned with operational metrics than pilot welfare? A disciplinary meeting could end his career. Halvorsen immediately understood he might be court-martialled. He later wrote, 'That long thin thread leading from the sugar beet field in Garland, Utah to Berlin was about to break.' It was the end – and not just of the sugar drops.

He was ushered into the meeting with Lieutenant Colonel James R. Haun. A reporter, investigating the mystery of falling chocolate around Tempelhof, had almost been hit on the head by a candy bar – but not before he jotted down Halvorsen's tail number.

Haun told Halvorsen in no uncertain terms that he was going to meet Tunner. 'The General called me with congratulations and I didn't know anything about it. Why didn't you tell me?'

A wave of relief washed over Halvorsen, but he replied sheepishly that he didn't think Haun would approve. What the chocolate pilot did not realise, and what was already obvious to his superiors, was the enormous propaganda value of his ad-hoc operation. What would spin out from those chunks of sugar, cocoa, and milk powder – gliding into the hands of children, or pirouetting to the foreheads of staff reporters – would become legend.

Tunner, recognising its value, sent Halvorsen to New York for two weeks of television, radio, and newspaper work. The big chocolate manufacturers got involved, including the confectioner Huyler's, along with layers of American civic life. Churches, schools, and charitable societies began collecting chocolate, fruit drops, packs of chewing gum, gum drops, Life Savers, and tons of raisins from a bumper crop in California. These gave the name *Rosinenbomber* or 'raisin bombers' to the men scattering the Berlin skies with little parachutes.

Halvorsen became a sensation, on both sides of the Atlantic. He was mobbed by children at airports and mail bags packed with thousands of thank-you letters overwhelmed US command. Over the next year, 23 tons of candy would be dropped on 250,000 parachutes over Berlin, collected by 100,000 children. But this was more than clever propaganda. For both American donors and their German recipients, the gesture suggested a transformation in the United States' relationship with Europe. Not only was it sweet, now it felt moral.

5

Mercedes Simon, as promised, followed her mother, zigzagging through the mounds of ruins, from Friedenau into Schöneberg, towards

Tempelhof airport, where the planes roared as they continually landed and departed. They waited on Tempelhofer Damm, just outside the fence, where a large group of kids, perhaps thirty, gathered. They waited, and then finally a plane took off, approached them, and wiggled its wings. The children cheered. As they watched the little white parachutes falling from the sky, Mercedes saw one coming her way and reached to catch it, but at the last moment a bigger boy knocked her out of the way and raced off with the prize.

Mercedes returned home to the apartment on Hähnelstraße in tears, where her grandmother took her by the shoulders, shook her, and said, bluntly: 'Don't cry. Do something.'

Mercedes wrote the chocolate bomber a letter. In no uncertain terms, the 7-year-old explained how the roar of the planes taking off and landing made her sad. It scared the white chickens in their yard so they wouldn't lay eggs. On top of it, she didn't get any of the chocolate the pilot dropped. Since there were no eggs, the pilot might as well drop her some chocolate instead. Mercedes added she didn't care if, while dropping chocolate, he scared her chickens. It would be worth it. Signed, your little friend, Mercedes.

Mercedes's letter was penned alone, without her mother or grandmother knowing. At the corner near their house was a mailbox. On the way to school, she walked over and posted her missive to 'The Chocolate Bomber, Tempelhof Airport' in a child's writing, without any stamps. Mercedes explains that she was good at writing letters as a 7-year-old. Since it was unsafe to wander Berlin for much of her childhood, she had plenty of time to stay at home, improving her penmanship.

A month passed, and October became November until Mercedes got a reply. Her mother was a little flummoxed, realising what her daughter had done. Mercedes still has the letter, which had reached Gail Halvorsen at Rhein-Main, and whose reply was typed and translated by a secretary who misspelled his name. Mercedes shows it to me. It reads:

Frankfurt, 4 November 1948
My dear Mercedes!

Thank you very much for your
little letter. I do not fly over your
house every day, but certainly quite

often. I didn't know that such a
lovely girl lives in Hähnelstrasse. If
I flew a few rounds over
Friedenau, I would certainly find
the garden with the white chickens.
But unfortunately, I do not have
the time. I hope that this gives you
a little pleasure.

Warmest wishes,
Your chocolate uncle
Gale Halversen [sic]

Inside the letter, she did not find chocolate, which was satisfactory enough because she did not like it, but instead candy and some chewing gum.

Childhood tastes and smells are rooted deep within us – they redolently evoke feelings later in life. Mercedes tells me of her first experience with peppermint. It was strange, but it stayed. 'I'd never had anything like it. You see,' she tells me, 'Toothpaste in those days came as tasteless powder.'

There was something else she admired about what had arrived in the post, which was the way Gail Halvorsen had signed his letter. Mercedes had grown up without a father, who perhaps became a war prisoner in Russia. She did not remember him. For this reason, at a young age, it was important suddenly to have a 'chocolate uncle'. But he became more than that although she had never met him; he 'became a father to me at that young age'. As Mercedes explained, 'The children of the post-war period grew up mostly without a father; the pilots and their companions were, especially among the children, models.' This was something new: an American pilot could be the father of a little girl who, a few years earlier, had been frightened such an American pilot would bomb her house.

But Mercedes, as a strong-minded young girl from Berlin, was also too sensible to lose her head over a few sweets. Instead of chewing all her gum, she took it to school. There, she deftly traded it for a large glass marble. Unlike the American chocolates, it was not perishable, and, when needed, it could easily be traded again.

Border sign of the American sector on Schillstraße in Berlin-Schöneberg. (Photograph by Henry Ries on assignment for the *New York Times*/Deutsches Historisches Museum, Ph 2007/990, Estate of Henry Ries)

Antenna installation on the roofs of Berlin, 1935. Henry Ries is pictured on the left. (Deutsches Historisches Museum, Ph 2008/1295, Estate of Henry Ries)

On board the SS *Bremen*, 14 January 1938. (Photograph by Henry Ries/Deutsches Historisches Museum, Ph 2008/104, Estate of Henry Ries)

Steffi Ries, 1937. (Estate of Steffi Ries, with permission from Vivien Fryd)

Election to the city council in the Western sectors. Ernst Reuter casts his vote at a polling station, 5 December 1948. (Photograph by Henry Ries on assignment for the *New York Times*/Deutsches Historisches Museum, Ph 009328, Estate of Henry Ries)

Performance by the Alexandrov Ensemble at Gendarmenmarkt, 18 August 1948. (Photograph by Henry Ries on assignment for the *New York Times*/Deutsches Historisches Museum, Ph 2007/1071, Estate of Henry Ries)

Cambridge Students in Berlin; featured in *Die Zeit* special edition, September 1948. (Public domain)

Alec Chambers. (With permission from Alec Chambers)

1st Lt Gail Halvorsen and the 17th Military Air Transport Squadron rig some candy bars to miniature parachutes for German children in Berlin as part of Operation Little Vittles. (US Air Force. Public Domain)

Mercedes Wild, in 1947, going to her first day of school, wearing shoes of two sizes. (With permission from Mercedes Wild)

Flower seller Martha Wolfert, of Anhalter Bahnhof, with her baskets in the compartment. (Photograph by Henry Ries/Deutsches Historisches Museum, Ph 009404, Estate of Henry Ries)

Ironing during the two-hour lifting of the power cut at midnight. (Photograph by Henry Ries on assignment for the *New York Times*/Deutsches Historisches Museum, Ph 009303, Estate of Henry Ries)

Cornell Borchers and Montgomery Clift in *The Big Lift*. Cropped screenshot from the 1950 trailer. (20th Century Fox. Trailer is in public domain)

Unloading aeroplanes during the Berlin Airlift. (US Air Force: 110124-D-7991K-003. Public Domain)

Frankfurt/Main, Airbridge, Transport. (German Federal Archives/Bundesarchiv, image 146-1985-064-09A/CC-BY-SA 3.0. (Creative Commons License))

Candy bomber approaching Tempelhof. (Photograph by Henry Ries on assignment for the *New York Times*/Deutsches Historisches Museum, Ph 013987, Estate of Henry Ries)

View from the roof of the Reichstag of the rally against Soviet policy during the blockade, 9 September 1948. (Photograph by Henry Ries on assignment for the *New York Times*/Deutsches Historisches Museum, Ph 2007/1013, Estate of Henry Ries)

Beginning of the construction of Tegel Airport, which was undertaken by mostly women, 6 August 1948. (Reinickendorf Museum and Archive, Li-Nr. 1402)

The Church of Stolpe. (Joseph Pearson)

Illus-Bratke: 'Over the past few days, the police have been checking all vehicles leaving the eastern sector to prevent various goods from leaving.' Berlin, 1948. (German Federal Archives/Bundesarchiv, Image 183-1983-0920-507/Bratke/CC-BY-SA 3.0)

'End of Blockade, 1949.' (US Air Force: 110111-D-7991K-001. Public Domain)

Frankfurt, den 4. Nov. 48

Meine liebe Mercedes!

Herzlichen Dank für Dein kleines Brieflein. Alle Tage fliege ich zwar nicht über Dein Haus, aber sicher recht oft. Ich wusste ja gar nicht dass in der Hähnelstrasse so ein liebes Mädel wohnt. Wenn ich mal ein paar Runden über Friedenau fliegen würde, fände ich bestimmt den Garten mit den weissen Hühnchen. Dazu fehlt mir aber leider die Zeit. Ich hoffe, dass ich Dir hiermit eine kleine Freude bereite.

Herzliche Grüsse

Dein Schokoladenonkel

Letter from Gail Halvorsen to Mercedes Wild, 4 November 1948. (With permission from Mercedes Wild)

WINTER–SPRING
1948–49

XIII

IN THE FRENCH QUARTER

1

In German, *stolpern* means 'to trip', and this is where the French tripped.

On a golden day in October, I take the Berlin S-Bahn train and a bus to Stolpe, the village of five hundred inhabitants, just across Berlin's border into former East Germany. The cobbled Dorfstraße runs the village length of fine two-storey houses, some neoclassical, one with Jugendstil plasterwork, and the old inn, here since the eighteenth century. The twelfth-century church's plastered interior ignores time. Its graveyard has buried generations of Stolpers who worked the land. What was the one-room schoolhouse sits across the street, teaching the young ones until the fourth year. Draping the façades are leaning autumn lindens, seasonal yellows and oranges that have seen it all.

Stolpe was not always part of the East. The village tragedy is that it used to be in the French zone but, during the Berlin Airlift, was abandoned because of an airport. At the end of the road is a field, the *Stolper Feld*. It's a great clearing – the Prussian woods distantly marking the perimeter – where the French planned the landing strips. Initially in the Soviet zone, Stolpe was assigned to the French on 29 October 1945, allowing them a place to build.[1] The field is now a golf course, and the no-man's-land of the Berlin Wall has seen new building. Young families live here who wish to be close to Berlin and play golf, but do not have much to do with the old village.

On the doorstep of the vicarage are potted musk mallows and geraniums, which still believe it's summer. The door is open to the house inside, as many of the village doors are. Traugott, the widower of the former pastor, Renate Vogel, has lived here since 1981. The interior is well swept and sparse, with books on tables and framed drawings of landscapes. With his wife, Traugott Vogel wrote a history of the village, which I found in the German State Library. A letter to the author brought me to Stolpe and introductions to its residents on the city's border – a place that ended up part of world history the winter the Airlift was at its height.

L'affaire de Stolpe was how it was known faraway, in the Parisian newspapers.

2

Why was France given a zone, despite having been defeated in the Second World War? General de Gaulle believed it would help restore French honour after the brutality of the occupation. The French socialists saw it promoting European integration. And the British supported them because they foresaw European stability in reconciling Germany with its nearest neighbour and former great power. The Brits were even willing to cede part of their Berlin zone to satisfy the French, although the gift consisted only of two small, and in places historically poor, neighbourhoods, Reinickendorf and Wedding in the city's north.

Berliners rightfully saw France, emerging from war's ruins, as the 'poor relatives of the Big Three'. Ragged uniforms and a few military parades did not project a great power status. Visible French institutions – a sailing club (Club Nautique), a French restaurant for the occupiers (Le Relais de Tegel), twenty cinemas showing French films, and a cultural centre – felt like soft power and ... soft.

The French were the only power without an airport in their zone and without aircraft to contribute to the Airlift, as these were tied up in the Indochina war. American and British pilots often complained that they were sometimes compelled to carry wine for the French along with coal and flour. Ken Slaker – the Presbyterian teetotaller – lamented: 'I had one load that really irritated me. It was full of French wine, flying up for the French. Here we were flying wine ... Hell, I don't like French wine.'[2]

So, when the French required respect – that German pedestrians salute the French tricolour or liberate the pavement for French soldiers – the Berliners grew impertinent.[3] When the French went about confiscating hundreds of houses from ordinary Berliners for their forces, the Berliners were up in arms. Meanwhile, the Soviets exploited their former ally's appearance of illegitimacy. Their newspapers insinuated that the French never really intended to remain in Berlin and were about to leave. After all, having just suffered one war, they would hardly stick around for another.

3

When the Airlift reached volumes that could no longer be supported only by Gatow and Tempelhof, the Americans and British approached the French with the idea of building a large airport in their zone. A facility with a long runway would make landings possible even in bad weather.

The Americans would fund the operation and temporarily direct Tegel's air control during the Airlift. German labourers would do the grunt work. All the French had to do was provide the land and supervise. They could assume full control of the facility when the Airlift was over. General Jean Ganeval, the French Commander of Berlin, jumped at the opportunity of a facility that would entrench the French presence in Berlin at little cost to them.

Stolpe had been chosen as the original site, but the authorities agreed it was not large enough and too far from central Berlin. An alternative was proposed in the village of Jungfernheide, on a former shooting range less than 4 miles as the bird flies from Zoo Station, compared to the more than 10 to Stolpe. The 37-acre area had been used in the first half of the century for various aeronautical experiments: launching airship blimps, and rockets at the dawn of space technology. The disadvantages were that the area was dedicated to garden allotments to grow food, and thousands would have to vacate. At the end of the proposed runway, and in the Soviet zone, was Berlin's highest structure, a 540ft antenna tower, along with other aerials belonging to Radio Berlin. The 100kW transmitter would pose a danger to incoming aircraft. The site too was full of craters, ruins, unexploded ordnance, flak guns, tree stumps, and sand dunes left over from the Ice Age. These were up to 40ft high and needed clearing to level the runway.

On 5 August 1948, German crews got to work. By September, nineteen thousand labourers were on the project to build the first of two planned runways in three round-the-clock shifts, illuminated at night with powerful lamps.[4] Klaus Scherff, who lived nearby as a child, recounted in 1976 'that almost all of Wedding and Reinickendorf were ... working on the airport'.[5] Every layer of society was involved: former Nazis, Wehrmacht officers, secretaries, grocers, academics, toiling side by side. Workers even came from the Soviet zone to toil – the city was only loosely isolated after all. As Klaus Hübner, a 24-year-old airfield labourer, remembered, 'Many of us commuted from East to West and vice versa. The borders in the city could still be crossed largely without issues. The neighbourhoods on both sides weren't yet sealed off fortresses.'

Together, the project would move roughly 70 million cubic feet of earth.[6] At first, completion was expected in February 1949, except General Clay wasn't happy with that forecast, grumbling it would be 'far too late'. The Airlift needed Tegel's capacity before the winter. But could an airfield really be built in ninety days? And could a runway be built in a city without the capacity to produce cement?

It could be if they used rubble. The half-mile-long airstrip – 1.4 miles with overrun areas – would rest on a 3ft bed, filled with 400,000 tons of bricks crushed from the remains of war-damaged Berlin buildings. Ten city blocks worth of rubble and ballast scavenged from decommissioned railway tracks would do the job. Nearby ruins of churches, such as Borsigwalde Church, were stripped of their blasted vaulting and buttresses for future landings. Hot tar would coat layers made of former schools and bombed rail stations, with ten thousand barrels of asphalt flown in on the Airlift flights. Vats of bitumen were rolled in through the fence, smuggled from the Russian zone.[7]

It was all a miracle, given the limitations of the isolated city. The FBI tracked down a specialist in the US Midwest who had cut down construction machines during the Second World War using an oxyacetylene torch. He had flown them to remote parts of Brazil to be reassembled. In Berlin, his practice was applied to eighty-one rock crushers and tractors. Eventually, an entire power plant was flown in parts, reassembled in Berlin, during the Airlift, and called 'Reuter'.

With the shortage of men, two-thirds of the labourers were women, working with picks and shovels. Many wore formal clothes, such as silk dresses, as they had only brought their best to the bunker.[8] The Eastern newspapers made the most of their working conditions, with *Neues Deutschland* reporting that 'no accommodations or toilet facilities are available. Girls under eighteen have been hired for heavy construction work, and small children of the female workers run around unsupervised'.[9] They wrote of explosions when incendiary bombs were accidentally detonated during construction, splintering the workers. An emergency worker reported to *Berliner Zeitung* how 'it seems as nature is working against human labour', as sand blew into workers' faces and the machines spurted hot liquids to make them 'walking tar-men'. Bricks were thrown into the crushers by hand, and the women only had useless gloves and were forced to wrap their hands in rags. In one comic, *Berliner Zeitung* satirised General Ganeval: 'The construction of Tegel airfield is comparable to that of the Egyptian pyramids', with a drawing depicting the women labourers as exhausted slaves.

But workers' testimonies tell us something different. Klaus Hübner remembered how, after a work shift,

> not a fibre of my battered body was pain-free ... Our work was based on the simple principle of collecting bricks from the endless stone deserts of the bombed houses and taking them to the construction site in Tegel. Since payment was based on quantity, it was important not to waste a single brick ... Three million bricks changed hands, often from the hands of those who were only used to dealing with typewriters, construction drawings, and files. Then the bricks were thrown into huge crushers to be ground into powder as material for the runways.

But did he feel like a slave? He replied in the negative and explained: 'We dug into the wild heathland because ... we neither wanted to starve nor surrender ... Like ants, we covered the vast area.' With few available jobs in Berlin, the 1.20 Mark per hour wage, plus 700-calorie hot meal with coffee, was considered good pay.

In the Reinickendorf Museum and Archive in Berlin, there are a series of photographs of the building of the airfield.[10] Tiny figures scatter the field's canvas like figures in a Brueghel painting or perhaps one by Hieronymus Bosch. The soldiers skim a metal detector for Second World War ordnance over ground soon to be torn up. Boilers steam with bitumen at one corner of the airfield. Young and old women alike, in dresses and fancy hats, scramble up the enormous dunes. In the close-ups, they seem puzzlingly to laugh and smile during the Babelesque work, even as three of them push a heavy skip full of sand. Then those piles disappear, lorries empty mountains of bricks into the holes, the ground is rolled flat, and it glistens black. The winter sky roils and threatens.

On 5 November, the first flight, a US Douglas C-54, landed with no one there to unload it. The field was mud, buildings were unfinished. But, remarkably, only ninety-two days had passed since construction began, when a plane could land.

November in Berlin was plagued by nearly unbroken fog, reducing tonnage and making flying dangerous. Down on the tarmac, engineers would have to get down on their knees around the planes, the fog had sunk so low. When Bob Hope came to entertain the troops, he said of Berlin weather: 'Soup I'd settle for – but this stuff has noodles in it.'[11]

But the fog lifted in early December. Flights at Tegel picked up. With the new airfield, tonnages quickly returned to the 4,500 mark. Soon, Tegel became Berlin's primary source of liquid fuel, brought in by Alec Chambers and his friends. By 30 December, there were record landings – 217 just that day, just as on 23 December the 50,000th landing was celebrated at Gatow. Then, just past Christmas, Tegel saw the Airlift's numbers explode. On 31 December the 100,000th flight of the Airlift was recorded.

Tegel was a miracle of land rendered flat – the most remarkable construction of the Airlift.

4

General Jean Ganeval was the forgiving sort. Imprisoned by the Nazis in Buchenwald for being in the French resistance, he emerged – like Léon Blum, the Socialist leader – as an advocate for the reconciliation of the Germans with the French. Better understanding with the Soviets was likely not on his mind when he invited a delegation of American brass to his office at the new Tegel Airfield on 16 December 1948.

The charming story is repeated in most sources on the Airlift, even if it is perhaps apocryphal: that drinks were served, and an air of celebration pervaded the occasion, but the guests still weren't sure why they had been invited. Then – at precisely 11 a.m. – explosions were heard at the end of the airfield, and the guests understood what had just happened.[12]

We do know that US Sergeant Donald Stensrud, an air traffic controller, was down by the runway, where the French military police had closed off the area and cut the telephone lines so the Soviet technicians couldn't call for help. There, he watched the action, reporting: 'We all got out of the control tower, and I saw the French grab the Russian guards and prepare the dynamite. I was wishing I had a camera. It was a neat, clean job; a big bang and the radio towers were gone.'

The French pointed out that they had given the Soviets plenty of notice. On 20 November, the director of Radio Berlin was informed that two antennas in the Soviet zone, half a mile distant from the runway, were a danger to incoming aircraft. The French wrote once again but received no reply. British intelligence later reported, 'This warning was apparently not taken seriously resulting in the French taking the necessary action.' Nonetheless, the Soviets were taken by surprise – perhaps they did not think the French would dare venture into their zone and destroy the strongest transmitter of their radio infrastructure.

Radio Berlin went off the air for the next twelve hours. The Western press bathed in the sudden silencing of Soviet propaganda.[13] As *Der Spiegel* reported, the medium wave signal had gone still. The Saxon accent of the SED director Heinz Schmidt, who called the 'demolition "cultural barbarism"', had been demoted to the long wave.

'You'll have no more trouble with the towers,' Ganeval informed the Americans as they finished their refreshments.

The next day, Clay congratulated Ganeval but also washed his hands of the matter, which would become the first major Cold War incident between the French and the East. The explosions were a 'matter between the French military government and German broadcasting, as the transmission facilities were the property of Berlin Radio and thus German ownership'.[14] The Soviets disagreed and were apoplectic. *Neues Deutschland* fumed about the 'outrageous deed at Tegel'.[15] And General Kotikov asked Ganeval: 'How could you have done this?'

The French general reportedly replied, 'With dynamite, *mon cher.*'

5

On an overcast and cold Saturday in December, the French zone chief of police, with a fellow officer, braced themselves against freezing temperatures on the outskirts of Berlin as Soviet soldiers approached. This must have surprised them, as they were 150ft inside their own zone near the village of Stolpe. More surprising was that the Soviets demanded they accompany them into East Berlin.

The senior Frenchman refused, but then, as the newspaper *Sozialdemokrat* reported a few days later, 'one of the Soviet soldiers fired a few shots into the air, while the others aimed their rifles at the Frenchmen'. The threatened men relented, were escorted to headquarters in Berlin-Mitte, and released only after a four-hour interrogation.[16]

The next day, on 19 December, there was an unusual amount of activity for a Sunday in Stolpe as the villagers emerged from their medieval church to see lorries arriving and departing from the town's large estate farm, a short walk up the Dorfstraße.[17] Nearly a fifth of the four hundred inhabitants worked on this 1,500-acre farm, along with many refugees who had come to Stolpe from German lands that were lost after the war. The estate was one of the largest producers of fruit and vegetables, and milk, in restricted Berlin, and the village was so food rich that the engineer who repaired the town's church tower clock could demand 110lb of potatoes and 55lb of grain in payment. Now, the French were emptying the farm, and a nearby depot of industrial materials. Still, as *Die Zeit* later reported, the villagers 'could not yet explain the unusual movement of trucks and passenger vehicles in their quiet heath village'.

Nor could they explain the spectacle in the fields, as the estate managers ordered that their herd of cows be driven south deeper into the French sector. Because the villagers refused, the French garrison took on the ungrateful job without the necessary experience to deal with the unpredictable, discontented animals, who bolted in all directions. 'The calves did not pay much attention to boundary markers,' wrote *Die Zeit*. The Russians waited on their side of the border, watching the absurdity, jumping at the opportunity to seize animals the moment they crossed into their sector. The French, meanwhile, had trouble removing all the goods they wanted – such as the 1,000 tons of potatoes left behind in piles on the estate.

Even if they could guess what was happening, the villagers remained uninformed of the reasons.[18] The village's mayor, Albert Wiese, however, knew precisely what decisions had been taken but was too afraid to tell his village or, as he said, did not want to spoil 'our Christmas celebration'.

The Stolpe villagers would learn the truth when everyone else did in Berlin – from the newspapers. The story broke three days later, on

Tuesday 21 December. By that time, the Soviets had occupied the village at dawn with a police and military force, erecting roadblocks and stopping all traffic.[19]

6

What General Ganeval had told the mayor already that Saturday was that Stolpe had been offered to the Soviets as compensation for the destruction of the radio towers. The Governor of the French zone in Germany, General Marie-Pierre Kœnig, was quoted in *Der Spiegel*:

> As General Ganeval has already offered the Soviet authorities on my orders, I agree to the return of the Stolpe site, which was made available to me by these authorities at the time for the construction of an airfield.

The Soviets had a strong claim: Stolpe was given to the French to build an airfield there. The signed protocol did not indicate that the transfer was permanent.[20] Now that Tegel was built instead, the French ownership of Stolpe was tenuous. Marshal Sokolovsky, so incensed about the explosions in his sector, was finally appeased.

The French were resigned to the situation. At a press conference, Ganeval later explained they had 'had to decide for the needs of two million people or those of four hundred. I decided for Berlin.' The French had proposed 3 January 1949 as the handover date. But the Soviets did not wait and took everyone off guard, something the French again accepted. What was the alternative – escalation, dispatching ragged French troops to face off the Soviets in open conflict? The answer to *Berliner Zeitung*'s headline, 'Is Stolpe worth a war?' was ... *non*.[21]

West Berliners did not accept the situation. On 5 December, the city had voted, confirming Ernst Reuter as seated mayor. Turnout was 86.3 per cent, and his SPD obtained two-thirds, while they were not allowed to vote in the East. As Ruth Andreas-Friedrich noted in her diary, it represented:

> one and a quarter million vote[s] against the politics of the Socialist Unity Party. An admirable result considering that this decision most likely will have to be paid for with an intensification of the blockade,

a winter without coal, nights without light and a permanent diet of dehydrated potatoes, dehydrated vegetables and canned meat. We feel as if we had wings. We feel it's great to be a Berliner. It is wonderful to live in a city that prefers death to slavery, that has decided to suffer more deprivations rather than dictatorship.[22]

The Stolpers voted too, almost unanimously on 5 December for the Western parties. This only increased the perception that they had been abandoned, and that they would be punished by the Soviets for their preference – although Ganeval was positive the Soviets would not discipline the townsfolk for their Western loyalty.[23]

Newspapers licensed in the British and American zones went on the attack. They had, until now, been slavishly obedient in their support for the West, but now there was no compunction in pillorying the junior partner. Things became much worse for the French when the Germans caught on to the idea that they had agreed to give Stolpe to the Soviets *before* the radio towers were detonated. As *Telegraf* wrote on 22 December, the transfer was 'obviously planned before 5 December', was 'executed hastily', and 'cannot contribute to strengthening the people's trust in the Western Allies'.[24] *Der Spiegel* explained: 'They have betrayed Stolpe', and *Sozialdemokrat*'s headline was 'What the French have done isn't nice' – a quote from a villager.

Concerned about losing the food production of Stolpe's large estate farm, Ernst Reuter's ruling party, the SPD, attacked the French. Otto Suhr, the president of the municipal assembly, declared that the 'ceding of territory without a plebiscite is a violation of human rights', and the party's executive committee voiced that 'this decision, made without consideration for the population and apparently without compelling reason, will not contribute to strengthening the trust of the population in the Western Allies'. Reuter himself was reported – but by the *Berliner Zeitung* – as wanting to send in a convoy into the town. What was at stake with the 'betrayal' was friendship itself between the Western Allies and the Berliners, which had been built painfully through the Airlift operation.

The tiny town of Stolpe meant much more to the Berliners than its four hundred villagers. It was Berlin in microcosm. Before their eyes, they witnessed the West delivering them to the East, selling them down the river. It was what could happen if the Airlift failed. Could the Allies be trusted?

Die Zeit wrote of *'preisgegebene Menschen'*, 'abandoned people' – that word *'preisgeben'* being a direct quote from Reuter's 9 September Reichstag speech when the leader promised: 'You peoples of the world! ... Look at this city and realise that you must not and cannot abandon [*preisgeben*] this city and this people!' On the day of Stolpe's occupation, Ruth-Andreas Friedrich wrote frankly in her diary about her fears of being betrayed: 'And what will we do if one day Berlin is incorporated like Stolpe?' some cynics ask. If only we knew! People around us look stunned and upset, and everybody has the same question: "Is that the future of those who voted for freedom?"'

British Intelligence reported at length on the Stolpe Affair, indicating that the French had been negotiating the return of Stolpe for a long time – well before the 5 December elections and the vandalism of the two radio towers. The officer noted:

> The most unsatisfactory aspect is that the population were allowed to vote in the recent city elections, unaware of the fact that the French were prepared to allow the area to revert to the Soviet zone. This aspect has not been missed by the Germans, many of whom have been most outspoken against the French, thereby causing some embarrassment to the Western Allies.

While the Berliners had been delighted by the tower explosions, those same explosions were later used to justify the transfer of Stolpe. *Der Spiegel*, who like the others had understood the French strategy, reported, 'Then why did they let us vote in the first place?' and the pro-West *Tagesspiegel* joined, 'The West has lost more than four hundred Stolpers.'

Meanwhile, as four geese crossed the road in the village and the church tower chimed, one woman in town laughed, 'Stolpe has never been this famous before.' That clock tower was being heard too in Paris – or was at least being transmitted by telephone on 23 December by the *Le Monde* correspondent Georges Blun, who rushed to Berlin to cover the unfolding 'L'affaire de Stolpe'. His article defended France against 'injurious articles that are detrimental to our national honour', asserting 'Stolpe was never part of Berlin' and that 'some Germans, eager to make matters worse, wanted to make a drama out of it'.[25] The *New York Times* was rather blunter in its assessment: 'French Abandon Town'.[26]

Even more disparaging than the American press was British Intelligence. They described the whole affair 'not very cleverly executed by the French', and 'on balance French prestige has lost rather than gained',[27] concluding: 'The Tegel-Stolpe incident ... will have two long-term results: a) The Russians will make use of it for propaganda purposes as a "violent act against democracy"; [b)] The German confidence in the western powers, particularly FRANCE, has had a severe jolt.'

7

The home of the Thiele farming family of Stolpe has the date 1884 nailed over its doorway and flourishes of neoclassical columns and pediments slung along its low façade. The granddaughters open the door for Traugott Vogel and me when we visit, preparing a big pot of coffee, carving up the plum tray cake, and settling us in the parlour stocked with East German furniture. It gives a sunny glow of teak wood and colourful cushions.

Frau Ilse Thiele, born in 1939, sits across, tough from years in the fields growing oats, barley, rye, and wheat, and rearing livestock. There is something in her upright expression like the lindens breaking through the cobbles outside her door. And although she was then only a little girl in the one-room schoolhouse across the street, she remembers the events of December 1948 and even more clearly the consequences for her family living in the Soviet zone instead of the French quarter.[28]

Ruth Andreas-Friedrich wrote on 22 December 1948, as Stolpe was occupied by the Soviets, that 'again people are fleeing across the border. Rather dead than enslaved. Rather dispossessed in the West than under the terror at home.'

But Frau Thiele's family stayed.

'Why did you not flee to the West when Stolpe was returned to the Soviets?' I ask. After all, the Western newspapers predicted an exodus of Stolper refugees.

She looks at me, a little confused: 'But everyone stayed!'

And it is true: the refugee camp for the Stolpers set up in Reinickendorf remained empty, and only two people left the town. Even Albert Wiese, Stolpe's mayor, stayed despite an invitation from the West for political asylum.

Even in 1948, some Western newspapers were realistic that the Stolpers would not budge and leave their productive farms for the 'half-destroyed apartment buildings' of Wedding. As one old farmer said: 'Out of the question! ... If it must be, and if they want to get at our women again, I'll take the pitchfork. But they cannot take this piece of land away from me.' At the local tavern, Krummen Linde, a village council decided that now they could not trust the Western Allies, 'we will have to look out for each other.'

'But did you not feel abandoned by the West?' I asked her, 'Didn't your lives change here on the farm because of the transfer?'

Again, Frau Thiele shakes her head. 'It did not change a lot. We had to produce and live from it. Even though we had to negotiate and trade between ourselves to get around the Soviets, life was a lot like before, and the smaller farms were not collectivised.'

I learn that the eight major farming families found their farms too small to be subject to the Communist land reform (*Bodenreform*).

For the farming villagers, always at work, politics felt far away. She says: 'We were tired when the evening came, got into bed, and in the morning got up again.'

But I insist: 'But could you, for example, still sell your goods at the markets in West Berlin?'

'At the market? Of course. They didn't have any policemen watching us there.'

The S-Bahn still ran into nearby Frohnau as usual, and the villagers continued to bring their crops there. After all, why abandon your home when the West was only a train ticket away? At least until the Berlin Wall was built in 1961 ...

Frau Thiele describes the flourishing black market between East and West: 'Yes, yes. They were all hoarding. The trains were overfilled with goods, with people returning [to Berlin] all the way from past Oranienburg, sitting on their goods like cushions. Life is hard, and they wanted to live.'

I'm wondering now what it was like to live without the assistance of the Airlift and its deliveries. When Stolpe was occupied, Western newspapers like *Der Spiegel* and *Sozialdemokrat* predicted that the children would soon go hungry on Eastern rations. 'Empty metal bowls are waiting for the warm soup' and 'who knows how long there will still be school lunches?'

'Do you remember not having enough to eat after you joined the Soviet zone?'

Again, Frau Thiele shakes her head, 'We were always full of food.' Farmers in the little village sat at the top of the food chain as producers of produce, grain, and meat. They were not the ones who went hungry. And they did not need the West's supplies.

'But don't you remember during the Airlift that you ate dried potatoes, dried vegetables, and other foodstuffs flown in by plane?'

'We did not get it, and we didn't eat it,' she tells me, 'We had potatoes fresh from the earth. We were self-providers, and when pigs were slaughtered, we got something from that, too. And then the Russians gave us extra, like sugar that the others did not get.'

Far from the feared reprisals against the Stolpers for voting for the West on 5 December, the Soviets did their best to calm fears and incorporate the Stolpers into their zone, with extra rations of potatoes as a Christmas present, in addition to the Western Christmas rations of raisins and dried fruit that had already been delivered to the village by the Airlift. Preferential rations, including coal, were then provided to 'pamper' the Stolpers so they wouldn't be tempted to cross the border. She remembers that in December 1948, 'We had a "Christmas plate" [*Weihnachtsteller*] here, and they filled it up twice!' referring to those double rations.

So far, things do not sound that rotten under the Soviets. So, I venture: 'In West Berlin, it could be eventually said that the Americans and British became friends with Germans. Can you say that the Russians became your friends?'

And now, the others laugh. I'm not sure if they are laughing at me or the question! There was no fraternising because the Russians were isolated from the local population in their barracks. From the summer of 1946, Soviet soldiers were forbidden anything but official contact with Germans, initially as a strategy to contain the spread of sexually transmitted infections and to protect Germans against sexual violence.[29] These rules ensured most Germans never really got to know their Russian occupiers as people. The Stolpers couldn't even practise the Russian they learned in their new school in the Soviet zone, except during required events. Then, they were afraid of what they could and could not say. And the Russians imprisoned their political enemies in camps.

The table before me moves with stories. And the granddaughter turns to me, 'You see, everyone here in Stolpe stuck together after the war. Family life felt much more intensive before. Friendships too, because we had to help each other.'

'So, no Soviet friendship –'

'– Friendship that was only a piece of paper.'

8

Ruth Andreas-Friedrich's world was different. What she said mattered, and she did not grow her own food. As an intellectual, she risked being considered a class enemy. How much the Soviets frightened you depended a lot on who you were.

Shortly after the events in Stolpe, Ruth decided to get out of Berlin. She was motivated to leave because there was no more paper for her magazine, so she could no longer work.

But the lack of paper didn't discourage those around her. Even her 'editor-in-chief looked at me as if I were a deserter', she wrote.[30] She walked through the city, touching every stone. She talked to strangers in a way she never had before. Perhaps these gestures, her 'affinity for them', were indications of regret.

Nonetheless, just before New Year, she arrived at Tempelhof airport. The fog was thick. She worried the plane would not fly. But then she heard, from the tarmac, the roar: *Das Brummen*.

'Outside, engines roar,' she wrote, and she took her seat. Each one of her motions was 'mechanical' as if she was forcing herself, against her will, to abandon the city and its solidarity:

> Mechanically, I start moving. Mechanically, I sink into my seat and fasten my seat belt. 'Toward freedom,' the person next to me says. Toward freedom, I want to respond. But the words are stuck in my throat. The engines roar. We are rolling down the runway, slowly at first, then faster and faster until, with a jerk, the plane rises into the air. Lawns, lights, building walls, railroad tracks, streets disappear in the fog … Somewhere down there, disappearing in the fog, lies the battleground of Berlin.

XIV

NEW YEAR

1

As deep winter gripped Berlin, the city cared most about heat and food. Adults who traded them got rich. They were the best dressed, capitalising on people's desperation, milling near the train stations, around the Memorial Church and Zoo Station, or Potsdamer Platz. These were popular places for the black market trade of the 500,000 tons of goods arriving from the East over the course of the Berlin Airlift in exchange for Western marks.[1]

Hoarders would take trains from the countryside into West Berlin and, before official searches, jump off or throw their goods to accomplices waiting alongside the frozen tracks. Mercedes Wild chuckled, telling me about all the Persian carpets from Berlin homes ending up in barns in surrounding Brandenburg in exchange for fresh milk, meat, and vegetables.

The black market proved an exceptional challenge to the authorities. In the British zone, infractions piled up. According to Foreign Office documents, the increase in black market trade was partly 'put down to Air Lift pilots who are bringing the goods into Berlin and selling them on the black market to obtain marks to enable them to have a night out in Berlin'.[2] But this was trifling compared to the third of Berlin's food supply coming straight from the Russian zone, as well as coal and wood.

The black market was so ubiquitous that goods were traded openly without much police interference, and sometimes even placed in shop windows. When there were checks of restaurants and bars, for example at Ali Bar on Meinekestraße, black market stocks were invariably confiscated, such as the 'spirits, liquors, and champagne found in the cellar, which were obtained at exorbitant prices from the Russian zone'. The archive lists hundreds if not thousands of variations on a theme, such as 'fresh perch-pike' fished in Potsdam in the East and served on restaurant plates. In one month, in the British sector alone, 300 short tons of sugar, 550 tons of flour, and 4,500 tons of potatoes were confiscated – a fraction of the total.

West Berliners turned to the black market because they had always done so since the wartime defeat and because the West did not provide enough calories.[3] But they also got better goods than the weight-efficient substitutes flown in with the Airlift – such as dreaded 'POM' dried potatoes. Fuel substitutes in the West were often dangerous. For the entire winter of 1948–49, only 28lb of wood or replacement coal was allowed per person. The latter was so-called *Branda-Platten*: a toxic mix of sawdust, tar, and coaldust. Berliners could thank their stars it was a mild winter.

But Berliners were offered another option other than the black market. While border guards vainly tried to control the illegal flow of goods, dumping piles of stones at intersections to impede traffic, and searching even cyclists to enforce the restrictions, the Soviet zone proffered an official route to East German foodstuffs. Already in August 1948, they offered West Berliners Eastern rations. There was enormous propaganda value in showing the Soviets were not starving the city. The offer was a blow to the heart of the West's narrative of a sealed city, in which people continued, in any case, to work on both sides of the border as *Grenzgänger* (Crossers) and where the subway system functioned city-wide.

Except the Soviets' universal rations proved a logistical nightmare of central planning. Initially, Berliners from the West could only shop in a designated 'sister district' that might be too far away. Crucially, getting Eastern ration cards involved long lines in the cold. Once inside a shop, people found them dirty with Stalinist-standard service. Compared to black market options, the goods were inferior, with the risk of mouldy bread, vile-smelling sausage made from innards, and inhalation of dangerous fumes from substandard petroleum.

If this was not enough to dissuade cross-border defections, registering for ration cards in the East carried the stigma of giving up one's Western ration card. This was a gamble on the future: who would Berliners want to depend on, West or East? And did they want a paper trail back to the

East? As a result, only 1 per cent of West Berliners took Eastern rations in August 1948 and, in the autumn and winter, as the weather deteriorated, only 3 per cent. Food came from the East, just not from Eastern rations.

When the Airlift began, Clay had asked Reuter whether the Berliners were willing to starve for democracy. At least one historian would later claim that: 'to go hungry for freedom and democracy was for the people of 1948–49 a question of rectitude. [Bertolt] Brecht's picture of humanity, that "*das Fressen*" [guzzling of food] comes before "*die Moral*" was turned on its head.'[4]

Except West Berliner behaviour was driven by something less lofty: the goods on the black market were much easier to acquire and of better quality than those obtained through official channels in the East or West.

2

One such entry point for black market goods, albeit a minor one, was Anhalter Bahnhof, the bombed Berlin train terminal. Wanda Ries told me her husband's favourite published volume was those photographs taken here during the Airlift. The space summed up so much of Berlin's pathos but miles away from the spectacular events on Tempelhof Airfield. Henry Ries used a Rolleiflex camera for the medium-format silver prints and a Leica and Zeiss lens for a few others.

Under a 110,000 sq ft iron and glass roof, the train station had once been continental Europe's busiest. For many Berliners, it exuded warmth as the train lines headed south. Anhalter was the beginning of voyages to Italy and the Mediterranean. Ries's childhood memories of the station were 'thoughts of vacations, friends and family visits ... it smelled of hot sausages and sweet lemonade, Havana cigars, and the aromatic mix from the carriages of leather and polished wood.'[5]

As Henry Ries entered the shell in the American zone, the station now resembled the crumbled brickyard of a Roman ruin. He recounted how 'dank mould and chilled ash, rot and decay, crept into my nose. From the vast roofless hall, silent screams sighed into the sky.' Trains left every six to five minutes before the war, carrying 16 million a year, but, by 1 April 1948, this was whittled down to eight departures a day. On the tracks, 'only a half dozen almost empty cars trundled to and from the Soviet zone', allowing Germans to travel to Erfurt and Halle but no longer cities farther West. The fact that trains still ran, just not very many, showed that the Soviet restrictions were largely focused on the military rather than civilians.

With his cameras, Ries wandered the hall, looking for subjects. He wrote of 'hungry, poor, confused' people but also how 'nobody was unfriendly' even if 'few wanted to talk to me, most didn't have the energy'. All the images he took were unstaged. Ries said, 'At the train station, I chose the people who animated me visually. I took them as they were, where they were. I didn't change anything. I didn't even let them comb their hair.'

Ries scoured their faces for the story. If the image could not tell it alone, he asked questions. Of the man in a suit hauling potato sacks on a small cart. Of the Russian soldier arguing with the Berliner pauper. Or the vendor with his 'four-wheeled skeleton of the Mitropa cart, promisingly offering diluted lemonade to the emaciated people'.

The German mother with two children expelled from their home in East Prussia – a china cup just visible in the crack of their suitcase – told Ries matter-of-factly she was raped by twenty-four Russian soldiers who overtook her refugee column in the snow: 'One was so young he could have been her son. He was timid, but since the others were doing it, he went along with it. She's sure he's the father of her little one.'

An ancient flower seller sat in a wooden train carriage. Her baskets now empty, she said, 'I come twice a week … it's not easy because the flowers are heavy … I always give the porter eighty pfennigs because he is always so kind to help me.' She told Henry her eldest child died a soldier in France, her next oldest sank in a submarine, and her youngest, Karl, was 'maybe dead too … every time prisoners of war arrive here, I ask the men about Karl. I ask every time.'

The one-legged war invalid on crutches, meanwhile, taunted Henry:

I know what you're thinking and why you want to take pictures! 'That poor soul with crutches and a suitcase on his back'. Well, you're wrong, my love. You're just like the others, feeling so crazy sorry for me.

Instead, the man explained to Henry that he's making money hand over fist on the black market since the Airlift began. After the war, he started by bringing nails to the countryside ('in the countryside everyone needs nails'), which he could trade for 'butter, eggs, meat and oil', which he'd then bring back to Berlin and trade back for more nails. With the currency reform and the stability of the West Mark, his money now had value: 'One thing I've learned all these years, no pity and no sympathy from anyone!'

Otto, the luggage porter, was stretched out on the steps of the main hall and said he was as old as the station. This was an exaggeration, since the station was opened in 1841. But Otto was dignified in his suit and numbered cap, his shoes polished, and he came here to work even though few had the money to have him carry their bags. He told Henry:

> Me and the train station are old friends. I could call it my home. We have experienced all sorts of things, good and bad ... Today the station is dead ... the only noise comes from the sky. You can imagine that both me and the station feel useless? The only thing that comes through the blockade these days is by the Airlift. Coal, wheat – everything flies to Berlin through the clouds.

Except, of course, what came by train.

3

For eleven months, Henry Ries's camera caught every aspect of the Airlift for the *New York Times*. Ries said he was less interested in the news than how Berliners experienced the news. In a 1973 catalogue of his work, Ries's Airlift photography is introduced not as a dry and 'chronological description of the time's political events ... [but] making visible the everyday life of contemporary Berliners and the human aspects that are often too hastily, superficially labelled with catch phrases such as "heroic"'.[6]

It helped that he knew the city intimately, that 'some things made my work easier; for the American who spoke both languages, for the photographer of one of the most important newspapers in the world, the doors to Clay or Kotikov, to Reuter and Ulbricht were easily opened'.[7]

One Airlift image from the clouds secured Ries's international reputation as a photographer. Ries described the photo in *Ich war ein Berliner*:

The most famous of all my photographs was the 'Candy Bomber' photo from the time of the Berlin Blockade: children crowding onto a pile of rubble near Tempelhof to greet an incoming plane. Although it has been shown and published many times, it obviously cannot be left out of my autobiography.[8]

Today, if you enter a search term for the Berlin Airlift, the image by Henry Ries appears. If you pull a book on the Berlin Airlift from a library shelf, again the same photograph is likely on its cover.

Was it a lucky snap or rather the logical consensus of his work as an artist: combining the urgency of the news with his attention to the everyday? The metallic weight of the aeroplane hovered just within the edge of the frame. The clouds weighed in as a competing density, perched on the houses and anchoring a corner, as the tippy-toed crowd rose from the rubble of past tragedies. One probing face turned from the spectacle to the photographer.

An extract from Ries's pocket diary tells us how he spent weeks just hanging around Tempelhof airport looking for the right shot – '12-2 Tempelhof – got excellent pics of dropping of parachuted candy'[9] – for an Airlift feature for the *New York Times*. Ries wrote such comments in leather-bound agendas, bought at Golde's Stationers on 6th Avenue and 57th Street near Carnegie Hall. Years of these volumes now sit in the archive of the German Historical Museum, and they tell us telegraphically about Ries's everyday life during the Airlift. Day by day is a list of photo-shoot locations: 'pic of barges', 'pic of C-47 crash', 'pic of new Tegel Airport', 'pic of airplanes in Gatow bringing food to Berlin', 'S-Bahn collision, no good for pic', 'got exclusive pics', 'all day in darkroom', 'pic to NY', or 'ship pic to F'Furt'. But he was also a mondain fellow, playing chess and tennis (usually losing), dining at the Press Club, and enjoying evenings of cinema, classical concerts, and operas,[10] followed by nights of cocktail parties. All these were glossed with comments 'wonderful', 'entertaining', 'much fun', 'very *fein*', 'got quite plastered', or maybe 'poor decision'. How else should he get through Berlin's dark winter?

The dated pages – in some places torn out – read of a full social life and many friends, but also how he bracketed amusements with more labour into the early hours, on his book project *German Faces*. Ries's artistic ambitions went well beyond the *New York Times* as he prepared this collection of portraits of everyday Germans living in poverty. To his disappointment, on 8 December the manuscript submitted to Simon & Schuster in New York was rejected. One day earlier, on 7 December 1948, however, his diary suggested that Berliners would see a large selection of his photos from the pages of the *New York Times*: 'exhibition of my pics seems assured'. Then in early January, whole days in his agenda were dedicated to the show's preparation.

The solo show organised by the US propaganda authorities happened between 19 and 28 January 1949 in an enormous 1920s cinema in the New Objectivity style. It had an otherworldly name: the Titania-Palast. Since the war had bombed out many venues, the palace became a usual venue of prestige in the West for the Berlin Philharmonic and others. His exhibition occurred when the Airlift was now a convincing success, Berlin was being fed, and even Stalin indicated in January that he was willing to budge diplomatically. The Soviets were not only concerned that their restrictions were not working. The so-called *Gegenblockade*, with which the West boycotted the Soviet zone, was having a surprising effect on East German industry, which needed some materials only available from the West.

So, when the 132 photographs by Ries[11] were placed on the Titania Palace's walls and the doors opened to the public for a week, it was in an atmosphere of confidence and self-congratulation. Many Berliners came – the Titania was a clever choice, as so many passed through on their way to see films or music – with one reviewer estimating more than twenty-six thousand visitors. *Der Abend* reported almost four hundred visitors in just the first four hours.[12] However, the true significance of these photos would be in the subsequent US response.

Ries did not provide exhibit labels for his photographs, and indeed 'no one asked about their origin' – he did not need to; Berliners knew precisely where the events chronicled had taken place and felt complimented that their city had been recognised by an eye that saw as they did. As *Der Tagesspiegel* reported of the exhibit: 'You walk past these pictures and, as if by magic, the texts to accompany them spring to mind, names, dates, contexts.' As Ries later wrote, 'Almost all of the many thousands of people who saw the exhibition ... were themselves affected and each had had to bear their own little fate during the blockade.'[13]

The public also had the opportunity to vote on their favourite photograph. The 'Candy Bomber' was Ries's most famous in the United States, eventually reprinted as a postage stamp. And the exhibit included many photos of C-47s delivering coal and flour – the men unloading caught in the frame of the wings – or the dozens of planes stalled by fog hovering over the tarmac. But for Berliners visiting this exhibit, the less spectacular images of daily life under the Airlift were even more popular: Berliner children playing in rubble, women clearing stones, large crowds watching officers divide their neighbourhoods between East and West, or a restaurant reopening before a broken façade on Kurfürstendamm. As *Der Abend* commented:

> Probably only a 'Berliner' could have an eye for the real Berlin without sentimentality or affectation. 'Which picture do you like best?' is asked on a slip of paper that each visitor receives. The answers will show, in addition to professional criticism, what interests Berliners most about 'their' blockade.

The photo that won the audience award was of a woman in a housecoat ironing in the middle of the night. Her family are sound asleep around her, suggesting the separate rooms they once slept in were bombed out. In one corner, a small child lies deep in one pillow with perhaps her grandmother next to her. In the foreground is the tired head of a younger woman, her hair parted. The sleepers look undisturbed by the stark illumination of the overhead lights in those few hours past midnight, when electricity was delivered and these domestic activities were briefly possible. The woman irons striped trousers on a lace-fringed tablecloth with an intent look. The image struck home because Ries recognised the everyday, muted heroics that reflected Berliners' problems, not just the grand gesture of a plane plunging from the sky.

4

The enthusiasm of the Berlin public paralleled the official response and suspicion that Henry's work could be very useful indeed. On 17 January, US Commander Frank L. Howley inquired with the *New York Times*: 'I am writing to you with two things in mind. First, to congratulate you

... and second, to selfishly ask permission to either reproduce some of these photographs for our own Military Government use or to get a set of the photographs.' Two days later, Mayor Ernst Reuter wrote to the newspaper urging 'the exhibition of these photographs in the United States, if it is possible to arrange their display there, would contribute greatly to an understanding of the Berlin situation'.[14] On the day of the opening, Ries wrote in his diary of many radio interviews, the 'terrific acclaim', and the propaganda interest from the highest levels: 'State Department calls for Washington'.

The exhibit secured his book contract for *German Faces*,[15] eventually published by Sloane Press in 1950, co-authored by his first wife Ann Stringer, with whom he had a tumultuous relationship ('Ann is great!!', 'Ann is difficult'). The volume, said Ries, gave 'the Americans for the first time an authentic impression of the life and thinking of the defeated Germans in their destroyed country'. Its power came from Ries's own explorations: 'I rediscovered my old city, through the lens and within myself. Since then, my lens has always been focused on the Berliners.' The photographer's interest in everyday people dovetailed neatly with the Western Allies' desire to humanise the West Germans. On 31 January, the *New York Times* wrote Ries a confirmation of their desire to support further visibility of his photos.[16]

Ries's photos were then flown to the United States and shown at the Library of Congress in Washington, D.C., the New York Public Library, and several US colleges and universities. The New York Public Library's exhibit, 'Berlin Story', opened on 2 May,[17] and their press release explained how 'the camera recorded not only the immediate answer of the Western Allies to the blockade and the steps that were taken but also, in a sweep around the partly ruined city, caught the impact of the crisis on the community'. His diary indicated only many meetings in New York. When the exhibitions opened, he was already on a steamer back to Europe – where he took the opportunity to catch up on sleep in relaxing, good weather. Then he got back to work.

Ries was astonished by the change in US public sphere reactions, comparing these to how 'immediately after the end of the war, the Americans deliberately avoided photographing the hungry, frightened faces of the people in the shattered ruins of Berlin'.[18] Now, the public displays of his photographs, focusing on individual faces, were meant to 'create a symbol of the future'.

But Ries had long had misgivings. His local knowledge meant he had quickly seen through German arguments that they should become allies of the West. As he had written to Dorothy Haller in 1945:

> What bothers me is that the majority of Berliners want to impress us with their losses in order to establish advantageous relationships with us Americans in their struggle for survival. They also want to prove how much more they value us than the evil, evil Russians.[19]

It would be tough for a man like Ries to reconcile with the Germans. It was ironic that he became *the* photographer of the Berlin Airlift, claimed as a Berliner by Berliners, and that he helped make that reconciliation possible – in the very city that had expelled and exterminated his family. Ries would wonder at this turn of events, writing: 'Certainly it was the first time, three years after such a war of annihilation, that the victor supplied the defeated enemy with food instead of firebombs, not to mention chocolate on tiny parachutes.' Walking around Anhalter Bahnhof, snapping his photographs, he reflected:

> I heard nothing, not a word, about responsibility or even guilt. It was probably too early; the pain and loss was still too strong. It was a time of deprivation, hunger, of homelessness, and widows and cripples. How could I have expected conversations about responsibility? Daily, hourly survival demanded exclusively the repression of what had just passed. I often remained silent, but memories I will never forget were captured by my camera.

Wanda Ries and I discussed why he focused on Berlin children in his photographs. He did not see them as guilty for what their parents had done. 'He felt his own generation had learned nothing,' she told me. A portrait of this 'perpetrator generation' would become the subject of his future book, *Goodbye to My Generation*. Ries remarked wryly in his autobiography: 'After the full extent of the Nazi crimes became known, we were bitter. But during the blockade, the West Berliners suddenly became friends. In fact, some of our best friends were Germans.'

Having made his name from the Airlift, Ries took the first opportunity to relocate himself out of Berlin to the *New York Times* office in Paris. He rented an apartment in the eighth arrondissement, where he lived for several years with his first wife, Ann Stringer. Each time he visited the French capital, the word 'Paris' was written in large letters on his agenda. As Wanda Ries told me, he was 'enchanted'[20] and 'happy to leave to Paris – he never wanted to go back to Berlin'. Then, returning to the *Times*' headquarters in New York in March 1951 (where he discovered that thousands of his negatives taken over these years had been destroyed), he turned his back again on Germany. As he wrote, 'My professional and private life took place exclusively in American circles. I knew no Germans here, spoke no German and lost interest in Germany until [for an exhibition] the Berlin State Picture Office contacted me in 1973.'[21]

Henry Ries would not set foot in Berlin again for a quarter of a century.

XV

WOLVES IN SHEEP'S CLOTHING

1

Henry Ries 'felt his own generation had learned nothing'. Such sentiments did not stop the Western Allies from working closely with his contemporaries to make the Airlift a success. The local population was unavoidably the only available workforce, and every German who remained from during the war had inevitably experienced the Nazi era, its crimes, and defeat.

Ries probably never met Ulrich Stampa. The engineer had built planes for the Luftwaffe during the Second World War. His family lost their home to the Soviets in Pomerania, and he was staunchly anti-communist. After a stint in the Wehrmacht, Stampa was interned in two French prisoner-of-war camps, where the Moroccan guards played violins. He opined: 'Creatures like them are not worthy of such instruments.' When interviewing Stampa at his home in Bremen, writer Richard Reeves reported the man said, 'There were no Jews killed in the camps. My father worked at Auschwitz. Those stories around the world are all Jewish lies.'[1]

After the war, Stampa spent time in Argentina in the German colony, building jet fighters for Perón, before returning to Germany in 1955, eventually to become a candidate for the extremist DVU (German People's Union), founded as a political party in 1987, before it merged with the neo-Nazi NPD (National Democratic Party). After he died in 2007, his daughter wrote how her mother 'suffered greatly' from his 'conservative attitudes' and 'she was sometimes completely desperate when malicious calls or letters came'.

The American authorities in Faßberg put Stampa's skill set first. It did not matter what he thought about Jews, North Africans, or Nazi Germany. He was a flight engineer and expert in aeronautical hydraulics. These competencies ensured he was one of the first German engineers employed by the Allies at the base. They used him just as they used old Luftwaffe bunk beds as ladders to climb up into the planes.

2

Harold Bowers, an 18-year-old from Scranton, Pennsylvania, describes how the legacy of the German Luftwaffe remained at the RAF base in Faßberg, where American planes and personnel were engaged. Like McAfee, Bowers had been in Hawaii; he was dispatched at short notice. The 94-year-old's eyes still light up when he tells me about his arrival at what he called a 'first-class Luftwaffe base', opened by the Nazis in 1934 as a military airfield and bomber pilot school. The ghosts of the Nazis' Air Force still haunted the 'marble wall of showers' or 'the old Luftwaffe dinner hall, where we sat at tables of four, feeling like the big shots'.

Bowers disagrees with many of the negative assessments of conditions at the base, saying he was 'happy for the whole thing, coming from the Pacific'. The food at Faßberg was comfortably a lot like home: sausages and potatoes. 'Breakfast was first class. Not powdered egg and milk, but fresh eggs and real meat. Toast and coffee.' Perhaps he didn't have high expectations as a young, lowly private: he joked that his official title in the Air Force was: 'Hey you'.[2]

The private would walk down the street to the hangar – everything was within walking distance – to bring in the plane for a total inspection, change the spark plugs, look at the tyres, start the engines. 'Not all the planes were too good. The tyres had to be exchanged frequently, because with those heavy loads they would run down. Twenty tons is a big full load, and landing was heavy. I admired the pilots. They worked hard.'

The massive operation required people to do all kinds of specialised ground crew tasks. There were fifty-seven thousand German civilian workers on the Airlift.[3] And who could do the technical jobs at the airports? Well, people who had worked with planes in the years previously. General Tunner, in his autobiography, *Over the Hump*, described meeting Lucius Clay one day at Tempelhof airport, telling him that they didn't have enough personnel and asking for more 'skilled German mechanics'. Clay was on board with the inclusion of former Luftwaffe mechanics despite fears they might sabotage planes or upset the Allied pilots. The Luftwaffe, after all, had totally destroyed two hundred thousand homes in Britain and killed fifty thousand civilians during the Blitz, just as Allied Air Forces had killed half a million and destroyed sixty German cities, many engulfed in the fire storms of incendiary bombs. Only a quarter of these Allied pilots survived the war unwounded.[4] Rancour was inevitable.

Nonetheless, Faßberg emerged from the war not only an architectural reminder of the Nazi years. It summoned back its Luftwaffe personnel who had seen the destruction of Germany. And not only would the Western Allies be feeding Germans, but they'd be working side by side with men who assisted in the bombing of Britain.

Bowers tells me, 'Particularly, the pilots were not fond of the Germans. They had bombed them.' But Bowers also said to me he didn't have as much difficulty relating to these men. The Luftwaffe people were professional and happy to be under his command. 'My grandfather was German – last name Bauer – and our family had emigrated to Pennsylvania in the late 1700s, so I had a connection to Germany.' At the hangar, the Germans called him 'the kid'.

'Never once, though, did they tell me that they had shot down a US plane' – this may be because most were mechanics and not pilots – 'No, they said instead, "we were out daily on patrol". They wanted to get along with us and us with them. I liked them. They never hesitated to get out of line a little when dealing with the pilots. But with me, I was accepted. I was Herr Bauer.'

I ask Alec Chambers what he thought of the Germans. How was it that they had come all this way to help a people with whom they had been at war so recently? Did they feel conflicted they were feeding them? Alec replies, 'No, they had only half our ration. Most lived in cellars. In rubble that could be seen from the air.' 'How could people survive? … In piles of rubble, bloody great piles.' In Hamburg, he 'had never seen such piles of rubble … they must have been four stories high.'[5] Chambers remembers seeing German housewives searching for usable bricks in rubble to rebuild their homes. He says, 'Most of us had no hard feelings; mine were sympathetic in view of the awful living conditions and general shortages of most essential commodities.'

Just as at Faßberg, Luftwaffe expertise was needed at Wunstorf: 'We had excellent relations with the ex-Luftwaffe air mechanics who we employed to assist in the servicing of our aircraft and engines. They were reliable and good at their job.' And Chambers describes how the Germans were grateful for the work and how one man had 'tears in his eyes as he took the first heavy sack. There was no need for words.'

'Did your enemies become friends?' I ask.

Alec says he never spent enough time around them for that to happen but insists they were excellent workers and describes Manfred, who 'was the elder. He'd served with Rommel in North Africa. We got on well. The enemy was remote. They were all bloody airmen. That's what mattered.'

3

The need for labourers with technical skills grew throughout the Airlift, especially with the building of Tegel airport. For this, the United States had been locally recruiting former military men. These programmes are familiar: the Industrial Police in their black uniforms and the related five thousand-strong Civilian Technical Service Groups (*Zivilen technischen Dienstgruppen*).[6] These Black Guard hires would greatly influence the logistics of the Berlin Airlift. Men from the Industrial Police helped form the first units of the US Labor Service that went to work for the Airlift at Rhein-Main. The enrolment was partly a cost-saving measure – Germans were cheap. What the Americans hid from the others was their numbers: nearly ten thousand in operation by 1949.

Back in the meeting rooms of the Kommandatura, in the months between July 1947 and 4 June 1948, the British and French had expressed worry about the rearmament of former German soldiers and airmen. The French spoke of the Industrial Police's 'controversial character', that it was a 'real military unit' and therefore illegal and worthy of investigation. The British agreed that they should both 'press for the absorption of Industrial Police into the Auxiliary Watch Police Force' and not 'solely under the Aegis of the US Occupational forces'.

At Rhein-Main and Wiesbaden, they worked long shifts loading and unloading aircraft, achieving the famed record times for turnarounds of five to six minutes per aircraft. A 1953 history by the Labor Service calls this 'an unforgettable testament to German efficiency'. Working side by side with Americans also meant the beginning of friendships: 'a good rapport also developed with the American occupation troops'.

The most serious allegation was that many were ex-Nazis. The British remarked in official documents that they 'won't comment on their character'. The Americans admitted they brought into the Industrial Police and the Civil Technical Service Corps men with expertise, 'regardless of their pasts'.[7] No doubt, the recruitment was a departure from the founding principle of denazification. The use of former Nazis was seen by US authorities as preferable to African-American soldiers. Representatives of the Negro Newspaper Publishers Association had already observed, on a research trip in 1946, that black soldiers were passed over for positions of 'trust and confidence' in favour of German prisoners of war. Their report argued that the segregation of black soldiers in the Army and their blanket exclusion from use in Berlin set a bad example for the Germans they were trying to democratise.[8]

The Soviets ran with their accusations: in a May 1948 memorandum of the Public Safety Committee, Kartmazov penned that 'former Nazis ... are also admitted into the detachments' and that their numbers included leaders of the Hitler Youth, 'military criminals', people who had 'worked in concentration camps' with 'many of them possessing Fascist Orders and medals' – all contrary to the laws and orders of the Control Council. The Soviets noted specifically – during the final meeting of the commanders on 4 June, whose report they refused to sign – that 'a notorious war criminal, the former Chief of Hitler's General Staff, General Halder, has been appointed by the US authorities to the post of the Chief of Staff of the "Black Guard" and had come to Berlin to inspect his units'.[9]

How much was smoke and how much fire? The Americans were hiring ex-Nazis: Franz Halder, the notorious ex-Nazi who helped plan the invasion of Poland, might not have been part of the Industrial Police but had been resurrected by the Americans for a consultant role with the US Army History Division. Industrial Police and US Labor Service members explained in their 1953 history the problem of former Nazi elements in their ranks and that the men in their black uniforms were 'widely misunderstood and misrepresented by the general German public'. The Labor Service's nationalistic language, like the Nazis', exalting national community – the forces working 'between two fronts – fulfilling their duty to their German homeland' – would not have improved perceptions. The 'misunderstandings' went so far that Black Guard men and their families were 'locally boycotted and even attacked' and 'in October 1948 ... a general purge was undertaken in the IP [Industrial Police] to remove undesirable elements who had repeatedly infiltrated due to the relaxed hiring conditions'. By 1955, these moves were deemed redundant and Waffen-SS, who had been part of the Industrial Police, finally became normalised members.[10]

The Berlin Airlift helped scrub clean the stigma of former Nazis and SS men in their ranks. As the Labor Service wrote in their history:

> For the first time, the American headquarters realised that the German people stood opposed to the Soviet system and, with open hearts, leaned towards Western civilisation, to Western, European values, and democratic forms of life. They gave the German people a new chance: the counteraction of the Soviet blockade through the Berlin Airlift – a gesture of true humanity, to save three million Berliners from starvation.

Putting these men in US Black Guard uniforms changed the dynamic: they became partners. The occupying army was no longer just foreign; it was also German. Those who participated in this project felt proud to be given back the dignity of a uniform, even if that uniform was of the former enemy. Just as many of the Allied pilots accepted former Luftwaffe as fellow airmen, former German soldiers bonded with the US Army, embracing military hierarchy and its trappings. The insignia, black uniforms, and badges have become stock items in the catalogue of post-war German army memorabilia collected by the alumni and admirers of the US Labor Service.

The failure of denazification in the Labor Service, and its precursor, the 'Black Guards', reflected the fiasco of denazification across Western German institutions. Nazi perpetrators, those in the mobile killing units of the *Einsatzgruppen*, were systematically recruited for German Intelligence from 1946 and, when the West German federal criminal police agency (*Bundeskriminalamt*) was formed in 1951, almost all its top members had Nazi pasts, many in the SS and the Gestapo. Parallel trends were observed at all levels of administration, not just in the German police.[11]

In their final meeting with the other Allied powers in June, the Soviet representative turned to the others and asked if they did 'not fear the resurgence of the German army and of militarism in Germany?' Were they going to give them guns?

The answer from the American point of view was, 'Yes, indeed.' At one investigative committee meeting on the Black Guards, the British joked that the Americans were not creating a 'Paulus Army' – referring to the German Field Marshal Friedrich Paulus, who joined the Soviets after the Battle of Stalingrad. But they were doing something similar: the Americans built an indigenous territorial army out of the expertise of the Nazi military, a force of old soldiers hardened on the Eastern Front that could easily be deployed against the Russians.

The Soviets were correct to be worried: already in 1947 and 1948, this looked like a unilateral paramilitary force that broke more than one tenet of the post-war peace. After the creation of West Germany, plans were made to increase their numbers to 100,000. Once the rules of the four powers no longer constrained the Americans, the Labor Force eventually became a US Army battalion – unthinkable at the war's end. In 1948–49, along with other local hires, it provided a massive workforce, dedicatedly anti-communist: a crucial pillar supporting the Airlift's logistical success.

4

'And how were things at the hotel?' I ask Alec Chambers.

Bad Nenndorf had an infamous reputation. In the region, it was called 'the forbidden village'. The little town and its spa buildings were used after the war by British Intelligence as a top-secret internment camp to interrogate some four hundred prisoners, both high-ranking and smallfry Nazis. The British ripped out the innards of the baths and turned the changing cubicles, with their tiled floors and smell of sulphur lingering in the air, into cells.[12] A British clergyman visited the camp at the beginning of 1947, having heard stories of torture, and was followed by British Labour MP Richard Stokes on a surprise visit. They observed abuse as a means of gathering intelligence.

Stokes reported in Parliament on the horrifying conditions, stating that the Chief of Intelligence, Major General John Sydney Lethbridge, 'ought to be sacked' for it. The camp was closed in July 1947 in the subsequent scandal widely reported in the British press, exposing the abuse of prisoners who were subject to extreme cold, hunger (several inmates starved to death), torture, solitary confinement, and assault, among other horrors, all of which was seen as very 'un-British'.

The British government was terrified of the fallout of publicity of having used 'German concentration camp methods' in Bad Nenndorf. Foreign Secretary Ernest Bevin took the case to court-martial in 1948 behind closed doors. Colonel Robin 'Tin-Eye' Stephens, the monocled commandant, was acquitted and reposted to Africa, despite the determination of the Court of Inquiry that 'our efforts to teach democracy in the British zone tally with an organisation in many respects resembling the Gestapo'. All this shows that the British were embarrassed by Bad Nenndorf, just when they began to curry West German public opinion in the looming Cold War with the Soviets. The camp was shut down, but its memories were fresh in the forbidden village.

Alec sensed something was wrong about town: 'At the hotel, everyone working there seemed like they'd just been released from prison, but nothing was pinched.' The men were housed in a hotel with the peculiar name of T-Force, where the female chief had apparently been involved in the Nazis' Strength Through Joy leisure organisation, suggesting even less affection for the English. The men did not often leave the hotel and perhaps had little exposure to the sordid events of the previous year. 'We were mostly home boozing in the hotel and didn't venture out,' Alec tells me. 'We were a bad bloody lot – nothing else to do but drink in the mess, which was in the hotel, or us going out looking for the ladies of the night.'[13]

Cyril Hagues, a civilian pilot involved in the liquid lift, was also housed in Bad Nenndorf and observed that after the fourteen-hour shifts, including travel to and from Wunstorf:

> There wasn't a great deal of time to do things in terms of leisure ... We weren't exactly popular in Bad Nenndorf, I mean, let's face it, we were the enemy. It wasn't considered very sensible to wander around the place after dark. Some chaps from British South American Airways were knocked over the head with a bottle, and things like that ... and a large part of Hanover was out of bounds to British personnel, and it's not surprising really, there was no reason they should like us really.

Then, in April 1949, the civilian crews were moved to Hamburg, where Alec says they were more popular. A year before, things had been quite different there, as reported by Hartmut Weil, writing for his university newspaper in the summer of 1948. He was shocked by the patrician attitudes of the British.[14] Buildings in Hamburg used by the British had notices, '"Germans not allowed in" – in one instance next to a shop window propagating Anglo-German friendship'. In a British hotel, he found copious meals, mod cons, and 'the shadows of hungry Germans behind window panes'. The experience was summed up by his Cambridge colleague in civilian clothes 'being pushed off the pavement by an officer, as Germans have to make way for Britons (Colleague's reply unprintable)'. All this was in the shadow of Hamburg having been brutally firebombed by the Allies only five years before his visit.

Chambers's account from Hamburg almost a year later, in the spring of 1949, was (according to Alec) 'very different indeed!' A whole city was now at their feet and not just a little town. The men were lodged in the centre, not far from the Alster.[15]

'The Germans thought we were heroes, bloody heroes. The Airlifters were something special!' he tells me, recounting going to the Hamburg opera to see *Carmen*. They showed up at the box office in uniform and were told they did not have to pay for the production if they showed a British passport. 'We had front-row seats. All in uniform. At the interval, the audience got up, put a spotlight on us, with tears in their eyes. There were other incidents like this with the Germans showing their appreciation.'

Chambers remembers nightlife hedonism very well, which was a little more risqué than the opera. Not far from their hotel was a house, where they'd go up to the top floor and spend time with the girls. He recounts, 'The nightlife in Hamburg was something else. I always remember descending into this nightclub and there was a row of bar stools, and there was a beautiful girl on every one.' He remembers them all swivelling in unison to size up the British men. 'That was my undoing in Hamburg!' he muses. The men were sexed up: in the work canteen, 'there was this lady in charge. All she wore was an overall. I remember that!'

Not only were there girls, but there was money to be made, and the British civilian crews got into the black market coffee trade. Sometimes, Chambers would meet his buyers under a tree in Hamburg's zoo and the money he made meant he did not think about his pay for a month.

Alec explains, 'At first, we returned to the UK every six to nine days [to Tarrant Rushton, near Blandford Forum, Dorset] for servicing and restocking the coffee! However, when it was established that the Airlift was a long-term commitment, our routine became a three-week rostered duty with two flights each day, then six days' leave in the UK.' To evade British customs, in Dorset they would mark the coffee as 'aircraft spares'.

All this provided ample opportunity to bring over products that could fetch a good price in starving Germany.

'One or two crews would go out with bottles of gin in the evenings,' he explains, 'Maybe twelve blokes with bottles of gin to trade. We were always mixing, boozing, at a nightclub, with the black marketeers. The flight engineers were told ("duty bound") to find the club's main switches and to turn them off and put the place in darkness if there was a fight.' If the Brits could get a black marketeer drunk, they'd try to empty his wallet.

'Were there fights?' I ask.

'Oh yes, they would tear up the furniture. Everyone would fight about the black market prices. The Brits were there to make some money. It was usually fairly orderly, but then the German black marketers would start bargaining for the coffee, for the gin. You got good money. You could sell rations for exorbitant prices.'

But bad behaviour on the streets of Hamburg was not out of the question for the men of Flight Refuelling Ltd. A presumably drunken group, after a night out, used a welding torch to vandalise as many of the city's tram points as they could find. And then one David Prowse, apparently a charmer of sorts, known for roguish off-duty antics, nearly choked an officer, hanging him from a window, for closing the company bar early. Prowse was removed by the chief of Wunstorf when he stole and drove a German steam train [sic] as far as his inexperience allowed him.[16]

Alcohol could also interfere with the job. Chambers recounts how, 'Drink was the main thing. Radio officers have a soft spot for booze: you could never find a bugger who was sober on many occasions. The mornings were especially painful: 'We did tend to drink too much. The next morning, we got into the aircraft and searched for the oxygen mask for a little relief from the headache!'

5

The civilian crews were 'aggravating' for the RAF. Despite their antics, Flight Refuelling Ltd was remarkably effective.[17] The company logged almost twelve thousand hours of flying and 1.7 million miles on 4,438 flights to Berlin. The 'Liquid Lift' transported almost 100,000 tons of liquid fuel. The men put in fourteen-plus-hour days.

Although Chambers and his men thought the Airlift was 'a bit of a joke' when they started, by the end he understood 'that having made a stand it did prevent Communism from spreading to the bloody Channel'. Willy Brandt would concur, calling 1948 'the year of the democratic counter-offensive which – at least in Europe – brought the further advance of Communism to a halt'.[18]

In August 1949, the civvies returned to the UK, and Chambers remained with the company until 1950, when 'flight refuelling took a dive'. He became a scientific civil servant and later lived in Shrivenham.

Alec insists on getting up from his wheelchair when I thank him to leave – he is solid, strong, awake, and merry – I think there are many more spicy stories he's not told me. But today, I got a hint. I suspect that's what's behind that little naughty smile of his: he had a good time, and he's glad of it.

But Alec Chambers does have one last anecdote for me: on 1 June 1949, he and his crew took off for Gatow from Hamburg on a midday flight. He remembers being told it would be a big occasion, and that VIPs were coming. This was because it was the occasion of the 100,000th tanker landing.[19] After they touched ground, loaded with motor spirit and domestic heating oil, and pulled into Gatow's ellipse, bunches of flowers confronted the men along with a photo shoot, a mention in the Official Diary, and a present that surprised them: 'US cigarettes. Lucky Strikes!' Perhaps the authorities knew too, as Alec already told us, that despite all that inflammable cargo the men smoked on board.

What is most startling about this story, documented in several sources, is that it is also a dead ringer for the first scene of the most famous film about the Berlin Airlift. A person with a story like Alec Chambers was played by the Hollywood actor Montgomery Clift.

XVI

THE HOLLYWOOD VERSION

1

In May 1949, Berlin became an enormous set for a film about the Airlift. Director George Seaton – who in 1947 had burnished his name with *Miracle on 34th Street* – stood behind the camera of *The Big Lift*. He had planned to shoot a night sequence on Potsdamer Platz but was worried about Russian interference, making do with Moritzplatz on the edge of the American Quarter instead.

Seaton had already had his fill of the Soviets. They had permitted him to film in their zone, provided they knew 'what, where, when, and how we planned to shoot'. Even if Seaton believed that *The Big Lift* 'wasn't really anti-Russian',[1] the Soviets didn't like the sound of an American film about the Airlift.[2] Their permission seemed suspiciously helpful. Armed with a *propusk* in Cyrillic decorated with official stamps, he wandered with his crew through the Brandenburg Gate to Unter den Linden to see what would happen.

The space in front of the gate was deserted – too deserted. Typically, soldiers or police were overseeing the action. The Americans got to filming when, suddenly, a Soviet loudspeaker piped communist propaganda at an intense volume onto their scene. They looked up and saw a newly installed loudspeaker.

The crew had been set up, and it was a production disaster. Later, the whole scene had to be dubbed.

Moritzplatz proved only marginally better. 'They were waiting for us,' Seaton later wrote, referring to 'hundreds of members of the Young Communist League' a half-block away from the shoot at the zonal boundary. The youths would begin to scream and whistle from the Soviet quarter every time Seaton signalled 'action' to the camera. They would stop when he cried 'cut'. It again made recording impossible despite a dozen attempts.

Except Seaton's crew was resourceful, and the assistant director whispered a solution in his ear.

Seaton got behind the camera and cried 'cut'. It was 'all quiet on the Eastern Front', and he successfully filmed the scene. Then he cried 'action', and 'all hell broke loose'.

The production team from 20th Century Fox did their best to look disappointed and not to let on that they had reversed the signals.

Seaton later told the *New York Times*, 'We didn't want the three hundred youngsters to feel they had come for nothing.'

2

At the time of the Airlift, Montgomery Clift was the hottest actor in Hollywood, on the cover of *Life* magazine, with a three-film contract in hand. The second of those projects was *The Big Lift*, with shoots in May, and in September before the last flight of the Airlift landed on 6 October.

Clift was a moody Method actor of the likes of James Dean and Marlon Brando, except more handsome. Out of New York's 1930s theatre scene, he rose to film stardom with two 1948 productions, *Red River* and *The Search,* for which he was nominated for an Academy Award for Best Actor. He went on to hits such as *A Place in the Sun* (1951), *From Here to Eternity* (1953), and *Judgment at Nuremberg* (1961), five years before his early death at 45.

20th Century Fox's press department played on him as the simple type: living in a 'cheap fifth-floor walk-up apartment in New York City. With his wardrobe just about what a boy working his way through college would have, the noted actor is forced to rent formal clothes whenever an occasion demands their use.' The press materials described him as 'always completely natural and convincing … It is hard to believe he is acting at all', 'always unpretentious and casual' and 'sloppy but handsome'.[3]

When he arrived from London, Clift was astonished by Berlin. The boy from Nebraska had spent his childhood travelling around Europe like an aristocrat with his mother, learning German and French. But the continent was now in places unrecognisable. Clift later told the actor Patricia Collinge how he was shocked by the poverty, the 'unbelievable conditions', when he walked through the former capital.[4]

Nonetheless, when the studio found him a villa in a leafy West Berlin suburb, fitted with furniture from Paris, Monty objected because he had 'visualised something with a garden'. Lucius Clay's office was reportedly called to convince a colonel and his family to give up their house for a few weeks.

3

At first, Clift got along well with George Seaton and thought the script's dialogue was 'fantastic', but good relations with the director did not last. One of the most conspicuous aspects of *The Big Lift* is that a film about falling in love with the enemy saw the real-life cast and crew making enemies with Montgomery Clift.

It wasn't just that Clift had caused trouble with his lodgings or was reportedly selling cigarettes on the black market. Clift's New York Russian émigrée neighbour, Mira Rostova, had been included in the actor's contract as his private secretary. Clift saw her as his 'artistic conscience', but the film crew observed something closer to a Rasputinian or Oedipal relationship with her constant presence on set.

Mira exerted an uncanny power over the young actor, who ceded to her his decision-making. She would nod or shake her head to indicate whether she liked a scene. As the de facto arbiter of retakes, she ensured shoots went on much longer than usual. The exasperated cameramen finally quipped, 'That woman is directing the picture!'

Seaton exploded and took Clift aside: 'I hired you, not Mira.'

With tears in his eyes, Clift replied, 'But *she* is Monty Clift!'[5]

Seaton wasn't hearing it.

So, Clift raised the stakes: 'If Mira goes, I go George.'

Clift might have been famous in Hollywood, but he was an unfamiliar face to most Germans who did not have access to a steady diet of American films. A backlog of 1940s classics would only become available in the 1950s.[6] So, when Clift was rehearsing one scene, singing with two German actors in a café, a photographer in the room was struck by his unfamiliar attractiveness.

He approached Clift and told him, 'You have a remarkable face.'

The photographer made an offer: he was photographing for a clothing line and could use a face just like that in his advertisements. Did Clift want a job?

'I pay well,' the photographer sweetened the pot.

Clift quietly thanked the photographer and said he didn't need the work.[7]

George Seaton had, after all, relented on Mira, and Clift was staying in Berlin.

Seaton remarked, 'I guess he was under a lot of pressure. But he could be very unpleasant.' When the director returned to Hollywood, he had nothing good to say about working with Montgomery Clift and spread gossip that the actor, with his many retakes, made filming expensive.[8]

4

Seaton almost certainly knew Roberto Rossellini's neorealistic *War Trilogy* and its final Berlin instalment, *Germany, Year Zero* (1948). These films were striking in their *chiaroscuro* photography of ruins, semi-documentary qualities, use of non-professional actors, and focus on everyday suffering. Many of the same qualities were found in Henry Ries's photographs.

Like *Germany, Year Zero*, *The Big Lift* is sometimes considered a 'rubble film' with neorealistic qualities. It was set in the spectacular destruction of Europe's war, with a similar focus on everyday life – that of lower-ranked servicemen and their relationships with everyday German women.[9] The action was also filmed during the actual operation of the Airlift, with real airmen, ground crew, and Berliners as non-professional actors. Seaton said, 'The backdrop of this blasted city is the most dramatic scene against which any man could ever pose a story ... these things gave us the drama we desired.'

The grandeur of the departures and landings made it, according to the *Los Angeles Times*, 'direct, forceful, and one of the attention-compelling photoplays of the post-war period'.[10] As a 'neorealistic' film, it fell rather short of its arthouse pretensions, with its formulaic Hollywood romantic plot and commercial considerations. But the period footage of the lift made *The Big Lift* the most important film document of the operation, one of enormous historical interest.

Only five professional leads were sunk into this real-world action, with Monty Clift playing the starring role of Danny MacCullough, a sensitive but gullible American pilot who falls for a German *Fräulein*, Frederica, played by Cornell Borchers.

Monty's character meets Cornell's when his plane lands at Tempelhof, the 100,000th of the Airlift. The horizon over the German landscape comes into view from the pilots' perspective, from the gritty filth of their cabin blackened with coal. Soon, we see the shattered rooftops of Berlin with the descent to the tarmac. As the film's production files describe, Clift's 'plane starts to descend, skimming over roofs. After she clears the last roof, she dips towards the runway. [They] wince, expecting to crash any minute. A "FOLLOW ME" jeep picks up the plane and directs it to a vacant spot.'[11]

As in the in-real-life version of events described by Alec Chambers, the airmen were surprised on the tarmac by flowers, reporters, and the kiss of a pretty girl – Frederica. As the production materials summarise, 'She speaks English quite well, and Danny, like any good American, gets her phone number.'

Originally, Hildegard Knef, famous for her role in Germany's first post-war 'rubble film', *Die Mörder sind unter uns* (*The Murderers are Among Us*, 1946), had been cast to play the role of Frederica. Like Clift, she was chosen for her naturalistic acting style. But the bright lights of Hollywood were sensitive to scandal, and Knef was fired when her relationship with a Nazi film giant, Ewald von Demandowsky, became public.[12]

Cornell Borchers, actress and singer, stepped in. The studio tells us that 'blonde, blue-eyed, and beautiful, [she] plays the German girl who twists Montgomery Clift around her little finger'. Known in Germany as something of an ice princess, she was nicknamed the *Eisente* (frozen duck) in the local press. Cornell explained, 'I'm just not an erotic actress,' but her English skills were an enormous asset, as was her edge of chilly sophistication. It proved popular with the American public – *froideur*, after all, makes a great femme fatale.

Born in East Prussia in 1925, Borchers survived the war in Heidelberg, where she saw horrors working in a military hospital as a nurse, after two terms studying medicine. She then found her way to Berlin for drama school, only to learn it wasn't an easier profession: 'don't think they give you presents', she quipped. At the time of the Airlift, Borchers's own story paralleled that of the film because she met an English officer and married him. In an interview, she explained: 'Mr Seaton looked at photographs of young German actresses – he interviewed quite a number and made tests of about ten. Then I finally got the part.' It was her big break, and she'd go on to make nearly two dozen films in Germany and the United States. While the Americans were arguing on set, this German made friends with the director and his wife, who became her acting coach. They all stayed in touch after the shoot.[13]

In the film, the plot continues with a newspaperman from St Louis wanting to write a human interest story about the progress of a sack of flour flown in with the Airlift to a Berlin bakery. The story would be even better with an American pilot as the protagonist. The journalist gets permission from the Air Force to give Clift's character a day off in Berlin for his article. Except our pilot is more interested in calling up Frederica, whom he finds clearing stones from a ruined building.

Borchers is the archetypal 'rubble woman', or *Trümmerfrau*. These women removing debris from bombed buildings became legends, a 'foundational myth' of West Germany popularised in the 1980s when they represented the 'phoenix from the ashes' of post-war society. At the time in occupied Germany, however, much of this hard work was regarded as punishment for former Nazis.[14] Seaton may have known this, as Frederica's biography – still hidden from our naïve American serviceman – will reveal later in the film. But first, Borchers takes Clift by the hand to explore her Berlin under the constant roar and spectacle of low-flying aircraft. The everyday hardships of the ice duck's compatriots will eventually melt his heart.

5

Yet more acrimony was seen on the set of this film about mending fences with your enemy. Clift's co-star Paul Douglas complained that he was pressured out of the camera frame during close-up shots. Exasperated, he warned Seaton he'd heard 'that this kid's a little shit' and that 'if he causes any more trouble during our mutual close-ups', he would have to respond. The next time the camera zoomed in, and Douglas felt Clift's insistent pushing, he stomped hard on his foot in retaliation. The younger man screamed, and it was the last time it happened. The two men were not friendly for the rest of the shooting.[15]

Douglas came from the voluble, wise-crack world of radio sports announcing and, according to the production's press materials, was 'voted by his theatrical friends as "the man least likely to be an actor"' before becoming the 'stage find of the year' and star in the 1949 film *A Letter to Three Wives*. At the age of 42, he was fourteen years Clift's senior. One female German journalist asked what all the fuss was about Montgomery Clift, 'Well, he's nice. But that other man, Douglas! He's so big and strong and looks so well-fed. He is the kind of man we like in Germany.'

Douglas's role was Clift's buddy, Henry 'Hank' Kowalski. The Polish-American spent the war in a concentration camp and is brash and anti-German. He 'figures [the Airlift] is a lot of trouble to feed a bunch of Krauts.' So it's a surprise when it's revealed he's fallen for a fiery and argumentative ('petite, vivacious, and charming' according to the pressbooks) German *Schatzi* named Gerda, played by Bruni Löbel.

The two men's parallel relationships – Clift with Borchers, Douglas with Löbel – explore the difficult 'sell' of the Airlift to the American public: could Americans and Germans reconcile after the war's bad blood? The stakes in this film are higher than just friendship – here, we are talking about the apotheosis of burying the hatchet: love.

Clift is the optimist, Douglas the pessimist, and their dialectic leads to surprising conclusions.

6

The majesty of the aerial footage is matched by everyday detail on the ground. The disputes off set were invisible in the action filmed. We follow that sack of flour from Tempelhof to a bakery, where it becomes bread. Through Clift's eyes, we peek through the bakery window when he says: 'Strange, you look in the store, and it seems like so little. Before you fly, it seems an awful lot.' Then our pilot loses his uniform – complicated story – and becomes a plain-clothed *flâneur* through the isolated city.

The scarcity of food is the recurrent theme. As a result, the film is full of paradox. The city is supposedly blockaded and dependent on the pilots' deliveries, but, nonetheless, we accompany Clift on a subway through the Soviet zone, where the friendly Berliners smuggle black market groceries from the East. Borchers explains a 'leaky blockade' to Clift: Berlin's zones are only a problem for the Allies, not for Berliners who go back and forth all the time. He then shares the locals' camaraderie as they survive a spot check on the train and celebrate their escape. Meanwhile, at street level, Soviet soldiers harass, spy on, and arrest Berliners. Monty shakes his head: 'I never realised that staying alive can be a twenty-four-hour job.'

The black market was also of fascination to the director. Seaton disguised himself as a German worker 'and went through a day of shopping in Berlin to learn all the tricks and dodges, which he later incorporated into the movie. Wearing shabby clothing, a peaked cap and the inevitable ragged muffler, Seaton was amazed to see the hours of bargaining and haggling for enough food for a meal.'[16]

Meanwhile, the lovers wander from ruined street to street and through a Tiergarten denuded of trees. The camera zooms in on faces and people's lives. The focus is on Berliners' humanity, their everyday deprivations, especially those of women and children. Implicit is the righteousness of America's operation to protect and save them from starvation and Stalin.

Monty and Paul pal around throughout the film – in a bar, in a jeep. This banter is a running commentary on how Americans should feel about the Germans. Monty plays good cop and Paul bad cop. Monty is sensitive and understanding. Paul quips they should have used the A-Bomb on Berlin, reminds the audience of the crimes at Buchenwald, the bombings of Coventry and Rotterdam, and beats up a German he recognises as the guard of the prison camp where he was interned – making clear, according to the pressbook, that 'the situation is now reversed'. Monty, on the other hand, is compassionate. When thinking dreamily about his love interest, he asks: 'What am I supposed to do? Blame all that on a girl who was fifteen at the time?'

In the end, Monty is too soft and Paul too hard. Borchers claims that the Nazis liquidated her father because he spoke out against them. But Monty grapples with the truth when he discovers she's instead the daughter of an SS officer. The stranded American pilot manages to forgive her when he is overcome with pity, wandering the broken streets of Berlin, watching people raid garbage for food. But Borchers is even more nefarious than he expects: she's also already married and using Monty as a one-way ticket and visa to America and her SS husband hiding out in

Omaha. Duplicity and the shadow of Nazism mean the end of the affair for Monty, but the American critics nonetheless saw allure in Borchers's deception, with *The Christian Science Monitor* lauding her 'striking good looks and unscrupulous Continental charm'.[17]

Paul's fortunes with Greta also turn out to be a surprise. She has been learning democratic values – mainly how to argue effectively with Paul. Despite himself, he discovers she's the girl he wants to marry when she shows Germans can be rehabilitated through democratic education. Gerda has her moment, explaining to Hank that not all Germans are like Frederica, and 'he shouldn't judge all by one'. Hank is convinced because he understands that Americans can only teach the principles of democracy that they follow themselves. Gerda will stay in Germany with Hank, who requests to remain, to promote that democratic future. The real-life actress Bruni Löbel, meanwhile, in an interview, stated that now that she understands what Hitler did, '*Yes*, I am ashamed.'

As the pressbook offers, *The Big Lift* 'suggests the answer of how to treat a conquered people, how to show them their errors, how to lead them into democratic ways'. While Douglas learns to see them as human beings, Clift understands 'they must not be forgiven too quickly'. Paul – who gets the happy ending denied Monty – concludes, 'We were both wrong.'

7

The Big Lift was candy coated, and not only because it needed to compete in the American film market. Originally called *Quartered City* and then *Two Corridors East*, it went through many layers of censorship and revisions of the text – not just those a punctilious Montgomery Clift made between rehearsals.[18]

The then Hollywood Code (Hays Code) required the filmmakers to self-censor to get the movie past moral authorities. Prohibitions on depicting violence or sex meant that fundamental realities of the occupation – such as the rowdy (or worse) behaviour of servicemen – could not be shown on US screens. The Code had the effect of sanitising and neutralising how Germans were depicted in the film – they became indifferent and harmless.

The Code Administration Records for the film indicate how these rough edges were sanded away. The word 'god' could not be spoken irreverently, breasts were always covered, and you couldn't see a hint of panties or brassieres. Sexually suggestive language, like 'That dame of yours must be awful hot to set a plane on fire at this distance', was expunged, along with the word 'poop', and even the sound of the 'Bronx cheer' (or 'raspberry'). Minimal drinking occurred, and only of wine. Even song lyrics *in German* were cut. There was no gambling, religion, adultery, illicit sex, sex work, or family problems in *The Big Lift*. Only romance! The Code-filing documents sunnily reported that Montgomery Clift was motivated by 'success in love', Paul Douglas by 'protection of others from harm', and 'idealism as a way of life', just like Gerda. All the characters ended up pretty likeable, and pretty flat.

The one scene of serious anti-Nazi retribution, when Douglas beats up his former camp guard Gunter, also needed attenuation. The censors warned against 'excessive, undue brutality' in the scene and instructed that Douglas should not pick up and use a marble fragment 'about the size of a gun butt, I guess' to finish the job. A character's confrontation with his Nazi tormentors became something of a childish tumble and only 'very incidental'. In the end, all US citizens were marked in the documents as being portrayed 'sympathetically', while the Germans emerged as 'indifferent'.

The next layer of censorship came from the military authorities. Certificates allowed the crew with their equipment to use US military aircraft and rail at locations such as Wiesbaden, Faßberg, Rhein-Main, and Berlin for ninety days from 12 May 1949 for the 'USAF approved motion picture'. In exchange for access to the spectacular military installations of the US Air Force, the directors needed to accommodate military goals. It was one of the Cold War's first and closest collaborations between Hollywood and the US military – namely the US Air Force Public Affairs Office, General Clay's office, and the Motion Picture Production Office. The military retained the right to ensure the script followed government propaganda interests and, in fact, changed it twice.

The resulting film – concerning one of the 'outstanding air achievements of all time' – had dividends for the US military. The press material from 20th Century Fox included information about military enlistment, including the locations of forces recruitment centres. They encouraged press outlets to use the slogan, 'Give your career "The Big Lift" by enlisting in the U.S. Air Force'. Meanwhile, the propaganda myths of the Airlift and justifications for its enormous expense were disseminated on screens worldwide: 'The two and a quarter million residents of the three Western-power sectors of Berlin, cut off from their sources of supply, were kept alive with goods from the air.'

Then there were the commercial interests. *The Big Lift* could tie in to sell products in stores ('Beardon's suits give a man that big lift in his woman's eyes'). But it also needed to sell itself with newspapers and magazine advertisements. These ads contained more sexual innuendo than the Code would ever have allowed in the film itself, such as when Clift says to Douglas in a speech bubble: 'I'll handle the women ... you take care of history!' or 'Wait until you meet this Schatzi ... she's marked dangerous!' Such ads pictured Clift lifting a buxom Cornell Borchers – a big lift of gender stereotypes.[19]

8

The final layer of sanitising revision was the remade German version. The most curious thing about it was it had a different ending.

Despite being sold out for several days after the April 1950 premiere in the States, six months after the Airlift officially ended, *The Big Lift* was no universal critical success. The *New York Times* thought that the love story – the 'comprehensions of one dizzy kid' – was a 'hodgepodge of impressions' against the big canvas of unfolding Cold War events. *The Big Lift* was 'in short, a big let-down'.[20] On the other hand, *Variety* loved the film, commenting on the dramatic value of

> the interaction of the American GIs and German civilians in the Cold War ... the mutual mistrust between the two peoples and the way the GIs discover American democracy for themselves by exposing it to their German girlfriends, all help punch across the story without resorting to the usual flag waving. It's a masterful scripting job.

The German public would have to wait until 1953 to see a much shorter version of the film called *Es begann mit einem Kuß* (*It Started with a Kiss*). 20th Century Fox cut any criticisms in the film of Germany and its Nazi past. Deleting scenes and dubbing to alter dialogue were the most common tools. This type of expurgation was common in the German versions of films released in the early 1950s. Alfred Hitchcock's 1946 *Notorious* (rereleased in German in 1951), for example, became a different film, with all mentions of Nazis hiding out in South America building atomic weapons removed. It was instead about a drug ring. *Casablanca* (1942, rereleased in Germany in 1952) also, incredibly, made no mention of the Nazis or resistance movements.[21] In 1944, the US State Department instructed its embassies that marketing and distributing American films were paramount over any ideological qualms. In the American zone, the Information Control Division could ensure Germans did not see films that might make them doubt their Hollywood consumption, because they controlled what films Germans could see. In this way, the expansion of the American film market was more important than presenting material that furthered the denazification process. Entertainment sells better than instruction, after all.

For *The Big Lift*, this meant that nearly thirty minutes of the film would disappear from the German version. For example, Paul doesn't beat up the concentration camp guard. The collective guilt of Germans is played down. Paul's mention of A-bombing Berlin is covered up with a voice-over. Most importantly, both Monty and Paul have successful romances with their German lovers, whom they will marry. Borchers isn't a trickster, after all. Any remaining sharp edges in the film were thus flattened. In any case, *It Started with a Kiss* bombed in the West German film market despite – or perhaps even because – of the many efforts to sanitise it.

9

The reality of occupied Berlin was obviously different from the film. At the time of the American premiere, the *New York Times* warned the audience not to think a 'film is "realistic" just because it is so photographed'.[22] Exploring Berlin was not something most pilots could do. The in-real-life Alec Chambers, after all, hardly remembers the Brandenburg Gate it was so dark. We also don't know much about what the real-life Monty got up to in Berlin (but, since he was bisexual, it perhaps wasn't with Cornell Borchers). The film too packaged fraternisation in occupied Germany as love, when it usually didn't always entail romance but rather just sex.

If you put thousands of US airmen on a base, presumably there was more to do than fly their planes. This was recognised when, from October 1945, rules on fraternisation between Western Allied soldiers and Germans were relaxed.[23] At least just as many so-called 'Veronicas' as soldiers showed up in Celle – the name coming from a military newspaper cartoon character 'Veronica Dankeschön', whose initials are more than explanatory. The US Army's medical journal reported on the excessive incidence of sexually transmitted infections due to

> persons suddenly removed from their established homes and placed in a new environment ma[king] hasty heterosexual adjustments [*sic*] ... When bases were expanded and new fields were opened, a large number of camp followers accumulated in the hope of gaining a livelihood from the American troops, self-support being difficult in a war-impoverished nation.

While some of the relationships were romantic – there were 3,500 marriages between Americans and Germans by June 1948, and closer to 10,000 by 1950 – as Walter Slatoff writing in *The New Republic* explained, GIs with cigarettes and food were magnets for frozen and hungry German women engaged in sex work. Slatoff appealed to parents: 'imagine your own 18 or 19-year-old son removed entirely from your supervision, given an almost unlimited supply of money, granted a power over women equal to that of ... Clark Gable'.

Montgomery Clift was more handsome. But *The Big Lift* was the Hollywood version, after all.

10

The denouement of the Airlift unfolded at the highest levels. Negotiations between Stalin and the West dragged on through February,[24] just as the flown tonnage increased in an upward spiral of optimism. On 15 and 16 April 1949, a daily record of 13,000 tons, 3,946 take-offs and landings, every twenty-two seconds, was recorded. Meanwhile, Ernst Reuter was visiting America to promote the Airlift as the 'living symbol of Berlin's struggle for freedom'. For the Americans, it was a roaring success. One British Intelligence officer remarked on the Russians' tremendous 'error in strategy'. 'Far from reducing America's influence in Europe, it resulted in America's throwing military power into Europe for the first time in peacetime.'[25] Putting an end to this mistake was now also in the Soviet interest.

Progress towards lifting Soviet restrictions on Berlin and creating the West German state happened simultaneously – both part of the same Allied success in defending their sphere of influence, ensuring the Soviets recognised the clear line between East and West. The apotheosis of Western alliances was the creation of NATO in Washington on 4 April by twelve founding countries, with the commitment to assist other members in case of attack. The NATO founding treaty was born of the Atlanticism of the Berlin Airlift.

A flurry of events occurred in May, the decisive month. On 4 May, the Soviets agreed with the Western Allies to lift their restrictions – and the 'Counter-Blockade' – on 12 May, although the Airlift flights would continue until October as a safety measure. Then, the Basic Law or Constitution of West Germany was signed on 23 May. With the division of Germany, the world of the Potsdam Agreement was over, the occupation yielding now to two Germanies formalised under two systems.

Everything changed at midnight on 12 May 1949. A minute later, the lights went back on and, throughout the Western zones, there was the spectacle of the lights being switched on and off, on and off, in the windows of houses and apartments.[26]

Not just the international press but scores of Berliners crowded around the first boat, first truck, and the first train from the West to arrive in the freed city. At the frontier on the *Autobahn*, they gathered, watching the scene illuminated by headlights and applauding the first vehicle to enter the city from the West – that of an American news agency. The first truck carried tons of cucumbers. Ten British lorries passed the boundary. And the first train arrived at 6.30 a.m. at Bahnhof Charlottenburg.

Meanwhile, electric light suddenly flooded the spaces of nightclubs across the city. Eyes found they were unused to the glare. Some establishments, like the Ali Bar – where so much Russian Zone liquor had been seized – preferred to revert to gentle candlelight after only one hour.

The day was declared a holiday, and masses gathered in Rudolph-Wilde-Platz – 300,000 to see Clay and Reuter and salute their victory. It felt like a festival, or a 'grand opening night', as journalist Curt Riess described it. 'Berliners stuffed themselves with fish,' he wrote, now that goods that could be bought with the new currency were suddenly available. Cakes were eaten in such large quantities that many stomachs couldn't take the sudden 'orgies of gluttony ... the result: the doctor's offices were jammed. Innumerable complaints of upset stomachs, rashes ...'[27]

Henry Ries also described the end of the restrictions, and how he was given the opportunity to photograph Lucius D. Clay, who had been recalled to America. When he ceremoniously took down his name plaque from his office door after his last press conference, the governor offered it to Ries as a memento. Clay was given a hero's exit, with Berliners lining the streets watching Reuter and him in a car.

The next day, Clay described to Ries how his family's Berlin apartment was under the flight path to Tempelhof airport. Journalist Curt Riess would later remark on the 'fundamental composure' of Berliners during the Airlift, 'as the planes of Operation Vittles roared over their heads at intervals of only a few seconds. That calm could never be forgotten by anyone who experienced the blockade of Berlin.'[28]

It meant something more for Clay. He told the photographer how he missed the sound, the *Brummen*: 'I got used to sleeping well under the constant roar. I only woke up when it was quiet.'

AFTER 1949

AFTER 1945

XVII

REFLECTIONS

1

The case of Kenneth Slaker's escape on foot through the Iron Curtain went unproblematically through the accident board.[1] A few days later, Slaker was given a fake name and sent up into the mountains to Garmisch-Partenkirchen to recover from his injuries. This would help him avoid the press, certain from their paid informant that there was a cover-up on the River Werra.

When he returned from the Alps, Slaker called the Central Intelligence Division at Hersfeld to get in touch with Rudolf, the East German who had risked his life to get Slaker across. The pilot found himself on the phone, unable to get any information about the German's whereabouts. 'This really disturbed me because I had promised to help him.'

A week later, Slaker was on the line again, but this time to the Army. Again, there was no information.

Finally, he contacted a close friend from his war days, Wiesbaden Commander Colonel Young, to see what he could find out.

A few days later, he got a call. Young had reached out to the Pentagon for help. It had worked. 'Come to my office tomorrow at 1 p.m. Rudolf will be there.'

Slaker remembered:

Exactly at 1 p.m., two Army military police escorted Rudolf into Colonel Young's office ... Rudolf and I rushed together, embraced, and shook hands. I stepped back and asked Rudolf what had happened to him during this time. He had tears in his eyes and said, '*Kannath*, Army CID beat me with rubber hoses! They wanted me to confess that I was a Communist, and I am not.' I was stunned: I looked at Colonel Young, who nodded his head in the affirmative.

Slaker was shocked: the man was now his friend. He had saved his life, only to end up in an Army prison, interrogated and tortured because he had no papers. There was another reason this case would be classified for so many years and why the press had to be so closely monitored. It was complicated that people were bribed. It was complicated that the Soviets had shot at an American officer. But the very existence of Rudolf was complicated after what had happened to him in an American jail. It was much easier to say Slaker simply 'walked through the Iron Curtain'.

The Air Force would now help Rudolf, set him up with a post office job in Wiesbaden, and get his family out from the East. Slaker would not stay long in Germany. His career eventually moved him north to Alaska, doing air rescue – again saving people instead of killing them – but, even from a distance, he stayed in touch with Rudolf's family, and he visited them in the years to come.

But what had happened to Rudolf haunted the pilot.

He had thought the Americans were his friends and the Germans his enemies: the world had been neatly ordered. Later, he observed, 'I could not believe that the American military would do that! I thought that we were the good guys.'

2

In 1985, Henry Ries got a phone call from a former classmate from the Schiller-Real-Gymnasium, Werner Mörlins, asking him if he planned to attend his high school reunion in Berlin. Mörlins told Ries how well he remembered when the Nazi teacher brought him to the front of the class and quipped how, again, 'We all want to stare at you a bit!'

Ries had been living in New York City for thirty-five years, having opened an advertising studio after leaving the *New York Times*. He returned to his American life, and, as his widow told me, 'He never wanted to come back to Berlin – his attitude only changed in 1973 when he was invited to the city for an exhibit of his photographs. It was then that he discovered the Wall and began photographing the city again. To fall in love with Berlin again.' That is when he met his new wife on a

Kreuzberg factory floor. Wanda had her artist studio there. Ries's first marriage had already failed, and Wanda moved to New York City in 1981. At this time, Henry lived at 3rd Avenue and East 35th Street, close to the Empire State Building, before building a house up the Hudson in Ghent, New York.

On the phone in Midtown Manhattan, Ries didn't immediately accept Mörlins's invitation but, eventually, he decided to go, unsure what to expect. The trajectory of his classmates under Nazism had been very different from their Jewish classmate who had been forced to leave.[2]

That first evening in West Berlin, he met up with ten of his fellow 68-year-olds in a bar: 'Man, Heinz, it's great that you've come across the pond to us. You haven't changed at all! Do you remember ...?' 'To be honest, I wouldn't have recognised you!' 'Boy, you've held up well! I wish Werner Lempke could be here – he fell in Stalingrad.'

The beer flowed, his peers got drunk, and they bonded over old stories. But the atmosphere for Ries was tense and uncomfortable. The men felt the need to mention how many 'nice Jews' they knew. How they had once a 'Jewish doctor'. How 'bad' the Nazis were. The high point of laughter was when the former schoolboys passed around old copies of their student newspaper, the *Klatsche*. It was not an official school paper, but one the students made clandestinely and circulated among themselves. Ries took a copy back to his hotel, read through it entirely, and was not amused by what he discovered in its 'Political Corner'.

The next day, the men gathered in a classroom of the Schiller High School on benches, as they had as schoolchildren. Ries asked them if he could read aloud something he found in the *Klatsche*. Of course, Heinz! Fifty years later – again conspicuously the Jew of the class – he stood at the front of the room to stare at his 'German peers with whom I had warmed the same benches, played the same pranks, learned the same useless names and dates and spoken the same language – except now we no longer understood each other'.

Henry opened the pages of the student newspaper and read from a passage praising National Socialist ideas and – here's the kicker – how 'they must be implemented so that we can remove the Jewish rubbish from our people as quickly as possible'. The passage ended with a quote by Adolf Hitler.

Ries described the first reaction from the room as a 'short silence'. And then Werner Mörlins – the classmate who invited Ries to the reunion

– piped up, 'Yes, of course, I wrote that.' He then started to make excuses: they were borrowed ideas, not even his style. Another peer added, 'Of course, the thing with the Jewish rubbish, that's idiotic, a *Stürmer* idea', but he went on to say 'people are always manipulated, at all times and everywhere. Me? No, I won't let myself be manipulated, neither this way nor that way. I read the *Bild* newspaper.' More reactions followed: 'We are a generation whose youth was stolen. After high school, we went to the Army, Labor Service, war. We had to be grateful that we came back at all! Then came the years when we were only concerned with bread. You can't understand us, Heinz. You had it easy. You left.'

It had occurred to Ries back in 1945 that he had been 'able to remain a human being' by leaving, but hearing it from a former classmate was intolerable. Of all the comments made at the reunion, the one that bothered Ries the most was this one: that somehow, because of the *Gnade* or 'blessing' of being Jewish, he had had the 'privilege' of avoiding the German tragedy of war, defeat, and the hungry times that followed, those events that 'resolved' into the Berlin Airlift and the establishment of East and West Germany, and the West German friendship with the Allies.

The intolerableness of the comment was reinforced by survivor guilt. Wanda tells me: 'His grandmother financed him to escape Germany. But she stayed, and she was exterminated.' Ries later travelled to Theresienstadt, guided there by a survivor, to find the bunk where his grandmother slept and the river where her ashes were dumped after her extermination.

Ries, for his part, could not make friends with that Germany. He returned to New York 'after three days of tiring, embarrassed and often ridiculous or disgusting conversations in classrooms and pubs, on city tours and steamer trips – only rarely interrupted by well-considered thoughts about the past'.

Ries's presence had been 'embarrassing to many', and he felt both a 'troublemaker and a confessor'. Even conversations about contemporary issues were confounded; he found his classmates were incorrigible in their views of diversity in Germany, especially regarding Turkish immigrants, and they also reacted confusedly to Ries's criticisms of Israel and its 'right-wing radicals or the evil of religious fanaticism'. They told him that as 'Germans, they could not afford to criticise or else they would immediately be branded as antisemitic'. As far as the Nazi years were concerned, Ries observed his peers either wanted to forget or suppress them rather than work through the past. Alarmingly, their attitude was laced with smugness, mixed with self-pity – 'as if they were proud of this burden'.³

Wanda Ries, a generation younger than her husband, told me he changed his attitude towards Berlin over time. He discovered a new generation who had rebelled against the wartime generation, whom he did not hold responsible for what had happened to his family. She told me, 'He began to digest what had happened to him thanks to the great relationship he had with the next German generation. He saw them as freed, and they challenged him to talk about his experiences and to open up. He felt differently about his own generation.'

Ries's photographic project, *Abschied meiner Generation* (*Goodbye to My Generation*), published in 1992, was an indictment of their attitudes. But it was not just a 'goodbye and good riddance' – but also a desire to understand. He photographed people his age and tried to recognise their separate trajectories under National Socialism. Again, Ries was interested in the stories behind each picture, the ones the image could not tell.

3

Arguably, Ruth Andreas-Friedrich was of Ries's generation. She was sixteen years older. We do not have many photographs of her, with her hair cropped short and modern, her angular, kite-like face, and her penetrating, alert eyes. She's not often caught smiling and seems to have the twentieth century stamped all over her visage – the battle lines and the détentes. Years after the war, she would be honoured as an example of the 'good German' – one of the few who had resisted.⁴

Ruth published her diary in America, with the intention of mending Germans' relationships with the West. Its first volume on her resistance activities during the Second World War appeared in 1947, a critical moment before the Airlift transformed the relationship. Critics have argued that her voice helped 'feminise' Germany as the defeated country, whose innocent surviving women (and children) needed provision by the male protector, the United States.

Her diary's introduction explains how, 'Germany today is the bad child of the world. The tendency is to identify the whole people with the outrages of its leaders. Yet thousands upon thousands had nothing whatever to do with those outrages.' She says she hopes the diary will 'go out into the world to testify that there were human beings living even under Hitler in Germany, human beings who do not deserve to be despised, along with their whole nation, because of an irresponsible government'.[5]

Most historians would disagree. Much ink has been spilt on why thousands enabled what she calls 'those outrages'. Historian Detlev Peukert helps us with the concept of 'internal emigration'. Many living in autocratic regimes retreat into private life, even if they object forcefully to the offensive government. These people are later faced with the question: what did you *do*? After all, good intentions are not the same as deeds. Emigration – internal or not – always asks that question. And 'inner emigration' helps stabilise the regime because it substitutes outward political acts of resistance. Another notion, articulated by Gérard Genette – focalisation – is about the tendency to see events of a historical moment from your perspective if you lived it. It's a phenomenon of everyday history: if we know an era, we tell it as we experienced it.[6]

Perhaps this is why Ruth Andreas-Friedrich was so forgiving of her fellow Germans. She did not see internal emigration negatively but applauded its intentions. She was forgiving because she could answer the question 'What did you do?' with a long list of her own resistance activities. She focalised others' experiences through her own.

Ruth's wartime biography is complicated. As the editor of *Kamerad Frau*, a women's magazine during the Second World War, she advised women how to hold up the home front. The magazine helped the regime, even if she resisted in her private life. Another perspective is that *Kamerad Frau* was a successful front to her resistance group, *Onkel Emil*. In 2022, she and her daughter were recognised by the Yad Vashem, the world Holocaust remembrance centre, as 'Righteous Among the Nations'. This was twenty-five years after her suicide in Munich, where she had worked as a journalist since leaving Berlin in the middle of the Airlift.

Ernst Reuter, too, cannot be called a perpetrator – Berlin was led into the post-war period by a convinced anti-fascist. He was not even present in Germany during the Nazi years, except as an enemy and prisoner of the regime. Indeed, what did it mean for him and Ruth to be *German* in a way that Henry Ries somehow was no longer? National categories solidify and individual stories blur when people are bitter.

In September 1953, Reuter found himself on the border of the Soviet zone, waiting to pass through to reach Hamburg. The East German *Volkspolizei* stopped him. They no doubt knew who he was – the mayor of Berlin was a household name – but they told him he could not cross.

Reuter had made a few mistakes: the address on his interzone pass did not match his documents. And he did not know he could have a new one issued at short notice, even though it was night. Instead of travelling, he went home and unnecessarily waited until the next day.

The *Berliner Morgenpost* related in his obituary that, 'he was forgiven he did not know something because one trusted he had important things on his mind.'[7]

A few days later, the mayor came down with a cold. He was told to rest but, overnight, the illness progressed to bronchitis. On the afternoon of 29 September 1953 he died. The funeral was one of the biggest in Berlin's history.

Berlin was a city that never voted in great numbers for the Nazis. Perhaps so many Berliners came out in public to mourn him because Reuter, like Ruth Andreas-Friedrich, represented a sentiment they shared, even if these others could not – or rather did not – act.

4

I am back at Tempelhof. It's 12 May 2024, the seventy-fifth anniversary of the Berlin Airlift, and a hot day with tight security checks because of all the VIPs converging at the old airport. The German Defence Minister, generations of Berlin mayors, European representatives, German Parliament members, and Airlift witnesses have all assembled before the sloping Airlift memorial, the *Hungerharke*.

I see familiar faces in the crowd – Mercedes Wild, Alec Chambers, the family of Rex Waite, and Wanda Ries. Those lucky enough to be sitting to the left of the *Hungerharke* benefit from its pronged shadow, while those on the right hold up programmes and papers to shield themselves from the intense sun.

The oldest people are the veterans in their wheelchairs. The Americans wear casual clothes, bomber jackets, and baseball caps covered with pins for all the reunions they've had of the Airlift. The British are more formally dressed, in suits and ties or their uniforms.

A priest speaks of the message of 'Forgive thy enemy'. The Church was invested in the fight against atheistic communism and interpreted the Airlift story as a Christian one of enemies becoming friends. The priest has the crowd of hundreds stand in prayer at the civic ceremony.

A hymn by the military band is followed by speeches by the dignitaries about solidarity, humanity, freedom, and the eight-month-long 'struggle for survival' that the Airlift represented. A UK Embassy official says that the Soviets wanted to starve and freeze a city into submission. There are words about falling chocolate, and the middle-grade students of the Gail Halvorsen School in Berlin complete a dance routine with umbrellas, playing bongos to 'Blue Skies', the jazz standard used in the 1946 film of the same name.

German Defence Minister Boris Pistorius now stands and delivers a serious speech about the relationship of the Airlift to today's foreign policy matters. He says the Allies taught the Germans 'goodness' and 'forgiveness'. They did not leave Germans *im Stich* – or in the lurch – during the first event of the Cold War, just as Berlin didn't give up. Germany today would not be Germany without the Airlift – and he reminds the crowd that the Airlift anniversary is also that of the German *Grundgesetz* or constitution.

Pistorius concludes by outlining three lessons relevant to the present moment: cooperate with your Allies (here he means NATO, founded out of the Airlift experience), have solidarity over the Eastern border (here he means defending Ukraine, holding up the Eastern Front as the Allies did in 1948–49), and do the right thing despite the price (here he means the cost to the taxpayer for common defence – again Ukraine, just as billions in today's coin were invested for Berlin). The Airlift moment was when the US and UK committed unwaveringly to Europe's security to the East. Today, Moscow's sphere of influence lies much farther East than Berlin, but much still depends on American policies of isolationism, and future relations with Russia's authoritarian regime. Pistorius concludes: *Entschlossenheit lohnt sich* – conviction is worth it.

Wreaths are laid. The band plays the US, UK, French, and German anthems – and I reflect that I have never been in a situation where a country formally commemorates its former occupiers. The VIPs are then guided to the old terminal for lunch, spectacularly at long tables in the great arrivals hall, where, during the Airlift, many of the pilots had never been.

5

In front of the Tempelhof terminal is an exhibit. Minister Pistorius and the veterans have taken pictures in front of it for the Berlin press and, once they are gone, I wander through the panels and reflect on the narrative: period photos of planes in formation, women with pickaxes at Tegel, children chasing falling candy, and, of course, Henry Ries's most famous photograph.

Despite the careful research by the Allied Museum there are also tensions. Pictures of smuggling, hoarding, and the ubiquitous black market don't sit comfortably with a *Big Lift* humanitarian operation to rescue women and children from cold and hunger. The possibility that, in effect, there was no blockade comes up only when you ask. And, when it does, it pierces a hole, letting out air from the ballooning and still pervasive Cold War narrative. (Perhaps the myth of a sealed city remained unquestioned for so long because, in 1961, West Berlin actually was surrounded by a wall, creating the impression of long-standing impermeability.)[8]

The Airlift becomes an inexplicable event unless the emphasis is put somewhere other than the access to food: the self-interest of each power. Previous wartime antipathies were overridden because of need. Generations of Germans, exuberant about their rehabilitation from the ignominy of Nazism, still romanticise the Berlin Airlift and the visits of Presidents Kennedy and Reagan (their 'Ich bin ein Berliner' and 'Tear Down This Wall' speeches) as emblems of friendship between peoples, motivated by democratic ideals and America's messianic spreading of democracy. But during the Berlin Airlift, Americans' relationship with the Germans was not so different than it is today: not idealistic but transactional.

One panel of the Tempelhof exhibit is entitled 'The End of the Alliance of Convenience', about how Soviet–Western cooperation dissolved after 1945. But aren't all alliances about convenience? The French only stayed with the people of Stolpe as long as it suited them. Had Berlin been less useful to the other Western powers – as a satellite in the middle of the Soviet sphere – the story could have ended quite differently.

While the hunger narrative became a propaganda ploy to justify the public expense and to rally the West into the Cold War, the Airlift was not just a performance. Berliners' loyalty and their local resilience were, in fact, victorious in the face of Soviet expansionism. They held the line. With this buffer role to play, Germans saw US and British attitudes towards them change quickly.

Not everyone could forgive: the willingness was proportional to wartime suffering: the French were less keen on the Airlift, and Jewish survivors like Ries were most critical. For the Americans, conversely, the capitalist goals of the Marshall Plan trumped any promises made about German unity, demilitarisation, and denazification – as illustrated by the recruitment of the Black Guards and US Labor Force.

Unsurprisingly, the Airlift proved popular in right-wing, conservative German circles, especially during the Adenauer years. Making Germans partners of the West redeemed them from their ugly history until the children of '68 brought a reckoning to their parents' generation. At the time, the USSR and East Germany reasonably criticised West Germany for not cleansing itself of its old Nazis. This might have given the Soviets the moral high ground had they not created a state that resembled that of the fascists more than what was created in the West.

Ultimately, the dynamic between Germans, the West, and the Soviets was triangulation. The Germans and the West aligned because of the Soviet threat. The Soviet failure was that they did not win over the Germans. In the long run, Moscow's failure was complete, with the finale of the Cold War concluding in Berlin – just as it had begun there. The challenge is now to imagine a future in which Germany improves its friendship with both the East and West. At the time of writing, a central question is whether lasting peace with Russia over Ukraine can be achieved without an unacceptably high cost. Meanwhile, European stability, without reliable American security commitments as during the Airlift, will likely depend on a rearmed Germany, capable of defending itself in any direction, which is ironically what the signatories at Potsdam most feared.

When one returns to everyday history, one sees that, when governments take the initiative to promote a friendship narrative, there is the potential to create meaningful relationships on the ground. Slaker befriended Rudolf despite years of hating Germans. Wild met Halvorsen even though she lost her own father during the war. Cambridge students reached towards the humanity of the old foe when they played the Bard in the ruins. All had an effect from the ground up, because friendship between former enemies is not just a private act, but also a public and political one.

For when geopolitics allows, and the other is no longer designated as the enemy, humans will connect.

6

Henry Ries took a series of photographs at the Brandenburg Gate, Berlin's symbol. Some are from 1937, another from 1946, and the final ones from 2001.

Ries describes the 1937 photos as the first taken with his new Leica as a 19-year-old Berliner. As he walked up Berlin's grand boulevard Unter den Linden towards the gate, 'I started taking pictures. I photographed women and men, children and animals ... whatever my Leica saw, and my head thought was interesting.' In one photo, it has just rained – two figures are in the foreground, one holding an umbrella. The square is daubed dark behind, either the downpour half-evaporated or the gate's shadow.

The next photograph is a snapshot of a US soldier standing with two children before the ruined gate of the city Ries never wanted to visit again. The officer looks down with calm gentleness; he seems to guard the kids in their Sunday best, amused by something out of the frame. No one is looking at the camera, and certainly not at the gate. The image was published in the *OMGUS Observer* on 5 July 1946.

The final ones are more recent: after Germany was defeated, divided, and reunited. Wanda tells me the gate 'is where he began his photographic journey and also where he ended it'.

Ries wrote, 'All Berliners know this landmark of the old and new capital, and almost every visitor photographs it. Some even know that world history has marched through this gate for two hundred years.' It might not be possible to distil a country's history into a single space – it risks becoming rigidly axiomatic – but the Brandenburg Gate comes close. It has seen many conflicts. Its surmounting goddess and chariot, the Quadriga, were originally symbols of peace. But after they were captured by Napoleon, and returned with the wars of German Unification, she was armed with an iron cross. The gate miraculously survived the bloody twentieth-century wars, only to become the tense Cold War border between East and West. Here, the most famous images of the Berlin Wall's demise in 1989 were also taken.

The Jewish émigré wandered around the edifice and through its portals, wondering whether he belonged inside or out. As Wanda reminded me, 'Henry had problems with symbols', yet, to his surprise, he discovered a space inside, which was between things. In his private papers, he calls it a 'chick under its mother':[9]

> I discovered something completely unexpected at the northern gatehouse: a door with the inscription 'Room of Silence'. I opened the simple door and quietly asked a supervisor in the vestibule what the room was for. It has existed, as I learned, since October 1994 and was set up ... to revive the original purpose of the Brandenburg Gate as a gate of peace. 'In this room,' it says on a leaflet, 'everyone – women and men, regardless of origin, skin colour, religion and worldview – is invited to be quiet and reflect ... and thus promote tolerance – especially between religions and peoples.

Tolerance might not be the same as friendship. Does Ries find in this space – located in the heart of the heart, of the capital and country – the reconciliation he is looking for?

The émigré asks, 'Will humanity hear the message of peace in the Brandenburg Gate?'

Ries is not sentimental.

He stands up, shakes his head, and writes, 'I have hope, but even more doubt.'

7

In 1970, Gail Halvorsen returned to Berlin as the US Air Force representative in charge of Tempelhof Airport. This news threw Mercedes Wild into a panic. She had kept the letter he had written to her as a little girl in its original envelope. She lived in the same house where she had received it in 1948, except now she was married with two small children of her own. The chickens that wouldn't lay eggs were no longer in a coop downstairs.

When Mercedes's husband told her he was attending a reception at Tempelhof Airport, she did not go. It was all too much for her, especially because she had a secret. Her own father had never returned from the war and, like many German children at the time, the US officer had become what she called 'a substitute father figure'. (I met one old man at the Airlift anniversary who kept the baby shoes a pilot had given him for seventy-five years.) Mercedes also wasn't sure what Halvorsen would be like – how her imagination would align with reality.

Her husband recounted her story at Tempelhof, and the charming story of the little girl and the 'chocolate pilot' caught the attention of the Americans' press department. They wanted an official photograph, so Mercedes took a deep breath and went to the US Air Force base. When she met him, she found him as compassionate and sympathetic as she had imagined. She decided to invite her 'chocolate pilot' for dinner.

Halvorsen showed up at the door of her house with his children. She had asked him if he liked chicken fricassee in advance, and he replied, 'The chickens from 1948?'

One of the first things she did when he was in her home was go to her desk and pull out the letter he had written her.

The pilot must have understood then how much it meant to her – and he took a pen and added some lines to the bottom of it: '22 September 1972: I am very happy to greet you and your wonderful family after twenty-four years.' He wished her 'many sweet things to come'.

Over the years, Mercedes and the American met regularly and became part of each other's lives – at their children's weddings or on trips in Germany, where Mercedes translated. Their lifelong relationship that began with a letter in 1948 was the embodiment of the German–American reconciliation, one that in large part was helped by those 250,000 parachutes containing chocolate and candy that fell on Berlin during the Airlift. Later in his life, Halvorsen would drop candy on others affected by conflict, such as Bosnians and Kosovars.

Each time the pilot saw Mercedes, he would add to the original letter he had sent her until all the corners and edges were filled with script.

TIMELINE

1945
2 May   Battle of Berlin ends, Soviets occupy the city
4 July   US troops officially occupy their sector in Berlin
11 July   Allied Kommandatura first meets in Berlin
1 August   Potsdam Agreement signed

1947
1 January   Creation of Bizone (US and UK zones together)
12 March   'Truman Doctrine' outlined in Congress

1948
24 January   Berlin–Bielefeld night train detained by Soviets
23 February   London Six-Power Conference begins (for the creation of West Germany)
25 February   Communist Coup in Prague
20 March   Soviets leave Allied Control Council for Germany
2–4 April   'Little Lift'
3 April   Marshall Plan comes into force
5 April   Crash at Gatow airfield
12 June   Bridge over Elbe blocked
16 June   Soviets leave Berlin Kommandatura
20 June   Western currency reform in effect
23 June   Soviets introduce new currency
24 June   The 'Berlin Blockade' begins
26–28 June   Airlift begins, transporting 1,200 US short tons a day (4,500 required)
28 June   US moves B-29 bombers to Britain
20 July   Tonnage at 2,250 short tons a day
27 July   First civilian flight of Airlift

29 July	General Tunner arrives in Germany. Tonnage at 1,550 that day
1 August	Soviets provide access to Eastern rations to Berliners in West
5 August	Tegel Airfield construction begins
7 August	Tonnage at 3,800 a day
13 August	Black Friday aircraft crash
6 September	Communists sack Berlin's new town hall
9 September	Mass assembly in front of Reichstag, death at Brandenburg Gate
14 October	Tunner becomes commander of Combined Airlift Task Force
25 October	Soviets veto UN Security Council Resolution on Berlin
2 November	US election, Truman re-elected
5 November	First plane lands at Tegel, Berlin plagued by fog
5 December	Berlin State elections, SPD victorious
16 December	Destruction of Soviet radio towers
21 December	Stolpe occupied by Soviets
30 December	Record Airlift landings, tonnage at 4,500 a day
31 December	100,000th Airlift flight

1949

15 February	Soviet–US talks
26 February	Tonnage at 8,000 a day
4 April	NATO treaty signed in Washington
16 April	Tonnage at 13,000 a day
25 April	Soviets hint in news sources willingness to lift restrictions
4 May	Soviets agree to lift restrictions on Berlin
12 May	Traffic restrictions are lifted, electricity restored
23 May	West German constitution signed
29 August	Soviets detonate their first atom bomb
6 October	Last Airlift flight

ACKNOWLEDGEMENTS

I would first like to thank the many period witnesses who shared their stories with me. These include Alec Chambers (in memoriam), David Edwards, Harold Bowers, Wanda Ries, Ilse Thiele, and Mercedes Wild.

I am grateful to libraries and archives I consulted, the many kind archivists who helped me with my project, and other individuals associated with the history of the Airlift.

In the UK: Cambridge University Library; King's College Archive (Rylands and Annan papers, with thanks to Tom Davies); the ADC Theatre, Cambridge (thanks to Luke Dell); and the National Archives, Kew. Thank you also to Sue Campbell and the British Berlin Airlift Association, David and Susie Gillespie, and Romilly Waite and her family.

In Germany: the Airlift Appreciation Foundation (Stiftung Luftbrückendank); the Allied Museum (Alliierten Museum Berlin, with thanks to Uta Birkemeyer and Bernd von Kostka); the Berlin Central and State Library (Zentral- und Landesbibliothek Berlin) and their Berlin Collection; the Berlin Mayor's Office; Berlin Philharmonic Archive (with thanks as always to Katja Vobiller); the Berlin State archive (Landesarchiv Berlin); the Berlin State Library (Staatsbibliothek zu Berlin) where much of the writing and researching of this book took place; the Berlin Wall Foundation (Stiftung Berliner Mauer); the Ernst-Reuter-Archiv; the German Federal Archives (Bundesarchiv); German Historical Museum Archive (Deutsches Historisches Museum, with thanks to Joerg Frieß, Anne Dorte Krause, Ariane Oppitz, and Oliver Schweinoch); Geschichtskreis Hohen Neuendorf (with thanks to Dietrich Raetzer and Petra Schmidt); Museum Berlin-Karlshorst; the

Reinickendorf Museum and Archive (with thanks to Dr Dirk Wissen); and the Renaissance Theatre Berlin's archive (with thanks to Joachim Flicker). Special thanks to Traugott Vogel in Stolpe.

In the United States: Margaret Herrick, Library of the Academy of Motion Picture Arts and Sciences (with special thanks to Caroline Jorgenson and Genevieve Maxwell); the UCLA Film & Television Archive; Vivien G. Fryd.

Colleagues, friends and other kind individuals helped this project along logistically and in discussion: Natalie Clein, Jacob Eder, Gabriella Etmektsoglou, Angelika Maser, Brendan Simms of Peterhouse, Cambridge, Ayşe Zarakol of Emmanuel College, Cambridge, and many others, including Lapo Biasutti, who left his mark at the very beginning of the research. My thanks to my wonderful colleagues at the Barenboim-Said Akademie and New York University. And my thanks to my family.

This book came into being through inspiring conversations with Tim Binding and my marvellous agent, Annabel Merullo, both of Peter Fraser Dunlop in London. My thanks too to the CEO of PFD, Caroline Michel, and her foreign rights team, especially Rebecca Wearmouth. Thank you to my editors: Claire Hopkins and Rebecca Newton at The History Press (UK) and Claiborne Hancock at Pegasus Books (US).

Thank you to James Helgeson for everything.

BIBLIOGRAPHY

Primary source material from the many archives consulted and thanked in the acknowledgements section are specified in the endnotes. I have particularly relied on the Airlift documents from The National Archives, Kew.

Interviews

Bowers, Harold, 12 May 2024, interview with author in Berlin
Burkill, Margareta, 26 January 1980, Imperial War Museum, London
Chambers, Alec, 6 March 2014, Imperial War Museum, London
Chambers, Alec, 25 May 2024, interview with author in Berlin
Chambers, Alec, undated, Legasee Veterans' Video Library
Clay, Lucius, 16 October 1973, Columbia Oral History Project, New York
Edwards, David, 12 May 2024, interview with author in Berlin
Hagues, Cyril, 30 November 1999, Imperial War Museum, London
Keeffee, Bernard, 29 July 2014, Royal College of Music, London
Reuter, Gerd Edzard Harry, 28 September 1979, Imperial War Museum, London
Ries, Wanda, 5 April 2024, interview with author in Berlin
Slaker, Kenneth, 13 October 2007, Library of Congress, Washington DC
Thiele, Ilse, 23 October 2024, interview with author in Berlin
Wild, Mercedes, 20 September 2023, interview with author in Berlin

Press Sources

BBC
Bee-Hive
Berliner Kurier
Berliner Morgenpost
Berliner Zeitung
The Christian Science Monitor
Collier's Magazine
Culture
Der Kurier
Der Morgen

Der Spiegel
Der Tag
Der Tagesspiegel
Deutsche Welle
Die Neue Zeitung
Die Welt
Die Zeit
Guardian/Manchester Guardian
The Independent
Le Monde
Lilith: die Zeitschrift für junge Mädchen und Frauen
Los Angeles Times
Nacht-Express
Neue Zeit
Neues Deutschland
New York Times
Radford News Journal
Scranton Times
Soviet News
Sozialdemokrat
The Sphere
The Sunday Dispatch
Swindon Advertiser
Tageszeitung (Taz)
Tägliche Rundschau
Telegraf
The Times of London
Time Magazine
Variety
Varsity

General, Political and Logistical Histories

Anderhub, A. and J.O. Bennett. *Blockade, Luftbrücke und Luftbrückendank: zur Geschichte der Krise um Berlin 1948–49*. Berlin: Presse- und Informationsamt des Landes Berlin, 1984.

Bath, Matthias. *Die Berlin-Blockade 1948/49: Stalins Griff nach der deutschen Hauptstadt und der Freiheitskampf Berlins*. Berlin: Neuhaus Verlag, 2018.

Berlin Historical Sites Office/Landesdenkmalamt Berlin.

Clay, Lucius. *Decision in Germany*. New York: Doubleday, 1950.

Defrance, Corine, et al (eds). *Die Berliner Luftbrücke: Erinnerungsort des Kalten Krieges*. Berlin: Ch. Links, 2018.

Divine, Robert A. 'The Cold War and the Election of 1948'. *The Journal of American History*, Vol. 59, No. 1, 1972.

Erickson, Paul, et al. *How Reason Almost Lost Its Mind: The Strange Career of Cold War Rationality*. Chicago: University of Chicago Press, 2013.

Harrington, Daniel F. 'The Air Force Can Deliver Anything' in *A History of the Berlin Airlift*. Washington D.C.: USAFE Office of History, 1998.
Harrington, Daniel F. *Berlin on the Brink: The Blockade, the Airlift, and the Early Cold War*. Lexington, KY: The University Press of Kentucky, 2012.
Jähner, Harald. *Wolfszeit: Deutschland und die Deutschen 1945–1955*. Hamburg: Rowohlt Verlag, 2019.
Koop, Volker. *Kein Kampf um Berlin?* Bonn: Bouvier Verlag, 1998.
Lemke, Michael. 'Totale Blockade? Über das Verhältnis von Abschottung und Durchlässigkeit im Berliner Krisenalltag 1948/49' in Helmut Trotnow and Bernd von Kostka (eds). *Die Berliner Luftbrücke. Ereignis und Erinnerung*. Berlin: Frank & Timme, 2010.
Miller, Roger G. *To Save a City: The Berlin Airlift, 1948–1949*. College Station: Texas A&M University Press, 2008.
Miscamble, Wilson D. 'Harry S. Truman, the Berlin Blockade and the 1948 Election'. *Presidential Studies Quarterly*, Vol. 10, No. 3, 1980.
Naimark, N.W. *Stalin and the Fate of Europe: The Postwar Struggle for Sovereignty*. Cambridge: Harvard University Press, 2019.
Parrish, Thomas. *Berlin in The Balance: The Blockade, The Airlift, The First Major Battle of the Cold War*. Boston: Da Capo, 1999.
Prell, Uwe and Lothar Wilker. *Berlin-Blockade und Luftbrücke 1948/49: Analyse und Dokumentation*, Berlin: Verlag A. Spitz, 1987.
Prell, Uwe. 'Militär in ziviler Mission – Lucius D. Clay und die Berliner Luftbrücke' in *Berliner Geschichte*, No. 12. Berlin: Eisengold, 2018.
Riess, Curt. *The Berlin Story*, London: Frederick Muller Ltd, 1953.
Rodrigo, Roberto. *Berlin Airlift*. London: Cassell, 1960.
Schuessler, John M., Adam R. Seipp, and Thomas D. Sullivan (eds). *The Berlin Airlift and the Making of the Cold War*. College Station: Texas A&M University Press, 2022.
Smith, Jean Edward. *Eisenhower in War and Peace*. New York: Random House, 2012.
Smith, Jean Edward (ed.). *The Papers of General Lucius D. Clay: Germany, 1945–1949*. Bloomington: Indiana University Press, 1974.
Tunner, William. *Over the Hump*. New York: Duell, Sloan, and Pearce, 1964.
US Department of State, Foreign Policy Studies Branch, Division of Historical Policy Research.

Subject-Specific Sources

Kenneth Slaker, and Other Pilots

Bardua, Rob. 'Flying dog's parachute lands at U.S. Air Force Museum'. Air Force Museum Public Affairs, 21 September 2004.
Holden, Henry M. *The Legacy of the DC-3*. Stockton: Wind Canyon, 2002.
Reeves, Richard. *Daring Young Men: The Heroism and Triumph of the Berlin Airlift – June 1948–May 1949*. New York: Simon and Schuster, 2010.
Slaker, Kenneth. *A Military Pilot's Exciting Life and Visit from the Hereafter*. Raleigh: Ivy House, 2008.
Steber, Clarence. Obituary in *Florida Today*, 5 January 2008.

Vaughan, Don. 'Vittle the Berlin Airlift Dog 130 Missions'. *Military Officers Association of America*, May 2005.

Henry Ries

Alexander, Leo. 'The Treatment of Shock from Prolonged Exposure to Cold'. *Journal of the American Medical Association*, Vol. 130, No. 9, 1946.

Bruce, Gary. *Through the Lion Gate: A History of the Berlin Zoo*. Oxford: Oxford University Press, 2017.

Fryd, Vivien Green. 'An Inverted Detective Thriller: Henry Ries and the Quakers' Rescue of Stefanie Ries from Nazi Germany, 1939–41'. *Quaker History*, Vol. 110, No. 1, Spring 2021.

German Historical Museum/Deutsches Historisches Museum Archive (Estate of Henry Ries).

Milton, Sybil. 'Henry Ries'. *History of Photography*, Vol. 23, No. 4, 1999.

Office of Military Gov. for Germany (US), Office of the Director of Intelligence, *HFFH, Himmler's Files From Hallein*, No. 1, 8 November 1945.

Peters-Klaphake, Katrin. 'Die Photojournalischen Jahre von Henry Ries, 1946 bis 1951' in *Brennpunkt Berlin: Die Blockade 1948/9 Der Photojournalist Henry Ries*. Exhibition Catalogue, German Historical Museum, 2008.

Perger, Werner A. 'Henry Ries: Photographer, author, friend – and a Berliner'. Private papers Wanda Ries.

Ries, Henry. *Berlin vor 25 Jahren*. Exhibition Catalogue of the Landesbildstelle Berlin, 1973.

Ries, Henry. *Deutsche, Gedanken und Gesichter*. Berlin: Argon, 1988; first published as Henry Ries and Ann Stringer, *German Faces*. New York: Sloane, 1950.

Ries, Henry (ed. Alfred Gottwaldt). *Menschen am Zerstörten Anhalter Bahnhof: Fotografien von Henry Ries aus Berlin, 1948*. Exhibition Catalogue of the Museum für Verkehr und Technik Berlin, 1990.

Ries, Henry. *Abschied meiner Generation*. Berlin: Argon, 1992.

Ries, Henry. *Ich war ein Berliner: Erinnerungen eines New Yorker Fotojournalisten*. Berlin: Parthas, 2001.

Ries, Henry. *Kalender aus dem Jahr 1948 mit tagebuchähnlichen Eintragungen des Fotografen Henry Ries* (Englisch). Berlin: Deutsches Historisches Museum Archive, Do2 2016/533.

Ries, Wanda. 'Henry Ries' unpublished, 2011. Private papers Wanda Ries.

Yad Vashem Archives, Jerusalem. Testimony Rabbi Dr Max Nussbaum.

Ruth Andreas-Friedrich, and Everyday Conditions

Andreas-Friedrich, Ruth (trans. Barrows Mussey). *Berlin Underground, Diaries 1945–1948*. New York: Henry Holt and Company, 1947.

Andreas-Friedrich, Ruth (trans. Anna Boerresen). *Battleground Berlin, Diaries 1945–1948*. St Paul: Paragon House, 1990.

Andreas-Friedrich, Ruth. *Der Schattenmann, Tagebuchaufzeichnungen 1938–1948*. Berlin: Suhrkamp, 2000.

Barton, Deborah. *Writing and Rewriting the Reich: Women Journalists in the Nazi and Post-War Press*. Toronto: University of Toronto Press, 2023.

German Resistance Museum/Gedenkstätte Deutscher Widerstand.
Goebbels, Joseph. 'Aus Churchills Lügenfabrik' *Die Zeit ohne Beispiel*. Munich: Zentralverlag der NSDAP, 1941.
Landsman, Mark. *Dictatorship and Demand: The Politics of Consumerism in East Germany*. Cambridge, MA: Harvard University Press, 2005.
Laughlin, James. 'Report on a Visit to Germany, 1948 (American Zone): Poems'. Lausanne: Henri Held. King's College Cambridge Archive, GRB 1/5/7.
Merritt, Richard. *Democracy Imposed: U.S. Occupation Policy and the German Public, 1945–1949*. New Haven: Yale University Press, 1995.
Van Sweringen, B.T. *Kabarettist an der Front des Kalten Krieges: Günter Neumann und das politische Kabarett in der Programmgestaltung des RIAS 1948–1968*. Bern: Rothe Verlag, 1995.
Weil, Hans Hartmut. Entry, Wiener Holocaust Library.
Weil, Hans Hartmut. 'An Undergraduate's Visit to Hamburg: Here Are His Frank Impressions of What He Saw'. *Varsity*, 12 June 1948.
Yad Vashem Archives, Jerusalem. Righteous Among the Nations collections.

Ernst Reuter

Auer, Peter. *Ihr Völker der Welt*. Berlin: Jaron, 1998.
Barclay, David E. 'Beyond Cold War Mythmaking: Ernst Reuter and the United States' in Wolfgang-Uwe Friedrich, *Germany and America: Essays in Honor of Gerald R. Kleinfeld*. Oxford, New York: Berghahn, 2001.
Brandt, P. *1948-Jahr der Entscheidungen: Ernst Reuter und der Weg in den Kalten Krieg*. Berlin, be.bra, 2012.
Brandt, Willy. *My Road to Berlin, as told to Leo Lania*. London: Peter Davis, 1960.
Brandt, Willy and Richard Lowenthal. *Ernst Reuter: Ein Leben für die Freiheit*. Munich: Kindler, 1957.
Cambridge University Library. Margareta Burkill papers.
Ernst Reuter Archive, Berlin.
Ernst Reuter 1889–1953. Katalog. Berlin: Exhibit Landesarchivs Berlin, 2003.
Ernst Reuter. *Ein zerrissenes Leben*, 2010 Documentary Film.
Герман А.А. Революционная деятельность Эрнста Рейтера в Саратовском Поволжье (1918 г.). *История. Международные отношения*. 2019. Т. 19, вып. 2./German A. A., 'Revolutionary activities of Ernst Reuter in the Saratov Volga region (1918)'. *Historia. International Relations*, Vol. 19, No. 2, 2019.
Krause, Scott H. '*Neue Westpolitik*: The Clandestine Campaign to Westernize the SPD in Cold War Berlin, 1948–1958'. *Central European History*, Vol. 48, 2015.
Murphy, David E. *Battleground Berlin: CIA Vs. KGB in the Cold War*. New Haven: Yale University Press, 1997.
Reichhardt, Hans J. *Ernst Reuter*. Hanover: Niedersächsischen Landeszentrale für Politische Bildung, 1965.
Reuter, Ernst. *Schriften, Reden*. Berlin: Propyläen Verlag, 1973, Vols 1–3.
Schwenger, Hannes. *Ernst Reuter: Ein Zivilist im Kalten Krieg*. Munich: Piper, 1987.
Waite, Romilly. Speech, Berlin Airlift Anniversary, Tempelhof Airport, 12 May 2024, and correspondence with the author.

Black Guards, Bad Nenndorf, Denazification
Borgert, Heinz-Ludger, Walter Stürm and Norbert Wiggershaus. *Dienstgruppen und westdeutscher Verteidigungsbeitrag*. Boppard am Rhein: Harald Boldt Verlag, 1996.
Cobain, Ian. *Cruel Britannia: A Secret History of Torture*. London: Portobello, 2013.
Deml, Hermann (ed.). *Geschichte des Labor Service*. Heidelberg: USAREUR, May 1953.
Hansard House of Commons Debates.
Miller, Roger G. 'Tunner and the Luftwaffe Connection with the Berlin Airlift'. *Air Power History*, Vol. 56, No. 4, 2009.
Photiadou, Artemis Joanna. 'Un-British No More: Torture and Interrogation by Britain in Germany, 1945–54'. *Journal of Contemporary History*, Vol. 57, No. 4, 2022.
Sälter, Gerhard. *NS-Kontinuitäten im BND. Rekrutierung, Diskurse, Vernetzungen*. Berlin: Ch. Links Verlag, 2022.
Schroer, Timothy L. *Recasting Race After World War II*. Boulder: University of Colorado Press, 2007.
The National Archives. Kew, London (Black Guard files, FO 1012/738).

Alec Chambers
Chambers, Alec (ed. Vivian Moss). 'Alec Chambers and the Berlin Airlift'. Shrivenham Heritage Society, undated.
Chambers, Alec. Private papers.
Cruddas, Colin. *Sir Alan Cobham: The Flying Legend Who Brought Aviation to the Masses*. Barnsley: Airworld, 2018.
Moss, Vivian. 'Memories of Shrivenham, 1900–1960'. Shrivenham Heritage Society, undated.
Tarkovskaya, M. (ed.).'I Lived and Sang Once Upon A Time ...' («Я ЖИЛ И ПЕЛ КОГДА-ТО ...»), *Memories of the poet Arseny Tarkovsky*. Tomsk: Vodoley Publishing House, 1999.

Elizabethan Festival
Annan, Noel. *Changing Enemies: The Defeat and Regeneration of Germany*. Ithaca: Cornell University Press, 1995.
Biskup, Thomas and Marc Schalenberg (eds). *Selling Berlin. Imagebildung und Stadtmarketing von der preußischen Residenz bis zur Bundeshauptstadt*. Stuttgart: Franz Steiner, 2008.
Boecker, Bettina. 'Shakespeare in Blockaded Berlin: The 1948 "Elizabethan Festival"' in Holland P. (ed.). *Shakespeare Survey*, Vol. 68. Cambridge: Cambridge University Press, 2015.
Botschafter des Friedens. Film, DEFA, 1948.
Buffet, Cyril. 'Ganz Berlin ist eine Bühne: Die Kulturpolitischen Vorstellungen des Vereinigten Königreichs' in Hans-Martin Hinz (ed.), *Die vier Besatzungsmächte und die Kultur in Berlin, 1945–49*. Leipzig: Leipziger Universitätsverlag, 1999.
Cambridge University Library. Records of the Cambridge University Madrigal Society.
Clare College Cambridge, *Clare News*.

Cribb, Tim. *Bloomsbury and British Theatre: The Marlowe Story*. Cambridge: Salt, 2007.
Genton, Bernard. *Les Alliés et la culture: Berlin, 1945–1949*. Paris: Presses Universitaires de France, 1998.
Hearnden, Arthur. *Red Robert: The Life of Robert Birley*. London: Hamish Hamilton, 1984.
Historisches Lexikon Bayerns, entry Dr Adolf Braun.
King's College Archive, Cambridge.
King's College Cambridge, Annual Reports.
Magee, Patrick. 'A journal: the days of Patrick Connor Magee'. King's College Archive, Cambridge, 1991.
The National Archives. Kew, London (Elizabethan Festival Files, FO 1012/166).
Sheen, Erica E. 'The Mystery in the Soul of State: Shakespeare in Airlift Berlin' in E. Sheen and I. Karremann (eds). *Shakespeare in Cold War Europe: Conflict, Commemoration, Celebration*. London: Palgrave Macmillan, 2015.
Spiel, Hilde. *Welche Welt ist meine Welt?* Munich: Paul List, 1990.
Symington, Rodney. 'The Nazi Appropriation of Shakespeare: Cultural Politics in the Third Reich'. Lewiston, NY: Edwin Mellen, 2005.
We Must Save the Children, Greta Burkill and the Cambridge Refugee Committee 1935–45, Exhibit. Keystage Arts and Heritage, Cambridge, 2014.

Mercedes Wild, Gail Halvorsen

Halvorsen, Gail. *The Berlin Candy Bomber*. Madison, WI: Horizon, 1990.
Hicks, Paul. ... *Ich stehe heute hier als Berliner Luftbrückenkind*, self-published, undated.
Raven, Margot Theis Raven and Gijsbert van Frankenhuyzen. *Mercedes and the Chocolate Pilot*. Ann Arbor: Sleeping Bear Press, 2013.
McLean Ward, Barbara. *Produce and conserve, share and play square: The grocer and the consumer on the home-front battlefield during World War II*. Portsmouth, NH: Strawbery Banke Museum, 1994.

Tegel Airport and Stolpe

Archives de l'occupation française en Allemagne, Colmar.
Bayer, Michael. *Die Geschichte des ehemaligen Flughafens Berlin-Tegel*. Berlin: Arbeitsgemeinschaft (ARGE) Geschichtsforum Tegel, 2022.
Blöß, Wolfgang. *Grenzen und Reformen in einer Umbruchgesellschaft*. Berlin: BWV, 2014.
Buffet, Cyril. *Mourir Pour Berlin: La France et l'Allemagne 1945–1949*. Paris: Armand Colin Éditeur, 1991.
Brumter, Christian. *Les Français à Berlin 1945–1994*. Paris: Riveneuve Editions et Ministère de la Défense, 2015.
Danke, Tegel! Berlin Morgenpost Special Edition. Hamburg: Funke, 2020.
Flughafen Berlin-Tegel: Geschichts- und Erinnerungs Orte. Berlin: Orte der Geschichte e.V., 2020.
Führe, Dorothea. 'An den Rand gedrängt: Frankreich als Besatzungsmacht in Berlin' in *Berlinische Monatsschrift*, Vol. 12. Berlin: Edition Luisenstadt, 2000.
Führe, Dorothea. *Die französische Besatzungspolitik in Berlin von 1945 bis 1949, Déprussianisation und Décentralisation*. Berlin: Weißensee Verlag, 2001.
Koop, Volker. *Besetzt Französische Besatzungspolitik in Deutschland*. Berlin: be.bra, 2005.

'Luftbrücke Berlin 1948/49 Der Bau des Flughafens Tegel 12. Juni bis 1. November 1998'. *Museums Journal,* No. 11, April 1998. Berlin.
Museum und Archive Reinickendorf.
Nachnutzung Flughafen Tegel Grundlagenermittlung. Berlin: Senatsverwaltung für Stadtentwicklung, 2009.
Ortel, Kai. *Flughafen Tegel: Die Geschichte einer Legende in Bildern.* Erfurt: Sutton, 2022.
Pegler, Klaus. *Stolpe und sein Flugplatz.* Published on Pegler's website.
von Przychowski Hans, and Rainer W. During. *Berliner Flughäfen.* Munich: GeraMond, 2011.
Schröder, Meinhard. *Tegel Zwischen Idylle und Metropole.* Berlin: be.bra, 2015.
Vogel, Renate (ed. Traugott Vogel). *Stolpe im Oberen Havelland – ein Dorf und seine Kirche.* Leipzig: edition winterwork, 2020.

The Big Lift, Fraternisation

Academy Collections/Margaret Herrick Library, Academy of Motion Picture Arts and Science, Los Angeles. (*The Big Lift* (1950): Pressbooks, Cast Lists, Synopses, Production Files, Manuscript Files, Censor Reports, Correspondence, PCA Analyses and Reviews; Charles Brackett papers; Charles G. Clarke collection; Hedda Hoppers papers; Thelma Ritter and Joseph Aloysius Moran papers).
Bosworth, Patricia. *Montgomery Clift: A Biography.* New York: Harcourt Brace Jovanovich, 1978.
Carruthers, Susan L. *The Good Occupation: American Soldiers and the Hazards of Peace.* Cambridge, MA: Harvard University Press, 2016.
Goedde, Petra. *GIs and Germans: Culture, Gender, and Foreign Relations, 1945–1949.* New Haven: Yale University Press, 2003.
Hochscherf, Tobias and Christoph Laucht. 'Censorship, Scripts, Suppression, and Selection: Twentieth Century Fox and the Story of the Berlin Airlift in *The Big Lift* and *Es begann mit einem Kuß* (*It Started with a Kiss*), 1950–1953'. *Film History: An International Journal,* Vol. 31, No. 3, Fall 2019.
LaGuardia, Robert. *Monty: A Biography of Montgomery Clift.* New York: Avon, 1978.
Making Montgomery Clift, 2018 documentary film.
Maulucci, Jr, Thomas W. 'Cold War Berlin in the Movies: From *The Big Lift* to *The Promise*' in Peter C. Rollins, John E. O'Connor (eds). *Why We Fought: America's Wars in Film and History.* Lexington: University Press of Kentucky, 2008.
Moseley, Harry. 'Medical History of the Berlin Airlift'. *United States Armed Forces Medical Journal,* Vol. 1, No. 11, November 1950.
Reinisch J. *The Perils of Peace: The Public Health Crisis in Occupied Germany.* Oxford: Oxford University Press, 2013.
Slatoff, Walter J. 'GI Morals in Germany'. *The New Republic,* 13 May 1946.
Stern, Ralph. '*The Big Lift* (1950): Image and Identity in Blockaded Berlin'. *Cinema Journal,* Vol. 46, No. 2, Winter 2007.
Treber, Leonie. *Mythos Trümmerfrauen: Von der Trümmerbeseitigung in der Kriegs- und Nachkriegszeit und der Entstehung eines deutschen Erinnerungsortes.* Essen: Klartext Verlag, 2014.
Weiß, Florian. 'Es begann mit einem Kuss'. *Museum Journal,* Vol. 19, No. 4, 2005.

Additional Sources

Benjamin, Walter. 'Theses on the Philosophy of History' (Harry Zorn trans., first published 1940) in Hannah Arendt (ed.). *Illuminations*. New York: Schocken Books, 1968.
Friedrich, Jörg. *The Fire: The Bombing of Germany: 1940–1945*. New York: Columbia University Press, 2006.
Gérard, Genette. 'Discours du récit' in G. Genette. *Figures III*. Paris: Seuil, 1972.
Peukert, Detlev. *Inside Nazi Germany*. New Haven: Yale University Press, 1989.
Zemon Davis, Natalie. *The Return of Martin Guerre*. Cambridge, MA: Harvard University Press, 1983.
Zemon Davis, Natalie. 'Narrative as Knowing'. *Yale Journal of Criticism*, Vol. 5, No. 2, 1992.

Further Reading in English

Cherny, Andrei. *The Candy Bombers: The Untold Story of the Berlin Airlift and America's Finest Hour*. New York: Berkeley, 2009.
Harrington, Daniel F. *Berlin on the Brink*. Lexington: University Press of Kentucky, 2012.
Reeves, Richard. *Daring Young Men*. New York: Simon and Schuster, 2010.
Rodrigo, Roberto. *Berlin Airlift*. London: Cassell, 1960.
Schrader, Helena P. *The Blockade Breakers: The Berlin Airlift*. Cheltenham: The History Press, 2011.
Schuessler, John M., Adam R. Seipp, and Thomas D. Sullivan (eds). *The Berlin Airlift and the Making of the Cold War*. College Station: Texas A&M University Press, 2022.
Turner, Barry. *The Berlin Airlift: The Relief Operation that Defined the Cold War*. London: Icon Books, 2017.
Tusa, Ann and John Tusa. *The Berlin Airlift*. New York: Atheneum, 1988.
Tusa, Ann and John Tusa. *The Berlin Airlift: The Cold War Mission to Save a City*. New York: Skyhorse, 2019.

NOTES

I Introduction
1. The composite of scenes from the sources is not intended to suggest the events happened simultaneously. Kenneth Slaker recounts his experiences flying in and out of Berlin in an interview with the Library of Congress and in his memoir *A Military Pilot's Exciting Life and Visit from the Hereafter*, p. 114.
2. The scene and details from inside Ruth Andreas-Friedrich's flat: 23 July 1948 entry of her diary (R. Andreas-Friedrich, *Der Schattenmann, Tagebuchaufzeichnungen 1938–1948*). Throughout, English translations of her diary are either my own, or those mentioned in the bibliography.
3. Henry Ries describes his salary, car, and Berlin on pp. 96 ff. of his memoir, *Ich war ein Berliner: Erinnerungen eines New Yorker Fotojournalisten*. Ries's party habits, alternated with periods of hard work, are recorded in his agenda, *Kalender aus dem Jahr 1948 mit tagebuchähnlichen Eintragungen des Fotografen Henry Ries*.
4. For Ernst Reuter, see P. Brandt. *1948-Jahr der Entscheidungen: Ernst Reuter und der Weg in den Kalten Krieg*. Willy Brandt describes Reuter's worry when the planes don't fly: Willy Brandt and Richard Lowenthal, *Ernst Reuter: Ein Leben für die Freiheit*, p. 429.
5. My secondary sources are listed in the bibliography. I especially depend, among others, on: Corine Defrance, et al (eds), *Die Berliner Luftbrücke: Erinnerungsort des Kalten Krieges*. Berlin: Ch. Links, 2018; Uwe Prell and Lothar Wilker, *Berlin-Blockade und Luftbrücke 1948/49: Analyse und Dokumentation*, Berlin: Berlin Verlag A. Spitz, 1987.
6. I quote from Natalie Zemon Davis's *The Return of Martin Guerre*, pp. vii, 125, and her 'Narrative as Knowing'. *Yale Journal of Criticism*, p. 163, as well as Walter Benjamin (trans. Harry Zorn), 'Theses on the Philosophy of History', thesis v.

II Roar
1. Slaker's story again is sourced from his interview with the Library of Congress and his memoir *A Military Pilot's Exciting Life and Visit from the Hereafter*. His account of Lieutenant Shirmer's death, and the transcript of their conversation, starts at 32:00 of the interview. The description of his DC-3 and his crash is from 1:18:00.
2. For information on the planes, see H.M. Holden, *The Legacy of the DC-3*.

III The Unforgivable
1. Henry Ries's story is again drawn from the autobiographical sources listed in the bibliography, as well as my interview with Wanda Ries in Berlin on 5 April 2024.

2   Collie Small's account of Berlin: 'Berlin's Winter of Fear', *Collier's Magazine*, 21 February 1948.
3   The meeting with the one-armed man is also recorded in Henry Ries, 'Ein Amerikaner in Berlin', *Die Zeit*, 9 September, 1994, p. 12.
4   Ries's complicated relationship with Berlin is recounted in Ries, *Deutsche, Gedanken und Gesichter*, p. 7, also quoted in Sybil Milton, 'Henry Ries', *History of Photography*, pp. 359–63.
5   Ries's centrality as the photographer of the Airlift is claimed in his obituary: 'Henry Ries, 86, Photographer Who Captured Berlin Airlift', *New York Times*, 26 May 2004.
6   'Baptised by the Spree' is found in: Introduction to Henry Ries, *Berlin vor 25 Jahren*.
7   Ries's encounter with the Nazi teacher: Henry Ries, *Ich war ein Berliner: Erinnerungen eines New Yorker Fotojournalisten*, p. 13; and Werner A. Perger, interview with Henry Ries, 'Ein milder Störenfried', *Die Zeit*, 5 June 1992.
8   His childhood and ordeals to get his sister out of Berlin: Vivien Green Fryd, 'An Inverted Detective Thriller: Henry Ries and the Quakers' Rescue of Stefanie Ries from Nazi Germany, 1939–41', pp. 35–6.
9   Testimony of Rabbi Dr Max Nussbaum, Yad Vashem Archives, Jerusalem, Israel, Item 3549470, O.1/222.
10 His letter on deciding to become a photographer is: Henry Ries to Aunt Nat, 21 January 1945, Deutsches Historisches Museum Archive, Do2 2022/793.
11 The history and contents of the secret papers from Hallein: Office of Military Gov. for Germany (US), Office of the Director of Intelligence, *HFFH, Himmler's Files From Hallein*, introduction. See also: Barry Siegel, 'Can Evil Beget Good: Nazi Data: A Dilemma for Science', *Los Angeles Times*, 30 October 1988; *Journal of the American Medical Association*, 'The Treatment of Shock from Prolonged Exposure to Cold', pp. 572–73.
12 Himmler haunting Ries: Letter from Henry Ries to Dorothy Haller, 12 January 1946. Deutsches Historisches Museum Archive, Do2 2022/793.
13 His perspectives on the Germans (which he later softens): Ibid.
14 His letter on his 'luck' leaving Nazi Germany: Letter to Dorothy Haller, Berlin, 9 September 1945, Deutsches Historisches Museum Archive, Do2 2022/793.
15 On Ries's 'gifts to resist': Werner A. Perger, 'Henry Ries: Photographer, author, friend – and a Berliner', p. 4.
16 For the Berlin zoo in wartime: Gary Bruce, *Through the Lion Gate: A History of the Berlin Zoo*, p. 203.

IV Enemy of My Enemy

1   Ruth Andreas-Friedrich's magazine during the Airlift was: *Lilith: die Zeitschrift für junge Mädchen und Frauen*, Year No. 2 (1948), Vols 1–5.
2   Throughout, I refer to Ruth Andreas-Friedrich's diary, *Der Schattenmann, Tagebuchaufzeichnungen 1938–1948*, in particular the entries: 14 November 1947 (edge of volcano), 25 March 1948 (disappearance of Friede), 24 May 1948 (Germans fear of the Russians), 13 October 1947 (anti-communist US propaganda).
3   The disappearance of Friede: 'Berlin Journalists' Disappearance', *Manchester Guardian*, 6 November 1947; *Die Welt* (Hamburg), 6 November 1947; 'Kotikow weiß nichts davon', *Die Welt*, 20 November 1947 (Kotikov 'not aware of any such case'); and 'Enthüllungen im Fall Friede', *Die Welt*, 13 March 1948 (Dau's confession recounted).

4 Hans Hartmut Weil's background is described by the Wiener Holocaust Library. He reported from Germany in 'An Undergraduate's: Visit to Hamburg: Here Are His Frank Impressions Of What He Saw', *Varsity*, 12 June 1948.
5 James Laughlin wrote: 'Report on a Visit to Germany, 1948 (American Zone): Poems'. Lausanne: Henri Held. King's College Cambridge Archive, GRB 1/5/7.
6 The reports on Russian rapes, the joke about 'reconstruction begins with deconstruction', and Germany's victim narrative are in Curt Riess, *The Berlin Story*, pp. 17, 21, 33.
7 Joel Sayre recounts the death of Borchard in his introduction to the translation of Andreas-Friedrich, *Berlin Underground*.
8 Reportage on Friede's arrest: 'Friede in russischer Haft', *Die Zeit*, 10 June 1948.
9 Eastern reactions: 'Dieter Friede, Schwennide und Neumann', *Tägliche Rundschau*, 15 June 1948.

V *The Revolutionary*

1 Reuter's meeting with Jogiches and his relationship to his group: Hannes Schwenger, *Ernst Reuter: Ein Zivilist im Kalten Krieg*, pp. 13–15; and Hans J. Reichhardt, *Ernst Reuter*, p. 33. These, and other sources cited in the bibliography, are used throughout.
2 Curt Riess recounts his meeting with Reuter in *Berlin Story*, p. 95.
3 Reuter's childhood in Leer, his family, and education are also described in Willy Brandt and Richard Lowenthal, *Ernst Reuter: Ein Leben für die Freiheit*, pp. 16, 22; *Ernst Reuter 1889–1953*. Katalog, p. 9.
4 Reuter's son is quoted ('he was not bourgeois') in *Ernst Reuter. Ein zerrissenes Leben*, 2010 Documentary Film.
5 Many quotes come from Reuter's collected three-volume speeches and writings (*Schriften, Reden*). Reuter's letter to his family 'I am a socialist' is in Ernst Reuter, *Schriften, Reden, I*, 17. Correspondence with his father over his politics is in Ernst Reuter in *Scriften, Reden, I,*: Letter to father, 26 February 1913, pp. 204–5; and Letter to his parents, 7 March 1913, p. 209.
6 Reuter's 'arrogance': Willy Brandt and Richard Lowenthal, *Ernst Reuter: Ein Leben für die Freiheit*, p. 16.
7 Reuter's experiences in Russia: Герман А. А., Революционная деятельность Эрнста Рейтера в Саратовском Поволжье (1918 г.)./German A. A., 'Revolutionary activities of Ernst Reuter in the Saratov Volga region (1918)', p. 241; and Marc von Lüpke-Schwarz, 'Ernst Reuter an der Wolga', *Deutsche Welle*, 12 August 2013.
8 'Only commissar who sends us bread' is in many sources, such as Hannes Schwenger, *Ernst Reuter: Ein Zivilist im Kalten Krieg*, p. 23, which is also the source for Reuter's 'cold shower', on p. 124.
9 For Reuter's return to Germany and the trial against him for crimes in the USSR: Willy Brandt and Richard Lowenthal, *Ernst Reuter: Ein Leben für die Freiheit*, pp. 113, 103.
10 For quelling unrest: Герман А. А., Революционная деятельность Эрнста Рейтера в Саратовском Поволжье, р. 243.
11 The death warrant is produced and discussed in the film: *Ernst Reuter. Ein zerrissenes Leben*.

12 Greta Burkill's father is Dr Adolf Braun. See also: *Historisches Lexikon Bayerns*. Reuter's trip to Arosa and his relationship with England are explored in: Interview with Margareta Burkill, 26 January 1980, Imperial War Museum. Reel 1.
13 Edzard's memory of his father's arrest: *Ernst Reuter. Ein zerrissenes Leben*.
14 The story of Reuter's concentration camp release, his arrival in Cambridge, and his son's remaining there is in the second reel of the IWM Interview with Margareta Burkill, and Interview with Gerd Edzard Harry Reuter, 28 September 1979, Imperial War Museum. See also Papers of Margareta Burkill, Cambridge University Library, GBR/0012/MS Add.8433.
15 Reuter's shock at his son's naturalisation and his gratitude: Letter to A.L. Barber (27 April 1948) in Ernst Reuter, *Schriften, Reden, III*, p. 374; and IWM interview with Gerd Reuter. For the CCRC see the exhibit, *We Must Save the Children, Greta Burkill and the Cambridge Refugee Committee 1935–45*, Cambridge, 2014.
16 For Reuter's interviews with the OSS: David E. Barclay, 'Beyond Cold War Mythmaking: Ernst Reuter and the United States' in Wolfgang-Uwe Friedrich, *Germany and America: Essays in Honor of Gerald R. Kleinfeld*, pp. 127, 128, 130.
17 'Reuter as "inconvenient" and that he "loved the Russian people"': Willy Brandt, *My Road to Berlin, as told to Leo Lania*, p. 165. Brandt's ties to the US are in: 'Willy Brandt war Informant für US-Militärgeheimdienst', *Die Zeit*, 17 December 2021. See also: Willy Brandt, *My Road to Berlin, as told to Leo Lania*, p. 163; and Scott H. Krause, '*Neue Westpolitik*: The Clandestine Campaign to Westernize the SPD in Cold War Berlin, 1948–1958', pp. 79–99.
18 For Reuter's return to Berlin: *Ernst Reuter. Ein zerrissenes Leben*; and Ernst Reuter, Letter to Friedrich Stampfer, 20 January 1947 in *Schriften, Reden, III*, p. 104 ('works a half and a quarter'). How Berliners did not remember, and mocked him: Willy Brandt, *My Road to Berlin, as told to Leo Lania*, p. 163; and Ernst Reuter Archiv, Ernst-reuter.org.
19 Reuter on Turkish democrats: Hannes Schwenger, *Ernst Reuter: Ein Zivilist im Kalten Krieg*, p. 57.
20 On the Soviet veto of his mayorship and Soviet pressure: Letter to A.L. Barber (27 April 1948) in Ernst Reuter, *Schriften, Reden, III*, p. 374.
21 Reuter's attitudes to the USSR, the US, and the CDU: Peter Brandt, *1948 – Jahr der Entscheidungen: Ernst Reuter und der Weg in den Kalten Krieg*, pp. 16–17, quoting *Sundsätze und Ziele der Sozialdemokratie*, 27 April 1947, p. 199, Vol. 3 ('quislings' and 'not a humane society'); Letter to Louis Biester, 3 May 1948, in Ernst Reuter *Schriften, Reden, III*, p. 390 ('nothing more to do with socialism'); Speech to the SPD Rally on 24 June 1948, *Schriften, Reden, III*, p. 401 ('We're not going back!').
22 Reuter quoted on 'not everything that glitters', on social democracy, and Reuter's nationalism: Peter Brandt, *1948 – Jahr der Entscheidungen: Ernst Reuter und der Weg in den Kalten Krieg*, pp. 12–15. 'Bread alone' quoted in Hannes Schwenger, *Ernst Reuter: Ein Zivilist im Kalten Krieg*, p. 74.
23 The 'Father of Berlin': the Ernst Reuter Archive website.

VI The Breakdown
1 The New Year's article: *Lilith: die Zeitschrift für junge Mädchen und Frauen*, Year No. 1, 1948, Vol. 1.

NOTES

2 Clay recounts the wedding in an interview: Columbia Oral History Project, quoted in Jean Edward Smith, *Eisenhower in War and Peace*, p. 24. More wedding details are in: 'In Berlin ergraut', *Der Spiegel*, 30 July 1948; and Lucius DuBignon Clay, *Decision in Germany*, p. 136. (Clay wouldn't let his wife attend the wedding. Family travel to Berlin was banned at the time, and the American was a stickler for rules.)
3 Robertson on Sokolovsky: FO 371/55364/C3762. Letter to Sir Arthur Street, quoted in Noel Annan, *Changing Enemies*, p. 199.
4 Sokolovsky's worries about the currency reform: Willy Brandt and Richard Lowenthal, *Ernst Reuter: Ein Leben für die Freiheit*, p. 407. His interview is in *Soviet News*, 5 October 1948, n. 2028. London: Press Department of the Soviet Embassy in London, 'The situation in Berlin', pp. 1–4.
5 Willy Brandt on events in Prague: Willy Brandt, *My Road to Berlin, as told to Leo Lania*, p. 174.
6 Reuter's views on the 'chess piece' are quoted in Peter Brandt, *1948 – Jahr der Entscheidungen: Ernst Reuter und der Weg in den Kalten Krieg*, p. 10.
7 Soviet diplomatic correspondence and manoeuvres: N.W. Naimark, *Stalin and the Fate of Europe. The Postwar Struggle for Sovereignty*, p. 164. This source has been useful throughout.
8 The lead-up to conflict, including 'Let's do it', is discussed in: Ibid., pp. 164 ff.
9 Clay's worries of war: Cable, Clay to General Chamberlin, Chief of Army Intelligence, 5 March 1948 in Jean Edward Smith (ed.), *The Papers of General Lucius D. Clay: Germany, 1945–1949*, Vol. 2, p. 568.
10 Nearly all documents referring to meeting and investigations about the US Industrial Police are from the 'Black Guards' files in the British National Archives, FO 1012/738.
11 Claims of destruction of the union offices: 'Politischer Einbruch beim FDGB', *Neues Deutschland*, 20 April 1948.
12 US soldier violence is claimed in: *Berliner Zeitung*, 25 April and 29 April 1948.
13 Kotikov's 'Independent police force' is quoted in *Neues Deutschland*, 24 April 1948.
14 Black guard terror, referring to their uniforms: 'Schwarze Garde terrorisiert FDJ', *Neues Deutschland*, 5 May 1948, p. 1.
15 'Civil war': 'Polizei Gegen FDGB', *Berliner Zeitung*, 19 April 1948, p. 1.
16 On the 'big lie': Joseph Goebbels, 'Aus Churchills Lügenfabrik', *Die Zeit ohne Beispiel*, pp. 364–69.
17 'Paradise of freedom' quoted from: 'Boykott der Kommandantur?', *Telegraf*, 9 May 1948, p. 1. Biting episode in: 'Kotikow beschuldigt Westmächte', *Telegraf*, 24 April 1948, p. 1; and *Der Kurier*, 24 April 1948.
18 US press licences: Richard Merritt, *Democracy Imposed: U.S. Occupation Policy and the German Public, 1945–1949*, pp. 299 ff.
19 Neumann on cabaret: Corine Defrance, et al, *Die Berliner Luftbrücke: Erinnerungsort des Kalten Krieges*, pp. 24–27; B.T. Van Sweringen, *Kabarettist an der Front des Kalten Krieges: Günter Neumann und das politische Kabarett in der Programmgestaltung des RIAS 1948–1968*.
20 Polls on press reliability: Richard Merritt, *Democracy Imposed: U.S. Occupation Policy and the German Public, 1945–1949*, pp. 305 and 313.
21 Banning of Communist newspapers: 'Kommunistische Zeitungen verboten', *Telegraf*, 4 May 1948, p. 2. Response on 'equivalent' ban: *Telegraf*, 6 May, p. 3.

22 Kommandatura minutes and transcripts on 'Black Guards': British National Archives, FO 1012/738.
23 Source for Ruth's experiences is again *Der Schattenmann, Tagebuchaufzeichnungen 1938–1948*. I refer to: 21 March 1948 ('get out of Berlin'), 8 April 1948 ('a matter of pride'), 19 January 1948 ('permits by car'), 4 April 1948 ('another war'), 31 March 1948 ('X-rays'), 2 July 1948 ('water to Moabit').
24 US defence on 'Black Guards': FO 1012/738, 7 May 1948: Extract of Minutes, with Deputy Commander meeting, Soviet Statement. Translated from Russian, Public Safety Committee Russian Delegate Major Kartmazov.
25 'Rubbish pit of crime': 'Die Sorgen General Kotikows', *Der Kurier*, 24 April 1948.
26 Kotikov on the West being more dangerous: 'Wieder keine Einigung', *Der Tag*, 24 April 1948, p. 1.
27 Reuter's 'little cottage' and on his 'strange life': Letter to A.L. Barber (27 April 1948) in Ernst Reuter, *Schriften, Reden, III*, p. 374.
28 'Enjoying garden terrace': Letter to Oscar Weigert (22 April 1948) in Ernst Reuter, *Schriften, Reden, III*, p. 373.
29 The weaponisation of travel: National Archives, Report by the British Air Ministry on the Berlin Blockade (1950). (Catalogue ref: AIR 55/111).
30 Reuter's worries about Berlin economy: Minutes of the 15 April 1948 City Meeting in Ernst Reuter, *Schriften, Reden, III*, p. 372.
31 Reuter on 'sitting in a witches' cauldron': Letter to Oscar Weigert (22 April 1948) in Ibid., p. 373.
32 Reuter on 'Berlin is well worth a mass', again Letter to A.L. Barber (27 April 1948) in Ibid., p. 375 and p. 377.
33 Clay on not sending people home and US official on 'bomb under the economic structure': Reeves, *Daring Young Men*, pp. 19, 27.
34 Reuter's 'who has currency has power': Corine Defrance, et al, *Die Berliner Luftbrücke: Erinnerungsort des Kalten Krieges*, p. 10. Willy Brandt and Richard Lowenthal, *Ernst Reuter: Ein Leben für die Freiheit*, p. 407.

VII Crisis

1 Ruth Andreas-Friedrich on her Reichsmark notes: *Der Schattenmann, Tagebuchaufzeichnungen 1938–1948*. Diary entry dates are indicated in-text, and otherwise noted.
2 Henry Ries on being at the border: *Ich war ein Berliner: Erinnerungen eines New Yorker Fotojournalisten*, pp. 96, 133–4.
3 Sokolovsky on protecting his economy: Interview with Marshal Vasily Sokolovsky in *Soviet News*, 5 October 1948, n. 2028, pp. 1–4.
4 His office's happiness when traffic restrictions begin: David E. Murphy, et al., *Battleground Berlin: CIA Vs. KGB in the Cold War*, p. 57.
5 Reuter not using written notes: *Ernst Reuter. Ein zerrissenes Leben*. Film. Ernst Reuter's speech to the SPD Rally on 24 June 1948, *Schriften, Reden, III*, pp. 400–12.
6 On the West leaving Berlin: Uwe Prell and Lothar Wilker, *Berlin-Blockade und Luftbrücke 1948/49: Analyse und Dokumentation*, pp. 27, 32; A. Anderhub and J.O. Bennett, *Blockade, Luftbrücke und Luftbrückendank: zur Geschichte der Krise um Berlin 1948–49*, p. 18; N.W. Naimark, *Stalin and the Fate of Europe. The Postwar Struggle for Sovereignty*, p. 166.

NOTES

7   Reuter on holding out fourteen days: *Ernst Reuter 1889–1953.* Exhibition catalogue, p. 16.
8   For the history of Lancaster House, see the website of the Berlin Historical Sites Office (Landesdenkmalamt Berlin).
9   Interview with David Edwards occurred in Berlin on 12 May 2024.
10 Details about Rex Waite come from Romilly Waite's speech about her father, Berlin Airlift Anniversary, Tempelhof Airport, 12 May 2024.
11 Rations and reserves in Berlin: A. Anderhub and J.O. Bennett, *Blockade, Luftbrücke und Luftbrückendank: zur Geschichte der Krise um Berlin 1948–49,* pp. 11–12, 19; Corine Defrance, et al, *Die Berliner Luftbrücke: Erinnerungsort des Kalten Krieges,* p. 18.
12 David Lawrence quoted from the Frye Archive in Reeves, *Daring Young Men,* p. 95.
13 Note 'Operation Plainfare' was earlier known as 'Operation Carter Paterson', but the name was changed when the Russians pointed out Carter Paterson was the name of a removals firm.
14 Edwards on Waite's announcement of his plan: quoted in 'Bitter-sweet memories of Berlin Airlift', *BBC,* 19 May 2009.
15 Clay's chain smoking and love of coffee are in his obituary: 'Gen. Lucius Clay dead at 80', *New York Times,* 17 April 1978. The joke about Clay relaxing is quoted in Reeves, *Daring Young Men,* p. 7; see also Barry Turner, *Berlin Airlift,* p. 19.
16 The meeting between Reuter and Clay is recounted in Willy Brandt, *My Road to Berlin,* as told to Leo Lania, p. 186; Willy Brandt and Richard Lowenthal, *Ernst Reuter: Ein Leben für die Freiheit,* pp. 425 ff.; David E. Barclay, 'Beyond Cold War Mythmaking: Ernst Reuter and the United States', p. 133.
17 Clay's lack of German skills: A. Anderhub and J.O. Bennett, *Blockade, Luftbrücke und Luftbrückendank: zur Geschichte der Krise um Berlin 1948–49,* p. 9.
18 Clay telegraph to DC on not moving 'one inch': Peter Brandt, *1948 – Jahr der Entscheidungen: Ernst Reuter und der Weg in den Kalten Krieg,* p. 24. See also: A. Anderhub and J.O. Bennett, *Blockade, Luftbrücke und Luftbrückendank: zur Geschichte der Krise um Berlin 1948–49,* p. 19.
19 Truman's objection to Clay's convoy plan: Uwe Prell and Lothar Wilker, *Berlin-Blockade und Luftbrücke 1948/49: Analyse und Dokumentation,* p. 33.
20 Robertson on 'heads to fall': Robertson to Foreign Office, 4 December 1947, PRO, FO371/64463, quoted in David E. Barclay, 'Beyond Cold War Mythmaking: Ernst Reuter and the United States', p. 134.
21 Reuter's 'magnet theory': Peter Brandt, *1948 – Jahr der Entscheidungen: Ernst Reuter und der Weg in den Kalten Krieg,* p. 35.
22 Reuter on 'something was washed away' quoted in Uwe Prell and Lothar Wilker, *Berlin-Blockade und Luftbrücke 1948/49: Analyse und Dokumentation,* p. 39.
23 Fred McAfee and other pilots' stories: Paul Fisher, 'The Berlin Airlift' (*Bee-Hive,* United Aircraft Corporation), Vol. 23, no. 4 (1948), pp. 6, 14–15.
24 Origin of airplanes: Uwe Prell and Lothar Wilker, *Berlin-Blockade und Luftbrücke 1948/49: Analyse und Dokumentation,* pp. 35–6.
25 Conditions at airfields, like those in a 'concentration camp': Harry Moseley, 'Medical History of the Berlin Airlift', *United States Armed Forces Medical Journal,* pp. 1249 ff.
26 McAfee on 'hauling macaroni' in Paul Fisher, 'The Berlin Airlift' (*Bee-Hive,* United Aircraft Corporation, Vol. 23, no. 4 (1948), pp. 14–15.

27 Construction of the Sunderlands: Roberto Rodrigo, *Berlin Airlift*, p. 25.
28 Computational work during the Airlift: Paul Erickson, Judy L. Klein, Lorraine Daston, Rebecca Lemov, Thomas Sturm and Michael D. Gordin, *How Reason Almost Lost Its Mind: The Strange Career of Cold War Rationality*, p. 70.
29 Bennett's memories: A. Anderhub and J.O. Bennett, *Blockade, Luftbrücke und Luftbrückendank: zur Geschichte der Krise um Berlin 1948–49*, p. 64.
30 Polka music: Ibid., p. 70.
31 Ruth Andreas-Friedrich on the sound of the roar: *Der Schattenmann, Tagebuchaufzeichnungen 1938–1948*, 27 June 1948.
32 'Losing proposition': *New York Times*, 'Limitations Cited on Berlin Airlift', 18 July 1948.
33 For tonnage: Uwe Prell and Lothar Wilker, *Berlin-Blockade und Luftbrücke 1948/49: Analyse und Dokumentation*, p. 39.
34 On Tunner dressing down his men and dropping coal: A. Anderhub and J.O. Bennett, *Blockade, Luftbrücke und Luftbrückendank: zur Geschichte der Krise um Berlin 1948–49*, p. 67.
35 Tunner's success, and on 'propaganda weapon' quoted in Reeves, *Daring Young Men*, pp. 105–6, 116, 269.
36 Brandt's starvation legend: Willy Brandt, *My Road to Berlin*, as told to Leo Lania, p. 184.
37 Clay on 'mass starvation': Lucius DuBignon Clay, *Decision in Germany*, p. 365.
38 For the perpetuation of the hunger myth see, for example, NATO: 'Two million people were isolated, to be faced with the prospect of hunger, cold, unemployment and misery. No way in; no way out. The only element still open: the air above' from transcript of 'Background to Berlin' (film), NATO Information Service, 1962, www.nato.int; from the UK government: the Airlift 'prevented the starvation of the two and a half million inhabitants of Berlin', from 'Coal, Calories and Candy Bombers: the Berlin Airlift 1948–9', 18 June 2018, www.history.blog.gov.uk; from the German Bundestag: Berlin was 'completely cut off by land and water by the Soviet Union' from 'Ihr Völker der Welt', 10 September 2008.
39 *The Airlift: Only the Sky Was Free* (2005) is, in German, *Die Luftbrücke: Nur der Himmel war frei*.
40 For questioning of the hunger myth: Michael Lemke, 'Totale Blockade? Über das Verhältnis von Abschottung und Durchlässigkeit im Berliner Krisenalltag 1948/49'; Volker Koop, *Kein Kampf um Berlin?*; Jörg Echternkamp, 'Die Berliner Luftbrücke: Zur Vermessung eines historischen Themas, 1948–2018' in *Die Berliner Luftbrücke: Erinnerungsort des Kalten Krieges*.
41 Soviets on supplying city quoted in Willy Brandt, *My Road to Berlin*, as told to Leo Lania, pp. 188–92.
42 One-third of food was accessed from the East: Mark Landsman, *Dictatorship and Demand, The Politics of Consumerism in East Germany*, pp. 41–2.
43 Sokolovsky on the food situation: Interview with Marshal Vassili Sokolovsky in *Soviet News*, 5 October 1948, No. 2028. London: Press Department of the Soviet Embassy in London, 'The situation in Berlin', pp. 1–4.
44 The British propaganda campaign to perpetuate that Berlin was 'fully blockaded': FO 1012/215, Magistrat Control. 'Berlin Blockade and Airlift: Publicity Campaign'. Appendix to 2201/4/coma/1132, 3 November 1948; Deputy Chief. (Plans),

Information Services Division; From Public Safety Branch to Office of D.D.M.G., 12 November 1948.
45 Ibid.
46 US Department of State on propaganda advantage: *The Berlin Crisis, 1948*, US Department of State, Foreign Policy Studies Branch, Division of Historical Policy Research, Research Project No. 171. Washington DC, 5.
47 For the importance of the Berlin Airlift to the 1948 US election: Robert A. Divine, 'The Cold War and the Election of 1948', p. 109, and Wilson D. Miscamble, 'Harry S. Truman, the Berlin Blockade and the 1948 Election', p. 312. The Gallup poll is quoted in Divine.
48 Brandt on Reuter's reaction to Clay ('necessary sacrifices' and the 'severe test' of hunger for democracy): Willy Brandt, *My Road to Berlin, as told to Leo Lania*, pp. 185–6.
49 British Intelligence on not being in Berlin to feed Berliners: FO 1012/283, 'Germany – Berlin food situation.' Foreign Office to Berlin Intelligence, 22 July 1948.
50 'Inevitable implications' spelled out in: FO 1012/283 Foreign Office Weekly Summary, 26 July 1948. See also discussion in N.W. Naimark, *Stalin and the Fate of Europe. The Postwar Struggle for Sovereignty*, p. 188.
51 East blaming transport chaos on West, quoted in *Neues Deutschland:* FO 1012/229, Current situation in Berlin. Control Commission Germany to Foreign Office, 29 June 1948.
52 Ernst Reuter on RIAS (transcript), 30 June 1945, in *Schriften, Reden, III*, pp. 412–13.

VIII Champagne

1 I interviewed Alec Chambers in Berlin on 25 May 2024, and this conversation is the backbone of what follows along with materials quoted in the bibliography. Chambers also provided me with dozens of pages of typed notes in which he recounts his experiences. His quotes in the narrative come from all these sources.
2 'Flying circus': Colin Cruddas, *Sir Alan Cobham: The Flying Legend Who Brought Aviation to the Masses*, p. 180.
3 Roberto Rodrigo, *Berlin Airlift*, contains a long section about the 'Liquid Lift', including the opinions in the hotel bars (p. 155), how the kitchen caught fire (p. 155), the lantern ignited a tanker (pp. 102–3), the misunderstood word 'off' (p. 106), and plasticine on the floors (p. 4).
4 Kitchen fire: Alec Chambers (ed. Vivian Moss), 'Alec Chambers and the Berlin Airlift', pp. 9–10.
5 On having to climb over tanks and the Soviets as night 'stalkers' see IWM interview with Cyril Hagues 1999, Reel 2.
6 Chambers recounts seeing the 'chap in front of you', how 'spirits were high', and the image of 'pearls in the sky' to Dan Bell, 'Bitter Sweet Memories of Berlin Airlift', *BBC*, 12 May 2009.
7 Descriptions of Gatow: Alec Chambers (ed. Vivian Moss), 'Alec Chambers and the Berlin Airlift', p. 6.
8 Smoking: See for example, Alec Chambers interview, Imperial War Museum (2014): Reel 3, 09'00 ff.
9 Soviet memories of Perleberg: Alexander Radkovsky's later memories of the town in the 60s in M. Tarkovskaya (ed.), '*I Lived and Sang Once Upon A Time …*' («Я ЖИЛ И ПЕЛ КОГДА-ТО …»), *Memories of the poet Arseny Tarkovsky*, p. 87.

IX Culture War

1 The 1948 interview with Boris Alexandrov can be found on YouTube. Other video material includes the film *Botschafter des Friedens*. For Berlin press reactions to the festival and Alexandrov Ensemble: *Berliner Zeitung, Kurier, Der Morgen, Nacht-Express, Neue Zeit, Neues Deutschland, Der Spiegel, Tägliche Rundschau, Telegraf,* and *Die Welt* (especially the September 1948 special issue on the festival).
2 'Event of the century': Anatoly Kompaniets, 'Pastoral on the Ruins', in *Culture*, 2000.
3 Ries's experience during Red Army Choir performance: *Kalender aus dem Jahr 1948 mit tagebuchähnlichen Eintragungen des Fotografen Henry Ries (Englisch)*, Deutsches Historisches Museum Archive, Do2 2016/533; and Henry Ries, *Ich war ein Berliner: Erinnerungen eines New Yorker Fotojournalisten*, p. 151.
4 British 'lightweight' cultural politics is discussed in: Cyril Buffet, 'Ganz Berlin ist eine Bühne: Die Kulturpolitischen Vorstellungen des Vereinigten Königreichs', pp. 191 ff.
5 Birley on the efforts of other powers: FO 1012/166, Robert Birley to Mr Patrick Dean.
6 The observations of Félix Lusset are from Archives de l'occupation française en Allemagne, Colmar, GMFB, XC 1/10. Report of Félix Lusset of 19.12.1947, Nr. 3953/MC, quoted also in Bernard Genton, *Les Alliés et la culture: Berlin, 1945–1949*, pp. 313 ff.
7 Birley's plans for the festival are recounted in Arthur Hearnden, *Red Robert: The Life of Robert Birley*, pp. 127 ff.
8 York House minutes on 10 May 1948: FO 1012/166, 22/28. See also for plans of who to invite: Educational Advisor to Foreign Office, 19 May 1948, FO 1012/166, 121.
9 Preparatory plans for the festival: FO 1012/166, 139.
10 Reuter's impressions of Cambridge: Ernst Reuter, 'Englische Reiseeindrücke', in *Telegraf*, N. 194, 21 August 1947, in *Schriften, Reden, III*, pp. 246–7; and in Letter to A.L. Barber (27 April 1948) in Ernst Reuter, *Schriften, Reden, III*, pp. 374–8. See also Interview with Gerd Edzard Harry Reuter, 28 September 1979, Imperial War Museum.
11 Kaldor's report and the minutes of meetings on Berlin's currency: King's College Archive, Cambridge: Berlin Currency and Trade Committee: press report, 1949-01-21 File Reference Code: GBR/0272/NK/7/16-20.
12 Experience of former soldiers in King's College: 'A journal: the days of Patrick Connor Magee', 1991. Reference Code: GBR/0272/KCAC/1/6/Magee/1. King's College Archive, Cambridge.
13 Anthony Blunt's involvement: FO 1012/166, 139.
14 Beves cleared as the fourth man: Albums of photographs and newspaper cuttings, 1920–1977. Reference Code: GBR/0272/SC/BevesD/2. King's College Archive, Cambridge.
15 Wyndham working for MI6: Bettina Boecker, 'Shakespeare in Blockaded Berlin: The 1948 "Elizabethan Festival"', pp. 282–93.
16 Keeffe was confused as to why he should have to spy on Jews, but their nationality was considered of more importance to British Intelligence. Clare College Cambridge, *Clare News 2015–6*, Obituary, p. 12; and July 2014 Royal College of Music interview with Bernard Keeffe.

NOTES

17 Atmosphere at the Madrigal Society: Records of the Cambridge University Madrigal Society, 1924–1970, GBR/0265/UA/SOC.XXII are in the Cambridge University Library.
18 For discussion of the Schlegel-Tieck translation: Rodney Symington, 'The Nazi Appropriation of Shakespeare: Cultural Politics in the Third Reich'. See also: *Deutsche Welle*, 'How Shakespeare was turned into a German' (interview with Heike Mund), 22 April 2016.
19 Publicity materials from 1948 date the Marlowe Society from 1912, even though today's society date their history from 1907.
20 Apostle members: Card index of the Apostle members 1820–1952. Reference Code: GBR/0272/NGA/7/4/1. King's College Archive, Cambridge.
21 Noel Annan on Rylands as a 'Cambridge celebrity', interior decoration of his rooms, and friendship: see correspondence between G.H.W. Rylands and Noel Annan, 1940-04-01–1999-01-18, Reference Code: GBR/0272/NGA/5/1/889. King's College Archive, Cambridge.
22 Virginia Woolf on Rylands, and Rylands on Gielgud quoted in: Tim Cribb, *Bloomsbury and British Theatre: The Marlowe Story*, pp. 56 ff.
23 Robertson on the 'battle for the German soul': Senior Information Services Officer to GOC British Troops Berlin, 3 August 1948, FO 1012/166, 158. See also Bettina Boecker, 'Shakespeare in Blockaded Berlin: The 1948 "Elizabethan Festival"', pp. 282–93.
24 On posters in Soviet zone: press preparations are outlined in Information-Services Branch to Cultural Relations and others. FO 1012/166, 166.
25 On inviting a Russian lecturer: Letter from Benson to Wint, 21 July 1948, FO 1012/166, 135; Letter to Soviets (Col. Yelisarov) from Brigadier Benson is FO 1012/166, 148.
26 On 'falsified' performances: Richard Reeves, *Daring Young Men*, pp. 90–1.
27 Soviet Olympic stadium request: Letter from GOC British Troops Berlin to Political Division HQ GOC (BE), 20 August 1948. FO 1012/166, 179. And Letter from Deputy DDMG, 20 August 1948. FO 1012/166, Empty stands were visible in: *Botschafter des Friedens*.
28 Magee's memories: 'A journal: the days of Patrick Connor Magee', 1991. Reference Code: GBR/0272/KCAC/1/6/Magee/1. King's College Archive, Cambridge.
29 The smashed vinyl records: Beament's obituary in *The Independent*, 18 March 2005.
30 The future of Marlowe society members and female actors: Tim Cribb, *Bloomsbury and British Theatre: The Marlowe Story*, pp. 56 ff.
31 Memories of Gabriele Annan: Obituary of Gabriele Annan in *The Independent*, 15 February 2015; Noel Annan's memories of the trip, and of the visit to Gabriele's house, are in *Changing Enemies*, pp. 237 ff.
32 Plans and programmes of the events: FO 1012/166, 169 and 171.
33 Description of the concert in Grunewald, and of Airlift sounds marring a concert: *Manchester Guardian*, 23 August 1948.
34 That costumes were hired: 'A' Branch Headquarters, Troops for Elizabethan Festival. FO 1012/166, 177. And Foreign Office to Bercomb Berlin, 17 August 1948. FO 1012/166, 175.
35 Programme of the concert: Cambridge University Library: Records of the Cambridge University Madrigal Society, 1924–1970. GBR/0265/UA/SOC.XXII.

36 The involvement of the Berlin Philharmonic and Peppermüller: FO 1012/166 and with thanks to the Berliner Philharmonic archive.

X Through the Iron Curtain

1 Kenneth Slaker again recounts his experiences in an interview with the Library of Congress and in his memoir, *A Military Pilot's Exciting Life and Visit from the Hereafter*.
2 Steber's story, and that of his dog: Don Vaughan, 'Vittle the Berlin Airlift Dog 130 Missions'; Rob Bardua, 'Flying dog's parachute lands at U.S. Air Force Museum'. See also Clarence Steber Obituary in *Florida Today*, 5 January 2008, p. 16.
3 German soldiers manning the Soviet Occupation Zone border were governed by the 'Schusswaffengebrauchsordnung aus dem August 1948' [Firearms Regulation from August 1948], which permitted them to use firearms, after a warning shot, 'if the border violator flees'. The establishment of the GDR brought new regulations; an explicit order to shoot border violators ('*Schießbefehl*') returned only in 1961, with the building of the Berlin Wall. The 1948 Regulation is quoted on the website of the Federal Agency for Civic Education (Bundeszentrale für politische Bildung).
4 Slaker and Steber's escape through the Iron Curtain was widely reported – though mostly in small-town US newspapers – between 15 and 18 September 1948. The story was sanitised by authorities: Slaker 'suffered only minor bruises', the Soviets did not 'even pay attention to him' as he walked through their zone, but he was 'apparently escorted to Berlin by Soviet officials'. The press also noted that the authorities were 'silent on details', and that Slaker was 'banned' from 'telling exactly where or how he crossed the border' (see, for example, *Daily Nonpareil*, 16 September 1948, p. 6; *Tipton Daily Tribune*, 16 September 1948, p. 7; *Gaffney Ledger*, 18 September 1948, p. 1).

XI Students in the Ruins

1 Vachell's unofficial mission: King's College, Cambridge, *Annual Report 2019*, pp. 276–7.
2 GDR-era historians claimed the marble was not used in all these locations. See also my Berlin history blog, *The Needle*: 'Hitler's Bloody Palace', 17 July 2011.
3 Magee's visit to the Reich Chancellery: 'A journal: the days of Patrick Connor Magee', 1991. Reference Code: GBR/0272/KCAC/1/6/Magee/1. King's College Archive, Cambridge.
4 'Hunger for theatre': Bettina Boecker, 'Shakespeare in Blockaded Berlin: The 1948 "Elizabethan Festival"', pp. 282–93. See also: Erica E. Sheen, 'The Mystery in the Soul of State: Shakespeare in Airlift Berlin'.
5 The atmosphere in the Renaissance Theatre: *Manchester Guardian*, 20 September 1948.
6 Copies of the Berlin theatre programmes: King's College Archive, Cambridge: Programmes, 1940 – 1964 GBR/0272/GHWR/4/1/2.
7 Rylands' production, and 'semen': Tim Cribb, *Bloomsbury and British Theatre: The Marlowe Story*, pp. 56 ff.
8 Austerity suiting a siege and staging: *Manchester Guardian*, 15 August 1948, 26 August 1948.

9   The visit to the *Egmont* rehearsal and the cabaret: 'A journal: the days of Patrick Connor Magee', 1991. Reference Code: GBR/0272/KCAC/1/6/Magee/1. King's College Archive, Cambridge; and Noel Annan, *Changing Enemies*, pp. 237 ff.
10 The British 'chess move' in cultural politics: Cyril Buffet, 'Ganz Berlin ist eine Bühne: Die Kulturpolitischen Vorstellungen des Vereinigten Königreichs', pp. 191 ff.
11 *The Sunday Dispatch* is quoted in Tim Cribb, *Bloomsbury and British Theatre: The Marlowe Story*, pp. 56 ff.
12 For the audit and related correspondence: FO 1012/166.
13 For Berlin as a 'shop window': 'Berlin als doppeltes »Schaufenster« im Kalten Krieg' in Thomas Biskup/Marc Schalenberg (eds), *Selling Berlin. Imagebildung und Stadtmarketing von der preußischen Residenz bis zur Bundeshauptstadt*, pp. 227–44.
14 The observations of Félix Lusset are from Archives de l'occupation française en Allemagne, Colmar, GMFB, XC 1/10. Report of Félix Lusset of 19.12.1947, Nr. 3953/MC, quoted also in Bernard Genton, *Les Alliés et la culture: Berlin, 1945–1949*, pp. 313 ff.
15 Hilde Spiel reflects on the Soviet and British performances in *Welche Welt ist meine Welt?*, pp. 96 ff.
16 Soviets blaming the 'Black Guards' for chaos in the New Town Hall is reported in *Radford News Journal*, Vol. 65, No. 189, 8 September 1948.
17 Ruth Andreas-Friedrich describes the masses coming to Reuter's speech in *Der Schattenmann, Tagebuchaufzeichnungen 1938–1948*, 13 September 1948.
18 Reuter's speech is reprinted in Peter Auer, *Ihr Völker der Welt*, pp. 7ff.
19 Reception of Reuter's rhetoric in the West: Scott H. Krause, '*Neue Westpolitik*: The Clandestine Campaign to Westernize the SPD in Cold War Berlin, 1948–1958', p. 81.
20 Reuter pitching over the heads of the generals: David E. Barclay, 'Beyond Cold War Mythmaking: Ernst Reuter and the United States', p. 134.
21 Description of events at Brandenburg Gate, death of Scheunemann, and trials: Willy Brandt and Richard Lowenthal, *Ernst Reuter: Ein Leben für die Freiheit*, p. 452; R. Andreas-Friedrich, *Der Schattenmann, Tagebuchaufzeichnungen 1938–1948*, 13 September 1948; 'Der erste Tote der deutschen Teilung', *Berliner Kurier*, 9 September 2018; N.W. Naimark, *Stalin and the Fate of Europe. The Postwar Struggle for Sovereignty*, p. 188.
22 Photographs of Ries in the city hall: *Ernst Reuter 1889–1953. Katalog*, p. 5.

XII Sweet Victories

1 This chapter is based on my interview with Mercedes Wild, née Simon, from 20 September 2023 at her home in Berlin-Friedenau. Additional material on Frau Wild's life is from the children's picture book, Margot Theis Raven and Gijsbert van Frankenhuyzen, *Mercedes and the Chocolate Pilot*. Wild gave me a self-published book, Paul Hicks, … *Ich stehe heute hier als Berliner Luftbrückenkind*, recording the memories of children during the Airlift.
2 For rations: Uwe Prell and Lothar Wilker, *Berlin-Blockade und Luftbrücke 1948/49: Analyse und Dokumentation*, p. 42.
3 For Hershey chocolate rations: Barbara McLean Ward, *Produce and conserve, share and play square: The grocer and the consumer on the home-front battlefield during World War II*, p. 223.
4 Gail Halvorsen's memoir: *The Berlin Candy Bomber*. See also Petra Goedde, *GIs and Germans: Culture, Gender, and Foreign Relations, 1945–1949*.

XIII In the French Quarter

1 I visited Stolpe in late October 2024. My general sources for building the airport and events at Stolpe are listed in the bibliography.
2 Slaker on French wine, from his interview with the Library of Congress.
3 German disparagement of French occupiers, and housing confiscation: Christian Brumter, *Les Français à Berlin, 1945–1994*, p. 253.
4 Powerful night lamps are seen in photographs in *The Sphere*, 20 November 1948, p. 235.
5 Klaus Scherff and Klaus Hübner are quoted in Matthias Bath, *Die Berlin-Blockade 1948/49 Stalins Griff nach der deutschen Hauptstadt und der Freiheitskampf Berlins.*
6 Earth moved: Christian Brumter, *Les Français à Berlin 1945–1994*, p. 253.
7 Bitumen rolled in from the Soviet Zone: Roberto Rodrigo, *Berlin Airlift*, p. 33.
8 Fine clothes to the bunker: Matthias Bath, *Die Berlin-Blockade 1948/49 Stalins Griff nach der deutschen Hauptstadt und der Freiheitskampf Berlins.*
9 For conditions at the construction site, I quote: '7000 Frauen bauen Kriegsflugplatz Alarmierende Zustände auf dem Flugplatz Tegel', *Neues Deutschland*, 7 September 1948, p. 4; 'Explosion auf dem Flugplatz in Tegel', *Neues Deutschland*, 23 September 1948, p. 1; 'Wir bauen einen Flugplatz Erlebnisse eines Arbeiters beim Flugplatzbau in Tegel', *Berliner Zeitung*, 30 September 1948, p. 6; *Berliner Zeitung*, 8 December 1948, p. 2.
10 Photographs of the construction site described from images at: Museum und Archiv Reinickendorf, *Bau des Flughafens Tegel während der sowjetischen Blockade West-Berlins 1948/49*. TePla series photographs.
11 Bob Hope is quoted in: Thomas Parrish, *Berlin in The Balance: The Blockade, The Airlift, The First Major Battle Of The Cold War*. Boston: Da Capo, p. 295.
12 Reports on Ganeval's reception and the destruction of the towers: Daniel F. Harrington, *'The Air Force Can Deliver Anything' A History of the Berlin Airlift*, pp. 55ff, 245–6 (Stensrud is quoted). The source quotes Curt Riess, *Berlin Story*, but the story of the towers does not appear in his book. See also: Volker Koop, *Besetzt Französische Besatzungspolitik in Deutschland*, p. 261 ff; AIR 20/7808 HQ Intelligence Intelligence Staff Sitrep for BTB Commanders and Heads of Staff 17 December 1948; FO 944, German No. 1 Distribution. From Berlin to Foreign Office (German Section), Military Governor's weekly personal report to Secretary of State 22 December 1948; FO 944, German No. 1 Distribution. From Berlin to Foreign Office (German Section), Military Governor's weekly personal report to Secretary of State 22 December 1948.
13 Silence on the airwaves: *Sozialdemokrat*. 17 December 1948, No. 295; *Der Spiegel*, 'Wir waren ja nur verpumpt', 22 December 1948.
14 Quoting Clay's reaction: *Sozialdemokrat*, 'Nur eine französisch-deutsche Angelegenheit Clay und Ganeval zur Sprengung in Tegel – Folge der Blockade', 18 December 1948.
15 'Outrageous deed': *Neues Deutschland*, 'Die Untat von Tegel', 18 December 1948.
16 The arrest of French police: *Sozialdemokrat*, 'Zwischenfall in Stolpe Berlin (Eigenbericht)'. 21 December 1948.
17 The French evacuation from Stolpe is described in Dorothea Führe, *Die französische Besatzungspolitik in Berlin von 1945 bis 1949. Déprussianisation und Décentralisation*, pp. 374–80; Renate Vogel (ed. Traugott Vogel), *Stolpe im Oberen Havelland – ein Dorf und seine Kirche*; 'Das Dorf Stolpe und die Weltpolitik Verträge, machtlose Proteste

und preisgegebene Menschen', *Die Zeit*, 30 December 1948; 'Politischer Skandal um Stolpe Auslieferung an die Sowjets – Verletzung des Selbstbestimmungsrechts', *Der Tag*, 21 December 1948, p. 1.
18 Stolpe residents uninformed: 'Wir waren ja nur verpumpt'. *Der Spiegel*, 52/1948, 22 December 1948.
19 Mayor and Sokolovsky quoted, and situation in occupied Stolpe: Renate Vogel (ed. Traugott Vogel), *Stolpe im Oberen Havelland – ein Dorf und seine Kirche*; 'Auf »Sowjetische Art« besetzt Dorf Stolpe abgeriegelt – Ganeval will nicht protestieren'. *Sozialdemokrat*, 22 December 1948; 'General Ganeval über Stolpe', *Der Tag*, 22 December 1948.
20 The French–Soviet protocol: Wolfgang Blöß, *Grenzen und Reformen in einer Umbruchgesellschaft*, p. 87.
21 Stolpe not worth a war: 'Stolpe einen Krieg wert?', *Berliner Zeitung*, 30 December 1948, p. 6.
22 Andreas-Friedrich's quotes come from her diary: 7 December 1948.
23 Ganeval's optimism about Soviet discipline: 'Auf »Sowjetische Art« besetzt Dorf Stolpe abgeriegelt – Ganeval will nicht protestieren', *Sozialdemokrat*, 22 December 1948.
24 German press and political reactions to the transfer: 'Sowjets besetzen Stolpe Berlin (DPD)', *Telegraf*, 22 December 1948; 'Wir waren ja nur verpumpt'. *Der Spiegel*, 52/1948, 22 December 1948; 'Stolpe – ein Dorf zwischen zwei Welten, "Ist nicht schön, was die Franzosen gemacht haben"'. *Sozialdemokrat*, 21 December 1948; 'Stolpe einen Krieg wert?', *Berliner Zeitung*, 30 December 1948, p. 6; 'Das Dorf Stolpe und die Weltpolitik Verträge, machtlose Proteste und preisgegebene Menschen', *Die Zeit*, 30 December 1948.
25 French press reactions: Georges Blun, 'Le village que nous avons évacué n'a jamais fait partie du Grand-Berlin', *Le Monde*, 23 December 1948.
26 New York reaction: 'French Abandon Town: Return Stolpe to Soviet, Saying Airport Is Not Needed Now', *New York Times*, 20 December 1948, p. 12.
27 British Intelligence on the Stolpe Affair: AIR 20/7809. Intelligence Staff Sitrep for BTB Commanders and Heads of Staff, 24 December 1948: TECHL; FO 944. German No. 1 Distribution. From Berlin to Foreign Office (German Section), Military Governor's weekly personal report to Secretary of State, 22 December 1948. FO 944, German No. 1 Distribution. From Berlin to Foreign Office (German Section), Military Governor's weekly personal report to Secretary of State, 22 December 1948.
28 Interview with Ilse Thiele was on 23 October 2024 in Stolpe. For related events, I refer again to sources, including newspapers, mentioned in the bibliography.
29 On Soviet non-fraternising with Germans: J. Reinisch, *The Perils of Peace: The Public Health Crisis in Occupied Germany*.
30 Andreas-Friedrich describes her departure in three diary entries: 24 December, 26 December, 29 December 1948.

XIV New Year
1   Location of black markets and volume of goods: FO 1012/175, Black Market & Price Control Report, 29 September 1948; A. Anderhub and J.O. Bennett, *Blockade, Luftbrücke und Luftbrückendank: zur Geschichte der Krise um Berlin 1948–49*, p. 38; Mark

Landsman, *Dictatorship and Demand, The Politics of Consumerism in East Germany*, pp. 41–2.
2   Foreign Office speculation on origin of goods, confiscations: FO 1012/175, Black Market & Price Control Report, 29 September 1948; FO 1012/175, Black Market & Price Control Report, 30 October 1948; FO 1012/175, Black Market & Price Control Report, 27 November 1948.
3   Ration amounts for Berliners: Uwe Prell and Lothar Wilker, *Berlin-Blockade und Luftbrücke 1948/49: Analyse und Dokumentation*, p. 42; Soviet rations and complications obtaining them: Mark Landsman, *Dictatorship and Demand, The Politics of Consumerism in East Germany*, pp. 43, 45–6.
4   *Fressen* and *Morale*: Uwe Prell. 'Militär in ziviler Mission – Lucius D. Clay und die Berliner Luftbrücke', *Berliner Geschichte*, No. 12., p. 20.
5   Henry Ries's Anhalter Bahnhof series: Henry Ries (ed. Alfred Gottwaldt), *Menschen am Zerstörten Anhalter Bahnhof: Fotografien von Henry Ries aus Berlin, 1948*, Ries's introduction, p. 9; Henry Ries, *Ich war ein Berliner: Erinnerungen eines New Yorker Fotojournalisten*, pp. 107–8; Ries, *Deutsche, Gedanken und Gesichter*; Ries, *Abschied meiner Generation*, portrait nos. 16, 18, 32, 34.
6   Ries's style of photography: Dr Friedrich Terveen's introduction to Henry Ries, *Berlin vor 25 Jahren*.
7   Door opening: Henry Ries, *Ich war ein Berliner: Erinnerungen eines New Yorker Fotojournalisten*, p. 138.
8   Ries on the candy bomber photograph: Ibid., p. 138.
9   For Henry Ries's pocket agendas: *Kalender aus dem Jahr 1948 mit tagebuchähnlichen Eintragungen des Fotografen Henry Ries (Englisch)*, Deutsches Historisches Museum Archive, Do2 2016/533. *Kalender aus dem Jahr 1949 mit tagebuchähnlichen Eintragungen u.a. zur Aufhebung der Berliner Blockade im Mai 1949 und mit Notizen zu Interviews für das Buch 'German Faces'* – Nachlass. Deutsches Historisches Museum Archive, Do2 2016/527.
10 Ries noted of the 9 August performance of the Alexandrow-Choir in the Staatsoper: 'not very impressed – leave after intermission.' In his autobiography, he expresses a lifelong love for Henry Purcell. Henry Ries, *Ich war ein Berliner: Erinnerungen eines New Yorker Fotojournalisten*, p. 187. Also conversation on Purcell with Wanda Ries.
11 On the exhibition, see unpublished short biography of Henry Ries, written by Wanda Ries (2011), p. 3.
12 Press responses to the exhibition in Berlin: *Der Abend*, 'Blockade in Bildern', 20 January 1949, Vol. 4, No. 16, p. 2; Dr Friedrich Terveen's introduction to Henry Ries, *Berlin vor 25 Jahren; Der Tagesspiegel*, '100 aktuelle Bilder: Photoaustellung im Titania-Palast'. The exhibit was not widely reported in *Der Kurier, Der Tag, Telegraf*, and *Die Neue Zeitung*.
13 Ries on reactions: Henry Ries, *Ich war ein Berliner: Erinnerungen eines New Yorker Fotojournalisten*, p. 134; Which picture do you like best?: *Der Abend*, 'Blockade in Bildern', 20 January 1949, Vol. 4, No. 16, p. 2; Katrin Peters-Klaphake, 'Die Photojournalischen Jahre von Henry Ries, 1946 bis 1951' in *Brennpunkt Berlin: Die Blockade 1948/9 Der Photojournalist Henry Ries*. Exhibition Catalogue, p. 99.
14 US interest in acquiring the photographs: Letter from Frank L. Howley, Office of Military Government Berlin Section to Bruce Rae, *New York Times*, 17 January 1949.

Private papers of Wanda Ries. And Letter from Ernst Reuter, Mayor of Greater-Berlin, to *New York Times*, 19 January 1949. Private papers of Wanda Ries.
15 Contract for German Faces and relation with wife: *Kalender aus dem Jahr 1949 mit tagebuchähnlichen Eintragungen u.a. zur Aufhebung der Berliner Blockade im Mai 1949 und mit Notizen zu Interviews für das Buch 'German Faces'* – Nachlass. Deutsches Historisches Museum Archive, Do2 2016/527.
16 New York Times interest: Letter from Bob Rae, *New York Times*, to Henry Ries, 31 January 1949. Private papers of Wanda Ries.
17 Press release New York Public Library, 29 April 1949. Private papers of Wanda Ries. Reportage of US exhibit: See 'Times Pictures of Airlift Chosen', *New York Times*, 24 April 1949 and undated *New York Times* photo clipping and caption from Ries private papers.
18 Americans avoiding pictures of starving people and symbol for future: Henry Ries, *Ich war ein Berliner: Erinnerungen eines New Yorker Fotojournalisten*, pp. 136–7; Werner A. Perger, 'Henry Ries: Photographer, author, friend – and a Berliner'.
19 On supplying Germans and his attitudes towards them: Henry Ries writing in 1999, file of unpublished documents from Wanda Ries; Ries quoted in Werner A. Perger, interview with Henry Ries, 'Ein milder Störenfried', *Die Zeit*, 5 June 1992; Letter to Dorothy Haller, Berlin, 9 September 1945, Deutsches Historisches Museum Archive; *Menschen am Zerstörten Anhalter Bahnhof: Fotografien von Henry Ries aus Berlin, 1948*, introduction.
20 Attitudes to Paris: *Kalender aus dem Jahr 1949 mit tagebuchähnlichen Eintragungen u.a. zur Aufhebung der Berliner Blockade im Mai 1949 und mit Notizen zu Interviews für das Buch 'German Faces'* – Nachlass. Deutsches Historisches Museum Archive, Do2 2016/527.
21 Leaving Germany: Ries, *Abschied meiner Generation*, p. 11.

XV Wolves in Sheep's Clothing

1 Richard Reeves interviews and quotes Stampa: *Daring Young Men*, pp. 139–40, 282, and mentions bunk beds on p. 100. Stampa's political activity is in: Michael Weisfeld, 'Rüstungsingenieur mit deutscher Gesinnung', *Tageszeitung (Taz)*, 9 September 1987. His daughter comments in: Sigrid V. Engelbrechten, 'Nachruf für Ulrich Stampa' on the family website.
2 I interviewed Bowers on 12 May 2024. Quotes also come from: Melissa Janoski, 'Berlin Airlift Veteran Honored', *Scranton Times*, 5 June 2024.
3 Ground crew, Tunner's request for Germans, and Clay's reaction: A. Anderhub and J.O. Bennett, *Blockade, Luftbrücke und Luftbrückendank: zur Geschichte der Krise um Berlin 1948–49*, p. 44; William Tunner, *Over the Hump*, pp. 182–3; Roger G. Miller, 'Tunner and the Luftwaffe Connection with the Berlin Airlift', *Air Power History* 56, No. 4 (2009), pp. 28–35.
4 For bombing of German cities: Jörg Friedrich, *The Fire: The Bombing of Germany: 1940–1945*, and Imperial War Museum archive.
5 Alec Chambers on reactions to German crew: my interview 12 May 2024 (used throughout); Alec Chambers (ed. Vivian Moss), 'Alec Chambers and the Berlin Airlift', p. 6.
6 Industrial police inclusion in the Berlin Airlift crews: Heinz-Ludger Borgert, Walter Stürm, Norbert Wiggershaus, *Dienstgruppen und westdeutscher Verteidigungsbeitrag*, pp. 116–8;

Labor Force History: USAREUR/ Hermann Deml, *Geschichte des Labor Service*.
7   Reactions of British and French to Black Guards: FO 1012/738, Black Guards files.
8   Preference for Germans over Black Americans: Timothy L. Schroer, *Recasting Race After World War II*, pp. 71–2.
9   Soviet–Western Allies discussion about Black Guards: FO 1012/738, Black Guards files (quotes from official transcripts in this section come from these records in The National Archives).
10 Reflections on controversies and inclusion of Waffen-SS in Black Guards: USAREUR/ Hermann Deml, *Geschichte des Labor Service*.
11 Denazification and West German institutions: 'Germany's FBI Examines its Nazi Roots', *Der Spiegel*, 1 October 2007; Gerhard Sälter, *NS-Kontinuitäten im BND. Rekrutierung, Diskurse, Vernetzungen*.
12 Torture at Bad Nenndorf and court-martial: Phillip Whitrock, 'Das Geheimnis des verbotenen Dorfes', *Der Spiegel*, 23 December 2005; Artemis Joanna Photiadou, 'Un-British No More: Torture and Interrogation by Britain in Germany, 1945–54', *Journal of Contemporary History*, Vol. 57, No. 4, 2022; House of Commons Debate, 24 March 1947, Vol. 435, pp. 1026–7; Ian Cobain, 'The interrogation camp that turned prisoners into living skeletons', *The Guardian*, 17 December 2005'; I. Cobain, *Cruel Britannia: A Secret History of Torture*. Atmosphere in Bad Nenndorf: Cyrill Hauges interview (1999), Imperial War Museum, Reel 2, 6'50" following.
13 Flight refuelling's presence in T-Force is from this interview, Reel 2, 18'; Alec Chambers interview, Imperial War Museum (2014), Reel 2, 18'30".
14 Atmosphere in Hamburg: Hartmut Weil, 'An Undergraduate's: Visit To Hamburg: Here Are His Frank Impressions Of What He Saw', *Varsity*, 12 June 1948.
15 Nightlife, anecdotes, black market, etc., in Hamburg: other primary interview sources pertaining to Chambers mentioned previously in notes.
16 Prowse's antics: Colin Cruddas, *Sir Alan Cobham: The Flying Legend Who Brought Aviation to the Masses*, p. 179. On welding incident, see also, Roberto Rodrigo, *Berlin Airlift*, p. 124.
17 Success of the 'Liquid Lift': Daniel F. Harrington, *'The Air Force Can Deliver Anything' A History of the Berlin Airlift*, p. 63; Colin Cruddas, *Sir Alan Cobham: The Flying Legend Who Brought Aviation to the Masses*, p. 181.
18 Brandt on importance of Airlift: Willy Brandt, *My Road to Berlin, as told to Leo Lania*, p. 179.
19 Alec on 100,000th flight: Chambers sources and 'The Man Who Helped Stop World War III', *Swindon Advertiser*, 20 October 2013.

XVI The Hollywood Version

1   George Seaton on a not anti-Russian film: interview with David Cherichetti. The American Film Institute/Louis B. Mayer Oral History Collection, Part 1, 18/ The New York Times Oral History Program. Glenn Rock, N.J.: Microfilming Corporation of America, 1977, quoted in Thomas W. Maulucci, Jr, 'Cold War Berlin in the Movies: From *The Big Lift* to *The Promise*'.
2   Problems shooting in East Berlin: George Seaton, 'Of Small Headaches; Film-Maker Reviews Soviet "Cooperation" while Shooting "*Big Lift*" in Berlin Impediment New Angle', *New York Times*, 16 April 1950; Charles G. Clarke collection *The Big Lift* (1950).

Manuscript Files: Correspondence from Office of Military Government for Germany (U.S.) and United States Air Force in Germany, 1949, 71301304. Academy Collections/ Margaret Herrick Library, Academy of Motion Picture Arts and Science, Los Angeles.

3   Clift as 'Sloppy but handsome', etc.: Production Files, *The Big Lift* (1950). Pressbooks, 72092820. Academy Collections/Margaret Herrick Library.
4   Clift's reaction to Berlin's poverty: Patricia Bosworth, *Montgomery Clift: A Biography*, p. 171. The Clift family dispute some details in Patricia Bosworth's biography (see the documentary film, *Making Montgomery Clift*, 2018) but descriptions of his time in Berlin are corroborated by document in the Oscars Archive. She also worked closely with the family, had access to their personal recordings, and interviewed a large roster of the film industry in New York and Hollywood.
5   Clift's relationship with Mira and events on set: Patricia Bosworth, *Montgomery Clift: A Biography*, pp. 167, 172–4, corroborated by Charles Brackett papers. Diary, 71432527. Academy Collections/Margaret Herrick Library, 14 April 1950 entry, pp. 99–100.
6   Backlog of US films in Germany: Tobias Hochscherf and Christoph Laucht, 'Censorship, Scripts, Suppression, and Selection: Twentieth Century Fox and the Story of the Berlin Airlift in *The Big Lift* and *Es begann mit einem Kuß* (*It Started with a Kiss*), 1950–1953', pp. 83–111.
7   Anecdote about Clift offered a job: Production Files, *The Big Lift* (1950). Pressbooks, 72092820. Academy Collections/Margaret Herrick Library.
8   Seaton spreading gossip about Clift: Patricia Bosworth, *Montgomery Clift: A Biography*, p. 174; Robert LaGuardia, *Monty: A Biography of Montgomery Clift*, p. 77.
9   Neorealism: Ralph Stern, '*The Big Lift* (1950): Image and Identity in Blockaded Berlin', pp. 66 ff.
10 Seaton on Berlin as a backdrop: Production Files, *The Big Lift* (1950). Pressbooks, 72092820. Academy Collections/Margaret Herrick Library; and as a 'photoplay': Philip K. Scheuer, 'Movie on Air Lift Achievement, Too', *Los Angeles Times*, 11 May 1950.
11 Synopsis of landing: Production Files, *The Big Lift* (1950). Cast Lists, Synopses, 72092820. Academy Collections/Margaret Herrick Library.
12 Hildegard Knef's participation: Tobias Hochscherf and Christoph Laucht, 'Censorship, Scripts, Suppression, and Selection: Twentieth Century Fox and the Story of the Berlin Airlift in *The Big Lift* and *Es begann mit einem Kuß* (*It Started with a Kiss*), 1950–1953', pp. 83–111.
13 On Cornell Borchers: Production Files, *The Big Lift* (1950). Pressbooks, 72092820. Academy Collections/Margaret Herrick Library; 'Eisgekühlte Bezirke', *Der Spiegel*, 10 May 1950; Hedda Hoppers Papers, Interview with Cornell Borchers, 11 April 1956, 71318806. Academy Collections/Margaret Herrick Library.
14 On the myth of 'rubble women': Leonie Treber, *Mythos Trümmerfrauen: Von der Trümmerbeseitigung in der Kriegs- und Nachkriegszeit und der Entstehung eines deutschen Erinnerungsortes*.
15 Clift and Douglas's conflicts: Patricia Bosworth, *Montgomery Clift: A Biography*, p. 173.
16 Seaton exploring Berlin in disguise: Production Files, *The Big Lift* (1950). Pressbooks, 72092820. Academy Collections/Margaret Herrick Library.
17 Press reaction to Borchers: 'Montgomery Clift Starring in Story of Berlin Air Lift', *The Christian Science Monitor*, 19 May 1950. Löbel interviewed: Production Files,

The Big Lift (1950). Pressbooks, 72092820. Academy Collections/Margaret Herrick Library.

18 On revision of *The Big Lift*, and Code and military censorship: Tobias Hochscherf and Christoph Laucht, 'Censorship, Scripts, Suppression, and Selection: Twentieth Century Fox and the Story of the Berlin Airlift in *The Big Lift* and *Es begann mit einem Kuß* (*It Started with a Kiss*), 1950–1953', pp. 83–111; Motion Picture Association of America Production Code Administration records, *The Big Lift* (1950). Manuscript Files: Censor Reports, correspondence, PCA analyses and reviews, 71338698. Academy Collections/Margaret Herrick Library.

19 Use of film by military for recruitment and propaganda, and advertisements: Production Files, *The Big Lift* (1950). Pressbooks, 72092820. Academy Collections/Margaret Herrick Library.

20 Reviews of the film: 'Eisgekühlte Bezirke', *Der Spiegel*, 10 May 1950; Bosley Crowther, 'The Screen in Review; "The Big Lift", Fox Film Based on Air Operations Over Berlin, Is New Feature at Rivoli', *New York Times*, 27 April 1950. Actor Thelma Ritter, meanwhile, opined that too much was 'lost in the flying technique', and (a little nastily) that 'Clift, while looking the part to perfection is so inept and ineffectual'. Letter criticising Montgomery Clift's performance in Seaton's *The Big Lift*, circa March 1950. Thelma Ritter and Joseph Aloysius Moran papers, correspondence, file 263, 71574863. Academy Collections/Margaret Herrick Library; '*The Big Lift*: Review', *Variety*, 12 April 1950, p. 6.

21 Scrubbing of German films of Nazi references and cutting of German version: Tobias Hochscherf and Christoph Laucht, 'Censorship, Scripts, Suppression, and Selection: Twentieth Century Fox and the Story of the Berlin Airlift in *The Big Lift* and *Es begann mit einem Kuß* (*It Started with a Kiss*), 1950–1953', pp. 83–111.

22 On 'realism' in the *Big Lift*: Bosley Crowther, 'Realistic Romance', *New York Times*, 30 April 1950.

23 Sex work, marriages, and other relations between Allied soldiers and Germans: Florian Weiß, 'Es begann mit einem Kuss', pp. 82–3; 'Foreign News: Veronica Town', *Time Magazine*, 13 February 1950; Susan L. Carruthers, *The Good Occupation: American Soldiers and the Hazards of Peace*, p. 296; Walter J. Slatoff, 'GI Morals in Germany', *The New Republic*, 13 May 1946, pp. 686–7; Harry Moseley, 'Medical History of the Berlin Airlift', pp. 1249 ff.

24 Denouement of Airlift: Uwe Prell and Lothar Wilker, *Berlin-Blockade und Luftbrücke 1948/49: Analyse und Dokumentation*, p. 54; A. Anderhub and J.O. Bennett, *Blockade, Luftbrücke und Luftbrückendank: zur Geschichte der Krise um Berlin 1948–49*, p. 40; David E. Barclay, 'Beyond Cold War Mythmaking: Ernst Reuter and the United States', p. 137.

25 British Intelligence officer quoted in: Riess, *Berlin Story*, p. 177.

26 Flickering lights in apartments: United Press correspondent Walter Rundle, quoted in Reeves, *Daring Young Men*, p. 265.

27 Ali Bar candles and atmosphere of lifting of Soviet restrictions, such as consumption of fish and desserts: Curt Riess, *Berlin Story*, pp. 162–5.

28 'Composure of Berliners': Ibid., p. 113. Clay to Ries, in Ries's autobiography, p. 141.

XVII Reflections

1 This first section is sourced from: Slaker, *A Military Pilot's Exciting Life and Visit from the Hereafter*, and other Slaker primary interview sources mentioned previously.
2 Ries describes his class reunion: Ries, *Abschied meiner Generation*, p. 17 ff. The student newspaper is quoted from: 'Politische Ecke' from the Schiller-Real-Gymnasium 'Klatsche', reprinted in Ries, *Abschied meiner Generation*, p. 19.
3 Ries's remarks on right-wing radicalism in Israel: Ibid., p. 13.
4 Ruth's resistance: see Gedenkstätte Deutscher Widerstand (German Resistance Museum) exhibits; Deborah Barton, *Writing and Rewriting the Reich, Women Journalists in the Nazi and Post-War Press*.
5 Her attitude to German responsibility: Ruth Andreas-Friedrich, *Berlin Underground*, author's introduction, p. xiv. Her recognition as Righteous Among the Nations, see Yad Vashem website.
6 For 'internal emigration' and 'focalisation': Detlev Peukert, *Inside Nazi Germany*; Genette, Gérard, 'Discours du récit' in G. Genette. *Figures III*, pp. 67–282.
7 Death of Ernst Reuter: Utta Raifer, 'Wie die Morgenpost über den Tod Ernst Reuters berichtete', *Berliner Morgenpost*, 17 June 2018.
8 On the Berlin Wall and public acceptance of the Airlift: thanks to Angelika Maser for this suggestion.
9 Ries talks about his earliest photos of the Gate and the 'Room of Silence' in Ries, *Abschied meiner Generation*, pp. 20–1, 219; 'The Room of Silence', unpublished private papers, Henry Ries, from Wanda Ries; material on Mercedes Wild is from my interview with her.

INDEX

Italicised references indicate illustrations.

aircraft 93–4, 103–04, 111, *175–76*, 209–11
   B-17 plane 24
   DC-3 (aka C-47 or Dakota) 25–26, 27, 93, 133, 205
   DC-4 (C-54 Skymaster) 26, 93–4, 162
   fuelling 218–19
   French aircraft 184
   Halifax Bomber 93
   Lancaster Bomber 106, 109, 111
   US Douglas C-54 188
   see also Luftwaffe
Airlift: Only the Sky Was Free (television series) 96
airlift 27–29, 130, 210–11, 217
   and black market 198–99
   and Cold War 16, 244
   anniversary 101
   Black Friday 94
   British interests 99
   cargo 29, 158, 164–67, 249
   cost 98
   denouement 232–33
   French role 184–85, 188–94, 212
   Jungfernheide 185–88
   landing 28
   'Liquid Lift' 102–11
   'Little Lift' 78, 87, 219
   pilots 29–30, 231–32, 249
   planning 86–9
   preparation 26, 212–13
   propaganda 95–8, 202–06, 229–30, 244–45
   Tunner's role 94–5
   Western military reaction 25
   see also The Big Lift
Allied Control Council 50
American Airlines 26
Andreas-Friedrich, Ruth 11–12, 19, 45–6, 75–6
   and America 51–2
   and money 80–1, 83
   at River Havel 81–2
   black market 198–99
   diaries 51, 194–95, 241–42
   during war 45, 242
   leaving Berlin 197
   on Berlin 191–93
   on blockade 84–5, 94, 154–56
   on the West 68
Annan, Noel 120, 124–25, 127–28, 146, 148, 151–52
atomic weapons 16, 230–31

Bad Nenndorf 215–16
Baker, Richard 125
Battle of Berlin 49
BBC 125
Benson, Brigadier E.R. 124, 150
Bennett, Jack O. 93
Berlin
   Airlift 11–14, 16, 27, 205–08
   American HQ 32,
   and Allied forces 231–32
   and West 192–95, 207
   Andrews Barracks 69
   Anhalter Bahnhof 200, 207

attitude to French 184, 191–92
blockade 16, 77–9, 84–5, 95–7
British zone 198
climate of fear 47–8
cultural events 116–24, 127–29 *see also* Elizabethan Festival
'dark tourism' 47
division 15–17, 68, 232–33
election of Reuter 191–92
Hungerharke 96, 243
in wartime 14, 242–43
isolating of 19
Kommandatura 68
media 73–4
post war 33–6, 41, 47–50, 60, 65–6, 75–6, 127, 164, 200–01
Soviet sector 144–45, 198–201, 204, 220–21, 233
unrest 155–56
Berlin Wall 183
fall of 14, 247
Beves, Donald 126
Bevin, Ernest 118, 216
Big Lift, The (1950) 219, 223–32, 245
and Hays Code 228–29
casting 221, 224–25
German version 230–31
production 225–26
Russian objections to 220–21
Birley, Robert 118, 127
black market 88, 96, 109, 159, 195–201, 218, 227
see also food *and* rationing
Blum, Léon 188
Blun, Georges 193
Blunt, Anthony 120
Borchard, Leo 52
Borchers, Cornell 224–28, 231–32
Botschafter des Friedens (1948) 115–116
Bowers, Harold 210–11
Bradley, Omar N. 86
Brandt, Willy 59, 60, 67, 86
on airlift 95, 99
on Clay 90
on Reuter 91–2
Brecht, Bertolt 200
Brummen 12, 30, 157, 197, 234

Burkill, Margareta 58–9
Burroughs, Hank 153

Cambridge 119–26
Cave, John 104
Chambers, Alec *172*, 211–12, 215–19, 231, 243
and airlift 105–111, 188, 224
background 101–04
Charlton, H.B. 127, 146–48, 150–51
Checkpoint Charlie 133
Christian, Lieutenant Bill 163
Ciro nightclub 26
Collier's 33
Comintern 56
Control Commission Germany 105, 146
Clay, Lucius 26, 66–7, 86, 158, 186, 189, 200, 222, 233
and Reuter 77–8
character 89–91
on airlift 89–92, 98, 201–11
on blockade 95, 100
Clift, Montgomery 219, 221–23, 229, 232
see also The Big Lift
Cold War 14, 66
and culture 149–50
impact of airlift 16–18, 188–89
Creighton, Tom 118
currency 67, 80, 83–5, 153
Czechoslovakia 67

Dau, Peter 46–7
Davis, Natalie Zemon 18
de Gaulle, General 184
Der Abend 46
Die Welt 52

Eckstein, Käthe 49
Edwards, David 87–9
Eisenhower 66, 74
Elisabeth Hospital Schöeneberg 49
Elizabethan Festival 128–29, 144–56
motivation 148–49
planning 118–27
reactions to 128–30, 146–53

FDGB (Free German Trade Union) 71
Five Ds 50, 68, 74, 214

food 88, 226, 233, 249
  and airlift 94–98, 158–60, 164–66,
    at Faßberg 210
    at Hamburg 217–18
    at Stolpe, 190, 195–202
  see also rationing and black market
Forrestal, James 86
French zone, origins 184
Friede, Dieter
  disappearance 46–7, 51–2

Ganeval, General Jean 185, 187–89
  on Stolpe Affair 191–92
Gatow 16
Germans, attitudes to 211–12
Germany defeat 49, 60
  demilitarisation see 'Five Ds'
  and Russia 50–2, 66–8
  division 67
Goebbels 73, 121
Göring 107
Greek Civil War 67

Halder, Franz 213
Hallein 40
Haller, Dorothy 42, 207
Halvorsen, Gail 159–68, *173*, 248–49
Hamburg, 216–18
Haun, Lieutenant Colonel James R. 166
Herdt, Victor 58
Hershey 160, 165
Himmler, Heinrich 40, 41, 42
Hitler *and* Third Reich 15, 32, 40, 46, 98,
    123, 188, 210, 225, 241
  and airlift 25, 98, 186, 214
  and Ernst Reuter 54, 58
  antisemitism 35–6, 38, 126 see also
    racism
  atrocities 41–3, 50, 51, 209, 240
  Hitler, Adolf 15, 35, 41, 58, 145, 239
  Industrial Police 68–76, 212–15
  propaganda 73–4, 86, 121, 212
Hope, Bob 188
Howard, Elsie 58–9
Hübner, Klaus 187

inflation 80–1

Jogiches, Leo 53

Kamps, Herman 151
Kant, Immanuel 55
Kartmazov, Major 68–71, 213
Kindertransport 59
Kœnig, General Marie-Pierre 191
Kommandatura 15, 69, 74, 79, 212
Kotikov, General Alexander Georgievich
    47, 60, 72–3, 76, 189
KPD (German Communist Party) 57
Kun, Béla 56
Kuzubski, Mariusz 111

Laker, Freddie 93
Laughlin, James 48
Lawrence, David 88
Lemke, Michael 96
Lenin 56, 84
Lennig, Walter 153
Lethbridge, Major General John Sydney
    215–16
*Lilith: The Magazine for Young Girls and
    Women* 45–6, 65
Luftwaffe 88, 209–12, 214
Lusset, Félix 150

Magee, Patrick 125, 127, 129, 148
  in Soviet sector 144–45
Mann, Anthony 158
Marlowe Society 121–23, 126–27, 148
Marshall plan 50, 66
Marshall, Arthur 122–23
Marx 55
McAfee, Fred 92
McGraw, Major 70–1
Morgenthau Plan 50
Mörlins, Werner 238–39
Moseley, Harry 93

NATO 233
Nazis *see* Hitler *and* Third Reich
New York Times 193, 221, 231
  and Ries 34, 82, 205–06, 208, 238
  on airlift 94, 202–04
November Revolution 57
Nuremberg Trials 41

October Revolution 56
OMGUS Observer 82, 247
Operation Vittles 234
Ord, Boris 121, 129, 149

Paulus, Friedrich 215
Perger, Werner A. 43
photography 222–23, 241, 245
   see also Ries, Henry
Pistorius, Boris 244
Potsdam 50, 66, 133, 220, 233
Prowse, Dave 218

Quakers 38, 58

racism 213, 217, 239–40
radio and radar 93–4, 185, 189
rationing 88, 96, 120, 199–200
   see also food
Red Army Choir 115–16
Reeves, Richard 209
reparations 50
Reuter, Ernst 13, 19, 67, 126, *171*
   and airlift 89–92, 98–100, 200
   and Britain 59, 61–2
   and Cambridge 58–9
   and Greta Burkill 58–9
   as mayor 191–93
   background and character 53–5, 242–43
   in America 59, 232
   in Cambridge 119–20
   in Comintern 56–7,
   in First World War 56
   in Germany 57–8, 154–55
   in Turkey 58–9
   in Zehlendorf 77–8
   magnet theory 91
   on blockade 85–6
   on Reuter 154
   politics 55–6, 59–61, 85
   return to Berlin 60, 233
RIAS 12, 94, 100
Ries, Henry 12–14, 19, 153, *169*, 209
   as photographer 12–13, 34–5, 39, 43, 82, 117, 153–56, 205–08, 238
   at Helmstedt 82–3

autobiography 34
background 32–3, 35–7, 43–4, 200
begins military career 39–40,
character 38–9, 42–3, 61, 247–48
exhibition 200–05
German Faces 206
Goodbye to My Generation 207, 241
in America 37–9, 207–08, 238–39
in post-war Berlin 32–5, 41–3, 117, 156, 200–08, 239–40
posted to Berlin 40
sexuality 37–8
translating 40–2
Ries, Wanda 34, 38, 39, 43, 200, 207–08, 238–41, 247
Riess, Curt 49, 233–34
   on Reuter 53
   on Sokolovsky 66
Robertson, Brian 66, 89, 91
Rommel 24, 212
Rostova, Mira 222
Ruhr 29
Russia 216, 244
   and French 185, 188–94
   and Nazis 50
   and UN 98
   atrocities 49, 201
   attitudes to West 66–76, 84, 130, 149–50, 215–16, 232–33, 245–46
   formation of the Republic 56
   Red Army 49
   Soviet secret police 47
   Stolpe Affair 189–94, 196
   tactics 77–8, 85, 94, 97, 99–100, 107–11, 115–18, 131
Rylands, George Humphrey Wolferstan 'Dadie' 122–23, 125, 146, 150, 152

Second World War 24
   end of 15
   America joins 38
Scheunemann, Wolfgang 155
Schmidt, Heinz 189
Schnabel, Rudolf 134–41, 143, 237–38
Seaton, George 220, 222–23, 225
   see also The Big Lift
Six-Power Conference 67

Slaker, Kenneth Hawk (pilot) 11, 14, 19, 50, 61, 143, 184
   aircraft 25–6
   and airlift 26–7, 29–30, 92–3
   and Rudolf Schnabel 134–41, 237–38, 244
   crashing in Germany 31, 131–34, 237
   early life 23, 25, 161
   in 1948 25
   in war 23–24
Sokolovsky, Vasily 66–8, 85
   on blockade 96–7
   on occupation of Stolpe 191
Spartacus League 53
SPD (German Social Democratic Party) 55, 57–8, 60, 85, 191–92
Speer, Albert 144
Spiel, Hilde 146, 151
Stalin, Joseph 16, 57, 61, 149, 153, 164, 232
   and division of Germany 67–8
Stalinism 15, 151–52
Stampa, Ulrich 209–10
Steber, Lieutenant Clarence 26–27, 30, 142–43
   capture 132–33
Steglitz 11
Stensrud, Sergeant Donald 188–89
Stephens, Colonel Robin 'Tin-Eye' 216
Stokes, Richard 215–16
Stolpe 183–85, 190–96
Stringer, Ann 206, 208
Suhr, Otto 192

Tegel 16
Tempelhof 13–6, 108, 125, 158–67, 185, 197, 203, 224
   today 14–17, 26, 29, 101–02, 243–49
Thiele family 194–97
Time 56
Tito, Josip Broz 56
Truman, President Harry S. 16, 59
   and Russia 98
   Loyalty Order 90
   on airlift 91, 100
   Truman Doctrine 67
Tunner, William H. 26, 141–42
   and airlift 94–5, 210–11
Turkey 58–60

Ulbricht, Walter 86
Ullstein, Gabriele 126–28, 152
US Army 71–2

Vachell, Antony 144–45
Vittles 142–43
Vogel, Traugott 183–84

Waite, RAF Commodore Reginald 'Rex' 243
   and Little Lift 86–9, 91, 96
Weil, Hans Hartmut 48
West Germany, creation of 67–8
Western democracy and Russia 15–16, 245–46
Wiesbaden 29
Wiese, Albert 190, 194
Wild, Mercedes née Simon 157–60, 166–68, *173*, 198, 243, 248–49
Wilder, Billy 81
Wunstorf 107, 111

Young, Colonel 237–38

Zhukov 66